Studies in First and Second Language Acquisition

Fred R. Eckman
Ashley J. Hastings
University of Wisconsin
Milwaukee

Newbury House Publishers, Inc.
Rowley, Massachusetts 01969

Library of Congress Cataloging in Publication Data

Symposium on Language Acquisition, University of
    Wisconsin--Milwaukee, 1977.
    Studies in first and second language acquisition.

    Papers presented at the Symposium on Language Acquisi-
tion, held March 18–19, 1977 at the University of
Wisconsin--Milwaukee.
    Includes bibliographies.
    1. Children--Language--Congresses.   2. Language and
languages--Study and teaching--Congresses.   I. Eckman,
Fred R.   II. Hastings, Ashley.   III. Title.
P118.S93   1977   401'.9   78-27002
ISBN 0-88377-119-5

NEWBURY HOUSE PUBLISHERS, INC.

Language Science
Language Teaching
Language Learning

ROWLEY, MASSACHUSETTS 01969

Cover and book design by KENNETH J. WILSON

First printing: March 1979
                    5   4   3   2   1

Printed in the U.S.A.

Preface

On March 18 and 19, 1977, a symposium on Language Acquisition was held on the campus of the University of Wisconsin—Milwaukee. This volume represents the revised versions of the papers presented at the Symposium, with the exception of the papers by Melissa Bowerman and Sonia K. Aller, which were presented at the Symposium but do not appear in this volume.

The success of the Symposium owed a great deal to the participation of the invited discussants. While practical considerations do not allow us to present transcripts of the discussions of the papers, a number of the papers in this volume have benefitted from points raised by the discussants at the Symposium. For their valuable contribution, we would like to express our appreciation to the discussants: Michel Benamou (Center for Twentieth Century Studies, UWM), Phillip Connell (Speech Pathology and Audiology, UWM), Alan Corré (Hebrew Studies, UWM), Leopold Dicker (Exceptional Education, UWM), Irwin Feigenbaum (English, Purdue University), Sidney Greenbaum (English, UWM), Linda Haughton (Spanish and Portuguese, UWM), Larry Hutchinson (Linguistics, University of Minnesota), Edith Moravcsik (Linguistics, UWM), Bernhard Peters (German, UWM), Betty Wallace Robinett (Linguistics, University of Minnesota), Gerald Sanders (Linguistics, University of Minnesota), Linda Schwartz (Linguistics, Indiana University), Charles Scott (English, University of Wisconsin—Madison), Bruce Stark (English, UWM), Charlotte Webb (Linguistics, San Diego State University), Barbara Wheatley (Linguistics, UWM), and Jessica Wirth (Linguistics, UWM).

The Symposium on Language Acquisition was the sixth in the series of annual UWM Linguistics Symposia. The nearly-even balance between papers on first language acquisition and those on second language acquisition, as well as the inclusion of papers dealing with theoretical, experimental and practical aspects of language acquisition, reflect our view that these Symposia should be a forum in which theoretical linguists, psycholinguists and applied linguists can speak to one another on issues of mutual interest. We hope that this volume will continue and extend the dialogue among the various approaches to the study of language acquisition.

Fred R. Eckman
Ashley J. Hastings

Acknowledgments

This Symposium was made possible by grants from the following sources:

The Graduate School

The College of Letters and Science

The Center for Latin America

The Center for Twentieth Century Studies

The Bilingual/Bicultural Teacher Training Project of the Department of Curriculum and Instruction

Department of Spanish and Portuguese

Department of Linguistics

From all of these sources, we gratefully acknowledge the support.

We would also like to thank our colleagues in the Department of Linguistics, who gave freely of their time and energy in making this Symposium run smoothly: Irwin Feigenbaum, Greg Iverson, Peter Lee, Edith Moravcsik, Barbara Wheatley and Jessica Wirth.

Finally, but by no means least in importance, we would like to express our appreciation to Michael Schneider and Nancy Thurow for their assistance in compiling and typing the bibliography.

Contents

Introduction

Until quite recently, a symposium designed to address questions of both first and second language acquisition might well have been regarded as an artificial union of two superficially similar but fundamentally distinct species, from which only sterile issue could be expected. First language acquisition has traditionally come under the rubric of psycholinguistics, while second language acquisition has been the concern of applied linguistics. This division has reflected the generally-accepted view that two very different types of learning are involved in first and second language acquisition. Children, i.e., first language learners, appear to acquire their native language as a normal and automatic part of their development, effortlessly, without instruction, requiring only a reasonable amount of exposure to the speech of their community. By contrast, second language learners— typically adolescents and adults—may expend great amounts of labor (and require a corresponding amount of labor from their instructors) in formal, richly structured courses of study, only to achieve an imperfect mastery—and often, no mastery at all—of a foreign language.

However, in spite of the obvious contrasts between first and second language acquisition, a somewhat different view of their relationship has begun to emerge in recent years. According to this view, the *similarities* between first and second language acquisition are at least as important as the dissimilarities; and our progress in understanding either may depend, in part, on our ability to identify, elucidate, and explain these similarities. More and more researchers in both areas are therefore seeking to establish closer communication among all those interested in one or another aspect of language acquisition, and to develop a common agenda for the general field of language acquisition studies.

The papers in this volume contribute to the above goals in two ways. First, by the physical fact of being bound together, they invite specialists in both first and second language acquisition to acquaint themselves with the assumptions, methods, and purposes of their colleagues "on the other side." Second, several of the authors address themselves specifically to the proposition that the two kinds of language acquisition have much in common. On the other hand, each of the papers in this collection is focused primarily on one or the other of the two areas, and we have grouped them accordingly.

The first group of papers—those concerned mainly with first language acquisition—is headed by the contribution by Sheldon: "Assumptions, Methods, and Goals in Language Acquisition Research." Sheldon challenges a number of assumptions that have been widely accepted in language acquisition research: that children acquire a transformational grammar when they learn their first language; that this grammar is identical to the grammar that a linguist would write to describe the language; that all children accomplish this through the operation of an innate language acquisition device; that this device is no longer operative in adult second language learners. Citing studies which indicate that children do not initially acquire an optimal transformational grammar and that first language acquisition is not as remarkably uniform and independent of environment as had previously been believed, Sheldon outlines some promising avenues of research aimed at getting a more accurate picture of what it is that children actually learn as they acquire language, what role general learning principles may play in language acquisition, and how the differences between first and second language acquisition might be explained without appealing to the hypothetical atrophy of the hypothetical LAD. Sheldon's paper thus offers a survey of some very basic theoretical and methodological problems in language acquisition research. Many of the questions she raises are taken up in the papers which follow.

In "The Mother as LAD: Interaction between Order and Frequency of Parental Input and Child Production," Forner seeks to establish a causal correlation between the order of introduction and frequency of modeling of constructions in adult speech to children, and the order and frequency of children's productions of those constructions. Such a correlation would be of considerable interest, for it would indicate that first language acquisition is governed to some extent by the same kinds of factors that govern other forms of learning; this would count against the claim by Chomsky (1965) and others that language acquisition is governed by an innate, specifically linguistic device. Forner presents an exhaustive statistical analysis of data gathered from recordings of interactions between herself and her son, and demonstrates significant correlations in both order and frequency for various types of German questions. Furthermore, she shows that similar results are obtained when the same statistical methods are applied to an earlier study of the acquisition of questions in Serbo-Croatian (Savić, 1975).

Roeper, Stack, and Carlson explore the child's formulation of linguistic hypotheses in their paper, "Stress Acquisition: The Role of Homogeneous Rules." They argue that children initially overrestrict their hypothesis-space, i.e., that children do not initially consider certain types of rules which are allowed by universal grammar and which are presumably included in adult grammars. Examining the ways in which English-speaking children and adults stress nonsense words, the authors conclude that the early stress rules of children are *homogeneous*—that each rule is conditioned by one and only one factor such as the phonological environment, the syntactic environment, etc. They suggest further that the transition to the adult system may take place by a process of collapsing the child's set of homogeneous rules into a complex heterogeneous schema.

In "The Acquisition of Perception Verb Complements," Goodluck and Roeper are also concerned with discovering limitations on the early grammatical hypotheses formulated by children. While the grammar of perception verb complements in adult English involves both syntactic and semantic factors, the authors find that before the age of five, semantic factors do not appear to play any role in children's comprehension of perception verb complements. They argue that the early stage in the acquisition of perception verb complements provides support for the hypothesis that children obey the obligatory principles of universal grammar but do not initially explore the possibilities allowed by optional principles of universal grammar; in the case at hand, the early child grammars are consistent with a universal syntactic constraint on control rules but do not exploit the optional power, allowed by universal grammar, to impose semantic restrictions on subcategorization frames.

The paper by Solan, "The Acquisition of Tough Movement," is an interesting attempt to resolve an analytical dispute concerning adult English on the basis of data from language acquisition. Solan presents evidence indicating that children learn to understand sentences like *John is easy to please* before they are able to understand sentences like *Mary is pretty to look at.* He argues that this would not be true if the two types of sentences are both derived from similar structures via deletion, as claimed by Lasnik and Fiengo (1974). Solan concludes that the *tough movement* analysis of the first type of sentence is therefore supported. The crucial assumption here, of course, is that children do not subsequently restructure their grammars to give a unitary account of both types of sentence, once both have been mastered. In other words, Solan views the adult grammar as a reflection of acquisitional stages, rather than acquisition as a series of increasing approximations to a theoretically optimal adult grammar.

In "Children's Interpretation of Reflexive Pronouns in English," Read and Hare present a study of the interpretation of various types of reflexive constructions by children and adults. On the basis of their data, they test a number of hypotheses involving the difference between unambiguous reflexives (whose antecedents are uniquely determined by the clause-mate constraint) and ambiguous reflexives (for which the constraint is irrelevant or indeterminate). They find that adults and older children employ a comprehension strategy for ambiguous reflexives: identify the main-clause subject as the antecedent. This strategy is apparently acquired (by most children) after the clause-mate constraint is acquired, which is consistent with C. Chomsky's (1969) hypothesis that regular constraints are learned before strategies for exceptions. However, Read and Hare also found disconfirmation of C. Chomsky's suggestion that regular constraints are learned at a relatively uniform age: in their group of subjects, ranging from six to twelve years old, some of the younger children had already acquired the clause-mate constraint, while some of the older ones had not yet done so. Since the clause-mate constraint is a very straightforward, regular, structurally-defined principle, this lack of uniformity is particularly striking.

The next two papers take as their point of departure previous studies of the acquisition of specific syntactic structures in English; they seek to broaden our perspective on these matters by carrying out similar studies in other languages. Since these languages differ structurally from English, the methodological difficulties encountered in such comparative studies are formidable, but the potential gains are obvious: by observing the interplay of language-specific and language-universal factors in the acquisition of a number of languages, we may be able to discern more clearly the basic, invariant processes in language acquisition.

Aller, Aller, and Malouf-Saad, in "The Acquisition of Ask and Tell Structures by Arabic-Speaking Children," report a study which closely parallels that of C. Chomsky (1969), in which Chomsky found a sequence of stages in the acquisition of *ask-tell* constructions in English. These stages were based on structural complexity (number of elements deleted from the complement clause) as well as the child's mastery of *ask* as an exception to the Minimal Distance Principle. The authors show that the MDP appears to play a similar role in the acquisition of Arabic; however, they argue that complement clause complexity does *not* play a significant role. They do find a sequence of stages not unlike Chomsky's, with one particularly interesting difference: many of the Arabic-speaking children's errors consisted of *asking* when they had been instructed to *tell*, which is the opposite of what Chomsky had found for English.

The paper by Lust and Wakayama, "The Structure of Coordination in Children's First Language Acquisition of Japanese," compares the findings of Lust (1977), a study of English-speaking children's imitations of sentential and phrasal coordinations, with a similar study of Japanese-speaking children. They find that, while English-speaking children prefer sentential coordination over phrasal coordination, and forward reduction over backward reduction, the opposite generally holds true for Japanese-speaking children. With respect to one type of forward-reduced phrasal coordination, however, the Japanese-speaking children behave in a way quite similar to the pattern observed in English-speaking children. The authors discuss their findings from a number of perspectives: the general theory of conjunction reduction, the analysis of Japanese coordinations, and language acquisition universals which may be of a linguistic or a general cognitive nature.

The concluding paper in Part 1 is "The Acquisition of Action Representations in American Sign Language," by Steyaert and Ellenberger. This is a welcome addition to the growing literature on sign language acquisition, an area which has been largely neglected. The authors present some results of a longitudinal study of a child learning ASL as a first language. They show a developmental progression in the acquisition of action representations, an aspect of ASL which involves spatial modification and structuring. While this has no obvious parallel in spoken language, the developmental progression seems quite reminiscent of acquisitional patterns observed in children who are learning to speak. Studies of this sort, though still in the pioneering stage, may ultimately bring us closer to—in the authors' words—"the formulation of *true* universals of child language acquisition."

The first paper in Part 2 of this volume, which deals with second language acquisition, is Spolsky's "The Comparative Study of First and Second Language Acquisition." In this paper, Spolsky rejects the traditional notion of applied linguistics with its implication that linguistics is to be applied to something, in favor of an approach which begins with specific problems and turns to a theory of language for possible insights to solutions. This approach is exemplified with what Spolsky terms educational linguistics. The specific problem with which he concerns himself is that of increasing a student's ability to communicate verbally. In the discussion of this problem, which Spolsky treats from a broad perspective, the question of whether first and second language acquisition are similar is taken up.

In the paper by Gaies, the similarity of first and second language acquisition is pursued in terms of the input data to which the language learner is exposed. After reviewing the literature on the simplification of adult language when addressing children, Gaies shows that in the study he conducted syntactic adjustments in the direction of simplification were made by foreign language teachers in the classroom. These results suggest that the role played by the teacher is roughly parallel to that played by the parent in first language acquisition. Thus, the fact that the majority of second language learning takes place in the classroom does not actually constitute a difference between first and second language acquisition. To the contrary, in terms of the input supplied to the learner, the two are similar.

The next two articles, by Mougeon, Canale and Carroll on the one hand, and by Rey on the other, deal with bilingualism. The first of these deals with the acquisition of English prepositions by French-English bilingual children. The authors point out that the study of the acquisition of English prepositions is significant because it has been suggested that a speaker's proficiency in English prepositions can be correlated with that speaker's overall proficiency in English. The results of the study suggest that the order of acquisition of English prepositions among French-English bilingual children is the same as for monolingual children.

The paper by Rey deals with bilingual adults who are at different stages of second language acquisition. Using some of the same methodology developed by Lambert, specifically, the Word Association Test (WAT), Rey attempts to measure seven aspects of bilingual proficiency: associational fluency, free association, word order influence, stimulus provocativeness, associational stereotypy, vocabulary commonness and speed of primary response. Rey presents his results in the form of hypotheses which were either supported or not supported by the tests. Some of his findings support those of the Lambert study, others do not, and still others extend beyond it in some interesting ways.

Keel's paper deals with the phenomenon of phonological replacement. While the majority of the studies of this problem have dealt almost exclusively with phonological replacements in the learning of English, Keel's paper considers replacements of speakers of five different languages in the learning of German. Most previous accounts of phonological replacements have centered around the idea that the speaker replaces a sound segment in the target language with a sound in the native language which is "closest" to the target sound. Keel attempts to make this notion of "closest" explicit by appealing to the concept of *minimal complement segment.*

The final two papers in this section deal with some of the pedagogical aspects of second language acquisition. The paper by Cortina and Myers discusses some of the problems faced by teachers in a foreign language classroom when at least some of the students are native speakers of a dialect of the target language—albeit not the standard dialect. After outlining a number of special problems which are germane to this situation, the authors propose a way of dealing with these problems. Their methodology stems from linguistic analysis on the part of the students applied to the various forms of the target language which one will encounter in the classroom. The authors then conclude by exemplifying some of their proposed methods with respect to the various spoken and written modes of language.

The paper by Chela de Rodriquez takes up the question of teaching certain aspects of English stress to speakers of Spanish. After outlining some of the specific problems that Spanish speakers have in this area, the author puts forth some of the preliminaries which are involved in teaching English stress and in testing the results of this teaching. Her paper contains a number of suggestions and exercises which can be used in the classroom, as well as some tests which can serve to evaluate students' progress.

Contributors

Sonia K. Aller
Indiana University

Wayne K. Aller
Indiana State University

Michael Canale
Ontario Institute for Studies in Educat

Greg Carlson
University of Massachusetts

Susanne Carroll
Ontario Institute for Studies in Educat

Bertha Chela de Rodriguez
University of Kansas

Rodolfo J. Cortina
University of Wisconsin—Milwaukee

Ruth Ellenberger
University of Minnesota

Monika Forner
University of Minnesota

Stephen J. Gaies
Indiana University

Helen Goodluck
University of Massachusetts

Victoria Chou Hare
University of Wisconsin—Madison

William D. Keel
Indiana University

Barbara Lust
Cornell University

Lina Malouf-Saad
American University of Beirut

Raymond Mougeon
Ontario Institute for Studies in Education

Oliver T. Myers
University of Wisconsin—Milwaukee

Charles Read
University of Wisconsin—Madison

Alberto Rey
Howard University

Thomas Roeper
University of Massachusetts

Amy Sheldon
University of Minnesota

Lawrence Solan
University of Massachusetts

Bernard Spolsky
University of New Mexico

Barbara Stack
University of Massachusetts

Marcia Steyaert
University of Minnesota

Tatsuko Kaneda Wakayama
Detroit, Michigan

Studies
in
First and Second
Language
Acquisition

Part 1

First Language Acquisition

Chapter 1

Assumptions, Methods and Goals in Language Acquisition Research

Amy Sheldon

For a long time, one of the most central questions in language acquisition research has been "What is the role of linguistic theory in a theory of language acquisition?" Since acquisition research is concerned with characterizing not only *what* the learner has learned about language, but also *how* they have learned it, how strategies of language comprehension and production interact with linguistic knowledge and how the learner's capacities change over time, we are thus concerned with both the linguistic and psychological factors in learning. And it is not always easy to keep them straight. The fact that there is no agreement in psycholinguistic research about the relation between the grammar and the processes of language comprehension and production is a sign of the complexity of language behavior and of the methodological problems that we face in studying it. What I would like to do here is to examine certain assumptions and methodologies that have prevailed in language acquisition research and that have fashioned our mental set with regard to how we view acquisition. A good deal of acquisition research has attempted to fit its findings into the prevailing conception of acquisition. However, there is a growing interest in alternative models of language acquisition. If we can clarify what the issues are, we will have a better chance of seeing what some viable alternatives are. Thus, I hope that the outcome of these remarks will encourage people to consider alternatives and to explore new and promising avenues of research.

Let us start by looking at a common method of investigating child language and the assumptions that underlie it. The method is to collect data on the presence of a particular structure in the language of children, for example, questions. The next step is to take a linguistic description of the adult language and compare it with a linguistic description that is constructed to represent the child language. Usually it is the current transformational grammar fragment of this structure for the adult, which is compared to a transformational grammar fragment for the child or children that are being studied. One conclusion that such studies come to is that the comparison of the child's grammar and the adult's grammar reveals the difference and similarities in what children "know," e.g., about questions and what adults "know" about questions.

Thus, for a long time, a standard methodology that has been used to demonstrate what the child learns about language has been linguistic, that is, the method has been to write a transformational grammar for the child in light of a transformational grammar for the adult. For example, the transformational grammar writing methodology has figured in most studies of the acquisition of questions: Klima and Bellugi (1966); Gruber (1967); Brown, Cazden, and Bellugi (1968); Brown (1968); Brown and Hanlon (1970); Ravem (1974); and Hurford (1975). This methodology is a reflection of the extent to which current linguistic research has created a framework for acquisition research.

It is true that writing transformational grammars for children is less popular these days than it was, due in part to Chomsky's (1964b) remarks. He said: (emphasis is mine)

> *It seems that if anything far reaching and real is to be discovered about the actual grammar of the child, then rather devious kinds of observations of his performance, his abilities and his comprehension in many different kinds of circumstances will have to be brought to bear on the attempt to determine what is in fact his underlying linguistic competence. Direct description of the child's actual output is no more likely to provide an account of the real underlying competence in the case of child language than in the case of adult language, ability to multiply, or any other nontrivial rule governed behavior.*   (p. 36)

So even though we have broadened the data base to include other kinds of observations about child language than their productions, and we have begun to use multiple measures of our subjects' language ability, and while we are now accounting for behavior in terms of "perceptual strategies" as well as "rules," nevertheless, language acquisition research is basically conceptualized within the Chomskyan, i.e., linguistic framework and continues to reflect its mentalistic assumptions about grammar. In 1973, Slobin pointed out the need for a consideration of these foundational issues in the field. He said:

> *A problem of structural analysis which has barely been faced . . . is the feasibility of using linguistic theory as a model for the mental structures*

underlying child speech. The issue of "psychological reality" of linguistic models is a deep and general problem in psycholinguistics . . . arguments (about whether "mental grammar" equals "linguistic grammar") have yet to be fully elaborated in developmental psycholinguistics.   (p. 173)

Let us examine what the assumptions about language acquisition are in the current framework, including what the role of the linguist's grammar is in acquisition research, and then let's look at some alternative assumptions and new, productive avenues of research that are mindful of psychological considerations as well as linguistic ones.

For those of us who became interested in language acquisition research in the Chomskyan framework, certain assumptions "came with the territory" so to speak. I will mention seven of them.

First, a learner constructs a grammar. According to this conception of language acquisition, the grammar plus the psychological operations that we use to produce and understand sentences together form our linguistic and psychological competencies as a kind of "central intelligence agency."

Second, a learner acquires a *transformational* grammar.[1]

A third assumption is that the kind of grammar that learners construct, that is, an actual speaker grammar or a mental grammar is the same grammar that the linguist constructs. In other words, the linguist's grammar is psychologically real. It has selected from among the many possible generalizations that might be made about the sentences of a language certain ones that are linguistically significant and that correspond to the generalizations that a child hearing such utterances would actually arrive at in constructing her grammar.

A fourth assumption is that the learner constructs the simplest, optimal grammar capable of generating the set of possible utterances in the language. Thus the learner should be constructing the maximally general rule possible.

Fifth, the formal, *linguistic* simplicity criteria that a linguist uses to arrive at a descriptively adequate linguistic grammar will be the same *psychological* criteria that learners use in constructing their mental grammar.

Sixth, a transformational grammar that is written for a child and one that is written for an adult are equivalent even though the grammar writers use different evidence of knowledge. The adult grammar is based on speakers' intuitions of grammaticality, of sentence relatedness, and of ambiguity. No such evidence is ordinarily used for the child, because it is exceedingly difficult to get, for young children at least.

A seventh assumption is that all learners have the same language acquisition device, so that individual variation in actual speakers' grammars will only be due to environmental differences in input, not to different intellectual abilities, or to different learning strategies or styles.

Let's look at these assumptions more closely. The assumption that children learn a transformational grammar and that the linguist's transformational grammar is the actual speaker grammar, was articulated by Chomsky in *Aspects*:

> *On the basis of the best information available, it seems reasonable to suppose that a child cannot help constructing* a particular sort of transformational grammar *to account for the data presented to him.*
> (p. 59, emphasis mine)

Notice that this is an unsubstantiated claim. It is not an empirically supported claim since Chomsky does not say what the evidence is that does make it seem reasonable to suppose this. In addition, he does not present *any* evidence against the contrary claim—namely, that children do *not* acquire a transformational grammar. This then is an equally reasonable alternative to his claim, and will remain so until evidence to the contrary is given.

The assumption that children learn a transformational grammar is held by many linguists, e.g., Kiparsky (1968). And it has filtered down to acquisition research. Gough (1967) said:

> *The child . . . somehow develops phrase structure rules and transformational rules . . . he learns a transformational grammar.*   (p. 108)

Brown (1968) in his description of the development of questions in child speech says:

> *The first* wh *questions seem to be unanalysed routines or constructions not involving transformations. As wh- questions become more complex and varied several kinds of evidence of transformational knowledge emerge.* (p. 279)

In a more explicit mentalistic statement, when Brown is referring to the acquisition of the rule of question movement, which moves an interrogated NP to the front of a sentence, he says:

> *The derivational rules operate with abstract dummy elements (i.e., he's referring to the NP that gets fronted, in the rule of question movement) that function as symbols for an unspecified instance of a constituent. Therefore, the child must be able to form from linguistic data . . . the idea of an "unknown," an algebraic "x" that is of a given type.* (p. 287)

Brown (1973) reflects the same point of view:

> *Generative grammars have, as their ultimate point, a distinctly psychological goal. They are intended to represent formally the knowledge that the native speaker must somehow utilize in producing and understanding sentences. Insofar as a grammar has correctly captured this knowledge it does not seem unreasonable that the relative complexity of derivations will be a determinant of the order of their acquisition.* (p. 406)

Gruber (1967) discusses the child's acquisition of questions in the same mentalistic terms:

> But if we assume that the child has internalized an inversion transforma-tion . . . especially if it is a precurser of the adult transformation, then we would expect it to remain in some form as a part of his grammar at subsequent stages of development. (p. 426)

Slobin (1971b), discussing Bellugi-Klima's (1968) work on questions says:

> Bellugi-Klima found that at the same stage at which a child produced wh-questions like "What he can ride in?" he also produced inverted yes-no questions like, "Can he ride in a truck?" Thus the child was also able to perform the grammatical operation of inversion, or transposing. It seems, therefore, that both preposing and transposing are "psychologically real" operations for the child, for we have evidence that he can perform each of them singly. Apparently, there is some performance limitation, some restriction on "sentence programming span" which blocks the application of both operations together at this stage of development. The child's "error" thus reveals his use of grammatical transformations. (p. 51)

Hurford (1975) says:

> A child's mistakes (in repeating the copula in wh-questions, e.g., "Whose is that is") may in this case be very simply accounted for by postulating that he has internalized an imperfect version of an adult rule (of auxiliary inversion). If this is accepted, then the child's mistakes must be said to provide evidence for the existence of the (inversion) rule. (p. 301)

The assumption that learners acquire a transformational grammar is made in second language acquisition research as well. For example, Eckman (1977), in discussing the difference between German and English obstruents in word final position, says:

> It should now be possible to apply the Contrastive Analysis Hypothesis to the generative descriptions of German and English to determine the directionality of difficulty, since a generative grammar, unlike a taxonomic description, is a representation of what a native speaker has learned.

The second language learning literature also frequently assumes an innate language facility in humans. Thus, Selinker (1974) says:

> I will assume the existence of latent (language) structure . . . which, according to Lenneberg, (a) is an already formulated arrangement in the brain, (b) is the biological counterpart to universal grammar, and (c) is

> *transformed by the infant into the* realized structure *of a particular grammar in accordance with certain maturational stages.*   (p. 33)

Jenkins (1976) also assumes that there is an innate linguistic theory in humans that can be referred to in explanations of mistakes that second language learners do and do not make. He says:

> *Thus we are faced with a paradox, the second language learner makes certain kinds of errors, but not others, indicating that he knows that the rule of question formation is structure dependent rather than structure independent. And yet he has never been given the relevant instruction or evidence to know this. Thus, in a sense he "knows without experience." The task then for error analysis is to explain why the second language learner makes certain kinds of errors, rather than other logically possible ones. . . . If as we have seen, the learner knows that the principle of structure dependence holds (rather than some principle of structure independence) without having had any relevant experience to decide this, then it seems quite reasonable to assume that he knew it all along, independent of his linguistic experience; i.e., the principle is innate (=inborn), a part of his biological makeup. . . . We therefore conclude that the knowledge that rules like question formation are structure dependent rather than structure independent is genetically encoded in the child and that the knowledge that one is going to find structure dependent rules in human languages is much like the "knowledge" that one is going to have red hair . . . i.e., it is in large part genetically guided as is the growth of any bodily organ.*

If we assume that children learn a transformational grammar, there are a number of problems associated with this model of language acquisition and a number of psychological questions that are not dealt with in this framework. First, what reason do we have to assume that a transformational grammar, that is, a recursive rewriting system, an algorithm for computing or predicting the sentences of a language, is what speakers learn about their language? It has not been demonstrated that languages can *only* be described by a transformational grammar of the sort that Chomsky has in mind. How do we know that a child acquires a transformational grammar rather than another kind of grammar? And why should we assume this?

Second, if we accept that children acquire a grammar of some sort, then why do we expect that the grammar that a linguist writes as a nonmentalistic description of *language* will also be a mentalistic description of the actual rules that *people* have acquired? In what sense do we mean that a speaker "knows" a grammar? Do we mean "know" in the sense of knowing *that* or of knowing *how*? Do we mean explicit knowledge or tacit knowledge? And what criteria should we use to determine if children are *following* these rules? Since transformational grammar has not been demonstrated to have psychological content, we can only interpret a transformational grammar as a *metaphor* for the generalizations that speakers know about sentences. Thus, transformational grammars represent knowing *that* and not knowing *how*. If *any* kind of linguist's grammar is just a metaphor for what speakers know, then in order to do acquisition research and to compare the learner's language to the native adult language, all we need is a good reference grammar: one that expresses true generalizations about the sentences of the language in as direct, explicit and complete a fashion as possible. It is *possible* to use a transformational grammar as a reference grammar, *if* the generalizations about the language are stated straightforwardly in the grammar. Thus it is possible to interpret the standard transformational grammar of question formation as descriptive statements about the *structure* of questions rather than procedures for computing the derivation of a question. For example, the standard rules for question word preposing and subject-auxiliary inversion can be interpreted as generalizations about word order. The preposing rule, which in a transformational grammar moves an unspecified, interrogated NP to the front of the sentence, can be interpreted as saying that information questions in English have a *wh*-word in sentence initial position. The inversion rule can be interpreted as saying that in information questions as well as yes-no questions, the subject occurs after the first verb. Hutchinson (1978) discusses this difference between interpreting rules in a grammar as instructions for generating sentences, that is as rewriting rules, or as true generalizations about sentences. He points out that many generalizations about language are not stated directly in a transformational grammar, but depend instead on our using the grammar to prove or state them. For example, if in a grammar every deep structure has a subject and there is a rule that deletes subjects in imperative sentences, the grammar does not state the generalization that every sentence in the language except imperatives must contain a subject. This generalization is true of all sentences generated by the grammar, but it is the grammar *user* who deduces this from their knowledge of the rules of grammar.

A grammar that is a set of true generalizations of this sort need not be an unordered set of generalizations. As we all know from experience with ordinary descriptive reference grammars, there are more or less optimal ways of organizing and presenting these descriptive statements.

The point is, if there are alternative linguistic descriptions—all of which account for the facts—is this an empirical issue for language acquisition research? The answer is no, unless we have evidence that these linguistic descriptions describe speakers and not only sentences. If transformational grammars describe "knowledge" only in a very general metaphorical sense in which no claims are made that the *form* of the rules is what is learned, but only the substance of the rules, then these grammars have no psychological content. If transformational grammars are not actual speaker grammars, then the question of how a child should learn such an abstract formal system of rules is beside the point. The postulation of an innate linguistic theory—the Language Acquisition Device—is beside the point also.

If we put our mentalist hat back on and we assume that speakers *have* learned a transformational grammar and that a linguist's transformational grammar *is* the speaker's mental grammar, or at least it is intended to be, then there are a number of psychological considerations that should enter into the evaluation and construction of transformational grammars. This point has been discussed at length by a number of people in the last few years: Watt (1970, 1972), Derwing (1973), and Hutchinson (1974), to name a few. I would like to discuss what some of these considerations are.

The Chomskyan view of language acquisition is that of an "instantaneous process." It does not take into consideration how language learning takes place. All language acquisition takes place in stages, and for children, over a long period of time. We want to know what the *process* of change is like, not only what the facts are about each stage. How did we come to learn what we know? How did we get from one grammar to another? *If* the product of language learning *is* a mental grammar, then instead of constructing the adult grammar on the basis of synchronic data from the adult, shouldn't we start by writing the simplest (optimal) grammar for the child at each stage, until we reach the final, adult product? Why don't we construct a model of a child's grammar and then look at what we have to do to the existing grammar to get the optimal grammar for the next stage? Children don't construct grammars based on the same full corpus that the linguist works with. Why should we assume that they'll wind up with an optimal linguist's grammar if they don't have the full corpus from the beginning? If the child is constructing optimal grammars then the simplest way to get from the first grammar to the final adult grammar may result in a different final learner grammar than the linguist's grammar. The final learner grammar may be different from the linguist's grammar because of the stages that it takes to get there. While the learner and the linguist may be grammarians, we should not take it for granted that they will arrive at the same generalizations about the language.

If we assume that the linguist's grammar is the learner's final mental grammar, then there should be some way to decide if they match. One question that needs to be investigated, then, is whether children keep adding rules to their grammar or whether they restructure their grammar. It is usually assumed that children restructure their grammar rather than add new rules (e.g., Hall 1964). Ingram (1975) claims that children do not acquire many of the transformations in English until between six and twelve years of age, and at this time they restructure their grammar and construct the transformational component.

If we assume that children restructure their mental grammar, and if the grammar is different from their procedures for comprehending and producing sentences, then we are faced with a puzzling complication in our conception of language learning. For example, it is well known that children learn certain forms that in a linguist's grammar are derivationally late forms, before they learn the linguist's derivationally prior forms. One example of this is the acquisition of prenominal adjectives before the acquisition of relative clauses. A standard analysis derives prenominal adjectives in a construction like *the big truck* from relative clauses that contain adjectives like, *the truck that is big*, by a series of transformational rules. But if we assume that this is a psychologically real grammar, i.e., that the child is learning these rules, then we are forced to say that the child restructures their mental grammar, and abandons their first, presumably phrase structure, rule, which directly generates prenominal adjectives, for a more elaborate and abstract derivation. The linguist has formal reasons for preferring to generate prenominal adjectives in this fashion. But why should *learners* prefer this grammar? And if this is an empirical claim, there should be some empirical differences between a model that claims learning proceeds by restructuring rules or by adding rules, and it should be possible to test these claims with learners. In addition, if at the first stage when they don't have adjectives in relative clauses children have developed adequate psychological procedures for producing and understanding prenominal adjectives, then do they change these processing procedures if the grammar is restructured? What is the effect of grammar change on these procedures? We might well wonder, if the learner has the procedures for producing and understanding sentences, and if we can account for the facts of language with these procedures, then why do we postulate that the speaker also has a grammar, that is, something that is different from the operations that produce and understand sentences? If grammatical knowledge can be derived from our sentence producing or comprehending operations, then shouldn't we put our efforts into constructing a model of language processing?

We are beginning to get data that is relevant to the questions that I have been raising, and I would like to turn to what I consider some very promising and important avenues of research that can help us solve some of these puzzles.

There is already some evidence that shows that learners only slowly reach the maximal generalization possible about the data, and that psychological and semantic factors intervene and apparently prevent the learner from making the maximal linguistic generalization. For example, there is evidence that the passive-active relation between sentences fails to become syntactically general for many years. Maratsos and Abramovitch (1975) found that three year olds understood full passives that contained action verbs like *push* and *tickle* in which the surface, passive subject NP is acted upon, as in *John was tickled*, but they had difficulty with the verb *chase*, in a sentence like *the old lady was chased by Tommy*. Maratsos and Abramovitch point out that in the case of *chase*, the surface subject *the old lady* is not only being acted on passively, but she is also doing something active; she is also running around. Sinclair et al. (1971) found that passives with *follow* were difficult for five and six year olds. Notice that in the case of *follow*, as in *John was followed by Mary*, the surface subject *John* is acting with "more independence" than the NP that is the agent, i.e., *Mary*, who is following the movement that has been initiated by the surface subject. Similar differences in the comprehension of passive sentences depending on whether the verbs are actional, e.g., *push* or nonactional, e.g., *like* have been found by Maratsos and his colleagues. Maratsos (1978) concludes that:

> *Subjects appear to have acquired general knowledge about actional passive forms and knowledge of a few nonactional passives, but seem still to lack a general, semantics-free comprehension of passives in terms of underlying grammatical relations.*

Maratsos and Kuczaj (1976) used an elicited imitation task to determine the extent to which three and four year olds related the full negative form: *Aux + not* and the contracted negative form: *Aux + n't*. Adult grammars (Chomsky, 1957; Klima, 1964) have captured the relationship between sentences with the full negative form and those with the contracted negative form by means of an optional rule of negative contraction: *The girl could not find the toy → The girl couldn't find the toy*. The researchers discovered that there was a great deal of individual variation in the extent to which children's behavior reflected their knowledge of this generalization at all, and the extent to which they applied it in the environment of all auxiliaries. Thus some children appeared not to have had the rule at all, while some children did not have as general a rule as is postulated in adult grammars. The question is: Why don't some children have this rule? *If* they have been exposed to the data all along, why haven't they made the connection between *not* and *n't*? If the data has been in the environment all along for children, and some don't make the maximal generalization then why should we assume that all *adults* do?

Another example of undergeneralization in syntax by learners is the nongeneralization of *auxiliary—subject* word order from yes-no questions to *wh*-questions in the early stages of question acquisition. As yet we have no clear understanding of the reason for this undergeneralization.

Another example of undergeneralization in children's two-word utterances is the data noted by Braine (1976) that "size" adjectives such as *big* and *little* were the only ones to combine with nouns at a time when the child did have other adjectives but used them as one-word utterances only—not in combination with nouns.

Other examples of learning suggest that the development of syntactic generalizations interacts with psychological factors. For example, Sheldon (1977) found that the ease of comprehension of four types of subject and object relative sentences by both French- and English-speaking children depended on such factors as a parallel function strategy, an adjacency strategy and an extraposition strategy. The effect of these factors on comprehension was such that even ten year old French-speaking children had not mastered certain kinds of relative constructions. Other cases of the interaction between perceptual processes and grammar acquisition have been cited by Bever (1970). And many examples of undergeneralization can be found in children's acquisition of word meanings (Bowerman, in press; Bloom, 1973). Why do learners only slowly reach what in the linguist's grammar is a fully general linguistic representation? Why is there individual variation in how general learner's linguistic representations are at a stage in language learning? Why do some learners make generalizations that others do not? How general are the rules that they learn and is there individual variation in the generality of linguistic knowledge among fluent adult speakers also? The little evidence that we have suggests that child grammars at least may not be as Chomsky (1965:58) claimed, namely, "strikingly uniform and independent of intelligence, motivation and emotional state." We are just beginning to explore the evidence for individual variation, and it is important to continue to do so. Since it is the case that *extreme* differences in IQ and *extreme* differences in environment cause clear-cut language differences, as in the case of mentally retarded individuals (Guess and Baer, 1973), and individuals like Genie (Curtiss et al., 1974) who suffered severe environmental deprivation, then we can not take it for granted that less immediately obvious internal and environmental differences don't also play a role in language competence. And it is important to our conception of *how* learning takes place to know the extent and nature of that variation.

Many language acquisition studies have begun to examine the learner's linguistic input in an effort to find environmental factors that at least correlate with language development and possibly have a determining effect on it. Research has shown that the linguistic facts that are available to the first and second language learner are highly restricted, certainly more restricted than the facts available to the linguist constructing an adult grammar. We have evidence that more linguistically knowledgeable speakers, whether they are parents, adults who don't have children, older siblings, or classroom language teachers, all quite automatically provide a modified corpus as well as many intensive language training procedures involving the learner directly and requiring his/her participation. This modified corpus is gradually enlarged to include new structures (Phillips, 1970, 1973; Sachs and Devin, 1976). How long the learner's corpus remains restricted is an open question, and one that has a bearing on the nature of their grammar and the order of language development.

What is important in the study of these environmental factors is not to observe only the child's input but also what the *interaction* of child and parent, or second language learner and teacher, is. This will enable us to observe what the effects of input modification and language training practices are on the learner. For example, the correlation of variables such as frequency and order of input presentation with frequency and order of acquisition are important for both first and second language acquisition. Order of presentation and frequency of examples are factors in the presentation of data that form the basis of rule induction, and they have been shown to be important independent variables in controlled laboratory studies of learning (Palermo and Parish, 1971; Foss, 1968a, b). The role that frequency plays in parental speech is unclear. It has been downplayed by Brown (1973), but the data that he presents are not conclusive; for example, frequency of occurrence does correlate with the order of acquisition of certain forms such as the prepositions *in* and *on* in his data. Correlations between the parent's frequency of use and the child's have been found in other studies (Bowerman, 1973; Brown and Hanlon, 1970). Forner (this volume) discusses correlations that she found for both parental frequency and order of introduction with the child's order of acquisition.

In second language acquisition studies Hatch (1974) found a correlation between the questions that were most frequent in a learner's input and the ones that he used first. Larsen-Freeman (1976) found a significant correlation between second language learners' common morpheme difficulty order and the frequency of these morphemes in adult native speaker speech based on Brown's data for the three sets of parents he studied.

There are other factors—potential training procedures in the learner's environment—that may help draw the learner's attention to certain language facts, enable them to practice and memorize linguistic forms, and thus to construct certain generalizations and perhaps ignore others. In talking about second language learning Corder makes the distinction between "input" and "intake." That is, data may be present in the environment but not taken in by the learner. Certain ways in which language is *used* in learner-parent or learner-teacher interactions may cause a learner to notice language facts, or may make language learning easier or faster. While there may be certain universal characteristics in parent-child or teacher-learner interactions, we are probably going to find many differences also. We should therefore not underestimate the influence that this variation has on learners. We know that some teachers are more effective language trainers, and probably some parents are more effective language trainers too. We know that adult second language learners vary greatly in their learning styles and abilities. We need to know more about how first language learners vary in their learning styles and in their language development, and what the limits are of that variation.

A number of observations have been made of apparent language training practices in the learner's environment. Snow (1972), Broen (1972), and Kobashigawa (1969) found that repetitions are very frequent in parental speech to children. So are the pattern practice kinds of drills that are the stock and trade of most language teachers (Paulston and Bruder, 1976).

An illustration of the way teaching seems to be going on in parent-child interactions can be found in Brown's report (1968) of the acquisition of questions by Adam, Eve and Sara. Brown observed that at his Stage 3, the children were producing declarative sentences with subject nouns, main verbs, object nouns, and adverbials. However, they were not successful in answering questions that parents asked about these constituents. They were correct only about half the time. During this period, Brown noticed that the mothers would use what second language teachers would call a "sentence completion drill" or "substitution drill." The mother would use an occasional question form, that is, a sentence with question intonation that has the question word at the end. She would use this to ask the child to repeat an unintelligible word or to prod them to answer her:

> *say-it-again*
> *Child*:   I want !†%&*
> *Adult*:   You want what?
> *Child*:   Milk
>
> *prompt*
> *Adult*:   What do you want?
> *Child*:   (no answer)

> *Adult*:   You want what?
> *Child* :   Milk

These exchanges look like instructional routines that teach grammatical information, that is, they relate the question word—in this case—*what* to the NP that it refers to or replaces in a declarative sentence. This exchange provides information that can teach the child how to answer questions, and it actually prods him to *try* to answer. Brown found that the mother's routine of using an occasional question to prompt the children, or to get them to repeat an unintelligible constituent, was used very frequently in the stage when children were *not* answering the mother's ordinary question—which has the question word at the front. It is a form that was used *before* the child was able to produce and answer questions correctly. It usually was used by the parent when the regular form didn't get a response, since it was more likely to elicit an appropriate response from the child than the regular form. The parents differed in how frequently each used the occasional question form to their child. Brown found that the occasional question form was used "much more frequently by mothers of the two children (Adam and Eve) whose grammatical understanding developed more rapidly" than Sara's, and less often by Sara's mother (Brown, Cazden, Bellugi, 1973:331). Granted this is a rather rough measure of the effectiveness of this technique as a teaching aid. But what this example does show, however, is that parents differ in the extent to which they provide the learner with potentially useful linguistic data, and they differ in their persistence, and in their attention to child speech. We might guess that a listener who is supplying richer linguistic data to a learner, and who is actively training and engaging the learner in language use, would be *helping* the learner to learn language. Parents and language teachers can be so helpful that they will often ask the question and then turn around and supply the answer, as the following examples with Sean Forner illustrate:[2]

> *Adult (babysitter)*:   Now what did you do yesterday?
> *Sean (17 mos.)*:   Becky!
> *Adult*:   Yeah and Becky. What did you all do? Sean? Did you play games? or what did you do?
> *Sean*:   Games
>
> *(Translated from German)*
> *Adult (mother)*:   What's that?
> *Sean (17 mos.)*:   de
> *Adult*:   That's the clock. And what's that here, Sean? What's that?
> *Sean*:   And that
> *Adult*:   That's a balloon
> *Adult*:   What's that?
> *Sean*:   Egg
> *Adult*:   An egg. Exactly, very good.

Adult (babysitter):   What did you tell them? Did you tell them how old
      you were, Sean?
Sean (29 mos.):   Yeah
Adult: How old did you say you were? You say "two years old"? That
      what you told them?
Sean: Ah. In the balloon I draw

Clark, Hutcheson and Van Buren (1973) point out that their subject Adam almost always echoed the part of adult utterances that carried the major pitch change. If the adult's answer to their own question carries the major pitch change and the child notices it and repeats it, then this kind of adult-child interaction can be a very useful technique for teaching how to answer questions.

Discourse analysis as a method of studying the language acquisition process has been engaging the efforts of a growing number of workers in second language acquisition also. Hatch (1976) points out that discourse analysis shows that even though learners may be uttering one or two words at a time, if we observe their behavior in the framework of a conversation, they and their listener are partners in building more complex syntactic structure. Studying conversations can provide important data about how learners are taught about language and how they teach themselves.

Hatch points out that the learner will frequently start the conversation by establishing the topic. The adult subsequently builds a conversation with the learner that clarifies or comments on the topic. Here are some examples of very beginning child second language learners:

(Scollen, 1974)
Child: Hiding
Adult: Hiding? What's hiding?
Child: Balloon

(Huang, 1970)
Child: oh-oh
Adult: What?
Child: This (points to an ant)
Adult: It's an ant
Child: Ant

Many children at this stage will repeat and play with utterances, possibly to practice their language skills, or just to keep the conversation going.

(Itoh, 1973)
Child: This broken
Native speaker: Broken
Child: Broken. This /əz/ broken. Broken.

Native speaker: Upside down
  Child: Upside down
           This broken
           Upside down
           Broken

When the learner begins to decrease the number of immediate repetitions they nevertheless stay close to the data provided by the adult, restating it in another way or making corrections in their previous incorrect repetitions:

(Hatch, 1976)
  Adult: It's a garage. Come in garage
  Child: /kəmən/ garage. /nay/ your (=not yours)
  Adult: This is yours.
  Child: /nay/ yours (note morphology correction)
           Come back
           You do garage to here
  Adult: No. The garage is too small
  Child: Small garage?
  Adult: Mmm. I can't come in. Right?
  Child: Okay. You'll can.

Such repetitions or restatements give the learner much opportunity to practice and check their repetitions against the adult model, keep the conversation going, and hear longer stretches of the language before they can produce these longer stretches themselves. Some learners may need linguistic richness and helpful training more than others. And linguistic environments that are much less rich or helpful or repetitive could affect the rapidity and nature of the development of language. We don't know enough about these possibilities. Further research in this area could certainly have practical consequences for the improvement of adult language teaching and methodology. It also can tell us whether learners are different in important ways and what environmental factors play a role in their differences.

In conclusion, I have shown that the conception of language learning that comes from transformational linguistics makes certain unsubstantiated claims about learners: basically, that all children learn a transformational grammar and that they accomplish this by virtue of the same innate, specifically linguistic endowment. But there are equally reasonable alternative conceptions of language learning that have not been ruled out. Before we postulate an abstract formal system like a transformational grammar and a specifically linguistic genetic mechanism, we must *show* that language can not be learned by general principles of induction and cognition that develop in the normal interaction between the child and their environment. This means that we need to observe what learners actually do, how they learn their language. The little evidence that we have indicates that language learning may not be as fast, as easy, or as uniform for all learners, or as independent of environmental influence and assistance as we had imagined. The more we can account for learning on the basis of environmental factors, the less complex will be the psychological mechanisms that we will have to postulate for learners. If second language learning is different from first, it may not be because a linguistic Language Acquisition Device has shut down as has been claimed, e.g., Selinker (1974). It may be because adults have learned many things in their lives, and the combination of these learning experiences and their native capacities have produced different proficiencies in remembering, speaking, and understanding, as well as different strategies in how they go about learning.

We are beginning to explore some of these alternative conceptions of acquisition. There are many promising avenues of empirical research, and we can look forward to a deeper understanding of how we learn language, as well as what it is that we have learned.

Notes

I would like to acknowledge the helpful comments of L. Hutchinson, C. Ringen, J. Ringen, B. Robinett, and G. Sanders on earlier drafts of this paper.

1. Watt's coinage.
2. Data from tape recordings made by M. Forner.

Chapter 2

The Mother as LAD:
Interaction between
Order and Frequency
of Parental Input
and Child Production

Monika Forner

The empirical specter of frequency of modeling as a variable which at least to some extent determines language acquisition has persistently disquieted scholars of mentalist orientation. If the strong innateness hypothesis in the form first introduced in Chomsky (1965), which attributes to the child innate knowledge of universally valid formal (i.e., syntactic) properties of language embodied in a language-specific (as opposed to generally cognitive) acquisition device, were correct, modeling frequency should not be a variable relevant to the progress of language acquisition. It would have to be grouped, together with "semantic reference" and "use of language in real-life situations," under

> certain kinds of data and experience (which) may be required in order to set the language acquisition device into operation, although they may not affect the manner of its functioning in the least. (p. 33)

Such "external data," according to Chomsky, thus may serve "the function of initiating or facilitating the operation of innate mechanisms," but they should not serve "the function of determining ... the direction that learning will take" (p. 34). It follows that if it could be shown that such empirically observable variables as modeling frequency (or semantic reference, or situationally determined use of language) do indeed determine "the direction that learning will take," the abstract and elusive language acquisition device (LAD) as perceived by Chomsky (1965) and McNeill (1970) would be rendered obsolete and the theory of language acquisition of which it is a part would have to be modified or abandoned.

Unfortunately, for scholars of this particular theoretical orientation, differential frequencies of parental usage have been found to be related to the proportions of appropriate responses to different *wh*-questions and therefore presumably to their comprehension, to the order of emergence of structurally different sentence types and different prepositions, and to differential child frequencies of possessive constructions and different possible word orders in Finnish and Dutch (Brown, Cazden, and Bellugi, 1968; Brown and Hanlon, 1970; Bowerman, 1973; Klein, 1974).

Despite all efforts to the contrary, these apparent influences of parental frequency on child language have never been convincingly explained away. However, while Brown, Cazden, and Bellugi in 1968 still consented that "there is a small amount of evidence that modeling frequency does affect the acquisition of knowledge" (p. 332), Brown in 1973 concluded that "there is an approximate invariant order of acquisition, and behind this invariance lies not modeling frequency but semantic and grammatical complexity" (p. 379). Since Brown also remarks that for the particular aspects of the acquisition of English as a first language which he investigated it seems impossible to separate transformational[1] and semantic complexity, the above statement should probably read "semantic and/or grammatical complexity."

Brown's conclusion appears to have pronounced a death sentence upon studies of parental frequency in relation to language acquisition. Thus any study that attempts to revive this subject, as this one does, will first have to account for Brown's strongest argument, the apparent lack of correlation between parental frequency and order of acquisition of the fourteen grammatical morphemes he investigated. It is my contention that Brown here compared items which cannot be compared. Whenever a comparison was made between parental frequency and children's order of production or frequency of use of items that were part of a particular subsystem of the English language, a relationship was found between parents and children. There is, however, no system short of the English language as a whole that would include two prepositions, articles as a group, the copula and auxiliary, and a few selected inflectional endings. If parents adjust their frequencies when talking to their children, they must be able to systematically favor one form over another. Thus although it would be possible, for example, to favor *in* and *on* over other prepositions, or simple active affirmative declaratives over negative truncated yes/no-questions (or vice versa, for that matter), there would be no systematic basis for favoring, for example, the present progressive over articles or the preposition *in* over the uncontractible auxiliary. Bound morphemes, on the other hand, reflect different systems which the parents might favor. Thus strong emphasis on elaboration of the noun phrase on the part of the parent should yield a higher number of plurals and possessives, while emphasis on elaboration of the verb phrase might be reflected in a higher number of past tenses and third person inflections.

Table 2.1

Rank orders for parental frequencies and order of acquisition
for bound- and process-morphemes discussed in Brown (1973)

	Parental frequencies			Order of acquisition		
	Adam	Sarah	Eve	Adam	Sarah	Eve
Present progressive	2	3	1	1	2.5	1
Plural	3	1	2	2	1	2.5
Past irregular	1	2	4	3	2.5	5
Possessive	6	5	3	4.5	4	2.5
Past regular	4	6	5.5	7	6	4
3rd person regular	6	4	5.5	6	5	6
3rd person irregular	6	7	7	4.5	7	7

Table 2.2

Correlation coefficients for parental frequencies and order of
acquisition of bound- and process-morphemes discussed in Brown (1973)

Adam's parents—Sarah's parents	r = .704*
Adam's parents—Eve's parents	r = .560
Sarah's parents—Eve's parents	r = .721*
Adam—Sarah	r = .782**
Adam—Eve	r = .573
Sarah—Eve	r = .673*
Adam's parents—Adam	r = .636 (past tenses omitted r = .918**)
Sarah's parents—Sarah	r = .955****
Eve's parents—Eve	r = .927***

    * p < .10
   ** p < .05
  *** p < .01
 **** p < .001

Eliminating the prepositions, the articles, and the copula and auxiliary, which all can or must be used in any number of different subsystems, Pearson product-moment correlation coefficients on the ranks of the remaining seven bound or process-morphemes as if they were raw scores in order to eliminate the problem of ties[2] were calculated. These ranks are listed in *Table 2.1* and the resulting correlation coefficients in *Table 2.2*.

The most striking correlations found are between Sarah and her parents and Eve and her parents. And even if Adam does not correlate with his parents, mainly because of discrepancies in the past tense forms, the correspondence of the relative frequencies of single parents to the acquisition order of their respective children is strong enough to yield a highly significant correlation between the summed ranks of parents and the summed ranks of children, provided in *Table 2.3*.

Table 2.3

Correlation coefficient and summed ranks of parents and children for frequencies and order of acquisition of bound- and process-morphemes discussed in Brown (1973)

	Parents	Children
Present progressive	6	4.5
Plural	6	5.5
Past irregular	7	10.5
Possessive	14	11
Past regular	15.5	17
3rd person regular	15.5	17
3rd person irregular	20	18.5

r = .921, p < .01

Under the assumption that language is a system of subsystems rather than a collection of different functor morphemes, therefore, parental frequency does correlate with acquisition order. Acquisition order, on the other hand, has been demonstrated by Brown to be related also to semantic and/or grammatical complexity. The child's acquisition order therefore is related to parental frequency as well as to complexity. It follows that parents use simple forms more frequently than complex ones.

This observation is not surprising in light of another well-established phenomenon of parental speech, namely the increasing complexity of mothers' speech as their children grow older. Numerous studies of the nature of the input to language-learning children compared mothers' speech to children of different ages and in some cases also to adults (Drach, 1969; Pfuderer, 1969; Phillips, 1970, 1973; Remick, 1971; Broen, 1972; Sachs, Brown, and Salerno, 1972; Snow, 1972; Nelson, 1973; Fraser and Roberts, 1975). The findings are amazingly consistent: Significant differences according to age of addressee are found for various measures of complexity. Mothers' speech is simplest when the child is about one and a half years old; its complexity has increased considerably by two and a half years; and after this age it further increases more slowly but consistently. In all cases in which the mothers' speech to adults was also analyzed, it was found to be significantly more complex than their speech to children.

As interesting as these findings are, their interpretation presents difficulties since the studies on which they are based suffer from a common drawback: They cannot prove a direct relationship between what mothers say and what children learn, because most of them are group studies conducted in a laboratory only once. And even those two studies which are longitudinal (Pfuderer, 1969; Nelson, 1973) compared the same mothers talking to the same children at two different stages only, and despite an increase of complexity over the interval in both the mothers' and the children's speech, the former was still much more complex than even the most advanced child speech. It is thus not surprising that two different surveys of this body of research could yield diametrically opposite conclusions. On the one hand, Snow (1974) argues that these studies should lead to an abandonment of the strong innateness hypothesis because they indicate that language acquisition is guided by the cognitive development of the child and the result of a process of constant interaction between mother and child to which both contribute equally, a process of crucial importance not only to language acquisition but also to the general psychological development of the child. Farwell (1973), on the other hand, rules out the necessity and seems to question even the usefulness of parental input to the process of language learning. In her opinion, these studies seem to show only that the child's language highly affects and restricts the language of the adult, while

> it remains to be proven that this restricted language has any effect on the child's acquisition. In fact it remains to be shown that adult language, simplified or not, has any direct effect on the progress of acquisition.
> (p. 49)

In light of these inconclusive findings, which nevertheless are indicative of certain processes of interaction operative in language acquisition whose possible importance should not be ruled out a priori, this paper, accepting Farwell's challenge, is an attempt to fill the gap left open by the input studies mentioned above by directly comparing over time parental input in terms of frequency and order of introduction of different forms to frequency and order of emergence in child production.

This is not the first such attempt, however. Savić (1975) investigated the same variables, comparing month by month the acquisition of questions by a pair of dizygotic Yugoslav twins with the questions addressed to these children by their parents, and concludes that

> the order in which adults asked the children questions does not correspond to the order in which questions appeared in the children's speech. Nor did the children's frequency of specific question types correspond in any close way to the adults' frequency.   (p. 253)

However, even a superficial glance at Savić's raw data, provided in *Tables 2.4, 2.5,* and *2.6,* reveals a striking linear order of introduction as well as production, and the ranks of frequencies also seem to correspond rather well. Savić bases her claims in particular on the facts that the boy used *whose*-questions later than the girl and that the children asked more *why*-questions than the adults. Individual differences, in learning rates as well as in interests, should however be expected. The crucial question to be asked, in essence the one also asked by Brown, is whether or not relative frequency of modeling and relative order of introduction on the part of the parents are related to relative frequency of use and relative order of emergence in the child's speech.

Table 2.4

Frequency and order of questions addressed to children by adults (Reproduced from Savić (1975) with permission of Cambridge University Press, order of columns modified)

Age in months	Total number of questions	what šta	yes/no da/ne	where gde	how kako	who ko	whose čiji	what kind of kakav	which koji	why zašto	where to kuda	how much/ many koliko	when kada	where from odakle
13*	—	—	—	—	—	—	—	—	—	—	—	—	—	—
14	3	1	1	1	—	—	—	—	—	—	—	—	—	—
15	4	2	—	1	1	—	—	—	—	—	—	—	—	—
16	19	4	8	4	1	2	—	—	—	—	—	—	—	—
17	43	11	6	11	10	1	4	—	—	—	—	2	—	—
18	34	9	10	2	—	4	—	5	2	3	—	—	—	—
19	72	18	14	9	1	7	13	6	2	—	4	—	—	—
20	151	63	22	10	—	31	11	9	1	—	2	—	—	—
21	121	37	13	18	1	26	12	7	1	3	3	—	—	—
22	88	40	12	6	1	17	7	2	—	—	2	—	—	—
23	87	22	21	12	1	8	5	6	—	4	3	1	4	—
24	86	23	19	13	3	16	1	2	4	1	2	—	—	—
25	140	24	29	44	3	14	3	3	13	3	—	2	—	—
26	51	16	4	14	—	9	4	2	—	—	—	2	—	—
27	66	19	12	11	3	5	1	2	6	5	1	1	—	—
28*	—	—	—	—	—	—	—	—	—	—	—	—	—	—
29	88	29	19	8	1	7	2	1	2	18	1	—	—	—
30	70	17	14	11	4	9	2	4	3	4	1	—	1	—
31	57	11	13	10	—	5	1	1	6	1	2	1	5	—
32	42	8	9	3	2	7	2	2	4	1	—	—	4	—
33	52	17	10	6	1	8	3	1	3	—	—	1	1	1
34	74	19	24	11	6	6	2	—	1	3	1	1	—	—
35	63	15	20	2	2	9	—	3	4	3	—	—	4	—
36	37	12	12	1	2	5	—	2	1	2	—	—	—	—
Total	1446	417	292	208	43	196	74	58	54	50	23	12	19	1

*family on vacation

Table 2.5

Frequency and order in question production (Jasmina) (Reproduced from Savić (1975) with permission of Cambridge University Press, order of columns modified)

Age in months	Total number of questions	what šta	yes/no da/ne	where gde	how kako	who ko	whose čiji	what kind of kakav	which koji	why zašto	where to kuda	how much/ many koliko	when kada	where from odakle
13*	—	—	—	—	—	—	—	—	—	—	—	—	—	—
14	1	1	—	—	—	—	—	—	—	—	—	—	—	—
15	—	3	—	—	—	—	—	—	—	—	—	—	—	—
16	—	—	—	—	—	—	—	—	—	—	—	—	—	—
17	—	—	—	—	—	—	—	—	—	—	—	—	—	—
18	—	—	—	—	—	—	—	—	—	—	—	—	—	—
19	8	—	—	1	—	—	—	—	—	—	—	—	—	—
20	16	3	11	2	—	—	—	—	—	—	—	—	—	—
21	24	4	2	17	—	—	—	1	—	—	—	—	—	—
22	10	1	—	9	—	—	—	—	—	—	—	—	—	—
23	32	15	3	13	2	3	—	—	—	—	—	—	—	—
24	31	19	1	5	3	3	1	—	—	—	—	—	—	—
25	127	34	19	28	—	17	10	1	4	1	—	—	—	—
26	33	10	6	6	—	6	2	2	—	1	—	—	—	—
27	68	16	19	15	6	6	2	—	4	—	—	—	—	—
28*	—	—	—	—	—	—	—	—	—	—	—	—	—	—
29	58	12	5	5	5	7	4	2	—	18	—	—	—	—
30	47	8	4	8	5	3	1	3	3	12	—	—	—	—
31	71	20	11	6	7	5	5	2	1	12	—	2	—	—
32	52	12	7	5	3	5	1	1	2	15	1	—	—	—
33	64	12	14	7	3	9	2	3	1	9	—	—	—	—
34	54	9	12	7	8	3	1	1	—	12	—	—	—	—
35	90	19	23	6	9	4	3	2	1	23	1	—	1	—
36	39	5	13	5	2	4	3	2	1	5	2	2	1	—
Total	825	203	157	145	53	72	35	30	17	108	2	2	1	—

*family on vacation

Table 2.6
Frequency and order in question production (Danko) (Reproduced from Savić (1975) with permission of Cambridge University Press, order of columns modified)

Age in months	Total number of questions	what šta	yes/no da/ne	where gde	how kako	who ko	whose čiji	what kind of kakav	which koji	why zašto	where to kuda	how much/many koliko	when kada	where from odakle
13*	—	—	—	—	—	—	—	—	—	—	—	—	—	—
14	1	1	—	—	—	—	—	—	—	—	—	—	—	—
15	1	1	—	—	—	—	—	—	—	—	—	—	—	—
16	—	—	—	—	—	—	—	—	—	—	—	—	—	—
17	1	1	1	—	—	—	—	—	—	—	—	—	—	—
18	2	1	1	—	—	—	—	—	—	—	—	—	—	—
19	3	—	3	—	—	—	—	—	—	—	—	—	—	—
20	12	—	9	3	—	—	—	—	—	—	—	—	—	—
21	14	—	6	8	—	—	—	—	—	—	—	—	—	—
22	17	—	4	13	—	1	—	—	—	—	—	—	—	—
23	18	9	—	8	1	—	—	—	—	—	—	—	—	—
24	19	9	2	7	—	—	—	—	—	—	—	—	—	—
25	75	40	12	11	6	3	—	—	—	1	2	—	—	—
26	30	11	4	6	1	5	—	2	—	—	1	—	—	—
27	51	24	6	8	7	2	—	—	1	—	3	—	—	—
28*	—	—	—	—	—	—	—	—	—	—	—	—	—	—
29	69	17	7	7	4	5	—	1	4	18	5	—	1	—
30	63	16	14	4	4	8	1	1	—	12	2	—	—	1
31	53	12	9	3	3	3	1	2	—	18	2	—	—	—
32	36	12	4	2	1	4	—	1	—	11	1	—	—	—
33	67	5	15	10	—	9	1	1	2	18	1	—	—	—
34	58	11	17	5	3	5	1	3	2	9	2	—	—	—
35	70	19	19	10	6	6	3	3	1	2	1	—	—	—
36	27	6	5	1	2	5	1	—	3	3	1	—	—	1
Total	687	194	138	106	43	56	8	14	13	92	21	—	1	1

*family on vacation

Table 2.7
Correlation coefficients for parental frequency
and order of introduction and children's frequency
and order of production for data presented
in Savić (1975)

7A

Child Frequency	Parental Frequency	Parental Order
Child 1 (Jasmina)	r = .908****	r = .662**
Child 2 (Danko)	r = .912****	r = .609*
Child Order		
Child 1 (Jasmina)	r = .786***	r = .899****
Child 2 (Danko)	r = .854****	r = .641**

7B

Order	Frequency
Parents	r = .619*
Child 1 (Jasmina)	r = .822****
Child 2 (Danko)	r = .822****

* p < .05
** p < .02
*** p < .01
**** p < .001

This question can be answered by calculating correlation coefficients, which Savić failed to do. Since her data, contrary to Brown's, are continuous, it is possible to use raw scores rather than ranks and to calculate r, the Pearson product-moment correlation coefficient, which is both more accurate and more revealing than the Spearman rank order correlation coefficient rho used by Brown, because it is dependent not only on ranks but also on the relative distances between them. The results of calculating r for Savić's data are listed in *Table 2.7.*

Since every possible match and cross-match between the variables for single speakers as well as between the parents' speech and the children's speech yields a significant value of r, the null hypothesis that frequency and order are not related in the language of adults to children, in the language of children, and in the process of linguistic interaction between adults and children must be rejected on the basis of Savić's data.

A relationship, however, does not have to be causal. Since order of acquisition seems to correlate also with semantic and/or grammatical complexity, it might be complexity which determines the adults' as well as the children's frequencies and orders. Only if it could be shown that neither this nor any other variable could independently determine both, could a direct causal relationship between structured input and language learning be assumed.

Table 2.8
Class I: *Wh*-questions

8A   Frequency and order of *wh*-questions addressed to Sean by mother

Age in months	Total number of questions	what was	where wo	who wer	why warum	how wie	what kind was für	when wann	which welcher	excluded: wie macht X
17	494	253	215	14	4	5	②	—	①	66
18	467	267	181	5	5	8	—	①	—	41
19	380	269	73	32	2	3	—	—	①	38
20	422	274	73	58	3	10	4	—	—	7
21	423	317	40	49	6	7	4	—	—	2
22	423	270	58	29	7	24	33	—	2	2
23	410	264	46	48	15	3	30	1	3	8
24	276	182	34	31	9	5	8	3	4	1
25	255	138	46	30	12	2	22	1	4	—
26	274	187	35	27	9	3	10	2	1	—
27	295	189	35	17	25	7	10	—	12	—
28	199	114	32	19	16	5	12	—	1	—
29	228	125	39	29	21	5	8	—	1	—
30	182	83	32	31	16	8	9	2	1	—
31	168	101	17	13	21	3	10	3	—	—
32	76	46	13	4	5	1	4	1	2	—
Total interm.	2609	1650	640	187	27	57	43	1	4	156
Total	4972	3079	969	436	176	99	166	14	33	165

The grammatical intricacies of Serbo-Croatian questions in general and the semantic content of the questions in Savić's corpus are unknown to me. Furthermore, drawing a distinction between cognition (i.e., concept-formation and world-knowledge) and semantics (i.e., knowledge of the lexical and structural meanings of language),[3] I regard the nongrammatical distinctions between different question types to be predominantly of a cognitive rather than a semantic nature.[4] In order to investigate whether semantic and/or grammatical complexity or any other variable could be a direct cause of the relationship between the speech of parents and their children, I replicated Savić's study with a corpus with whose syntactic and semantic properties I am familiar, i.e., the German data I gathered during a longitudinal study of my bilingual son Sean's language development. This corpus consists of my interactions with Sean during weekly one-hour sessions tape recorded either on Saturdays or Mondays and manual transcriptions, which include situational and contextual information, of Sean's total language production on Sundays. In order to keep the size of the samples constant, the first four weekends of every month were included in the analysis, an occasional fifth weekend was excluded. The corpus thus comprises four hours of mother's speech and approximately 56 hours of child speech per month; it begins at age 17 months, at which time Sean spoke only holophrastically, and ends at age 32 months, after which time I discontinued the transcriptions on Sundays.

Table 2.8 (continued)

8B   Frequency and order in *wh*-production, Sean

Age in months	Total number of questions	*what* was	*where* wo	*who* wer	*why* warum	*how* wie	*what kind* was für	*when* wann	*which* welcher	excluded: wie macht X
17	—	—	—	—	—	—	—	—	—	—
18	—	—	—	—	—	—	—	—	—	—
19	—	—	—	—	—	—	—	—	—	—
20	—	—	—	—	—	—	—	—	—	—
21	—	—	—	—	—	—	—	—	—	—
22	—	—	—	—	—	—	—	—	—	—
23	5	2	3	—	—	—	—	—	—	—
24	95	4	88	3	—	—	—	—	—	—
25	150	11	139	—	—	—	—	—	—	—
26	191	103	87	1	—	—	—	②	①	—
27	281	169	108	1	1	2	—	—	—	—
28	373	234	90	2	7	1	39	—	—	—
29	233	123	88	7	2	1	12	—	—	—
30	356	157	130	2	53	1	12	1	—	—
31	376	160	91	11	92	9	9	2	2	—
32	285	116	79	9	56	10	3	8	4	—
Total	2345	1079	903	36	211	24	75	11	6	—

The present analysis is restricted to *wh*-questions, since they form a narrower system than questions as a whole, and in particular to those *wh*-questions which contain a main predicate; thus questions like "What?" or "Oh, why not?" are not considered. Omitted also are echo-questions like "You ate the what?". Three different classes of full *wh*-questions are analyzed. Class I, for which the raw data are listed in *Table 2.8*, includes *wh*-questions as a group and compares with Savić's data. Because of their different cognitive, semantic, and syntactic properties, *what kind*-questions are treated as distinct from *what*-questions, although both utilize the same interrogative morpheme.

Within the *how* column, two particular questions are excluded from the analysis. The first is the familiar routine for matching animal names and sounds, e.g., "Wie macht die Kuh? Muh!" (literal translation "How makes the cow? Moo!", the German form of "What does the cow say?"). These questions are very frequent in the early data, but they soon completely disappear and apparently do not function in the process of acquisition of *wh*-questions. The second question omitted is "How's that called?". *How* here alternates with *what* in German in most instances, and *heissen* (to be called) is the only verb in the corpus with which this alternation does not result in a difference in meaning. As will be seen later (*Table 2.9*), Sean used questions containing *heissen* initially with *what* exclusively, which is not surprising considering the high saliency of *what* at this time, and only two months later he used *heissen* with *how*. These questions

Table 2.9
Class II: *What*-questions

9A   Frequency and order of *what*-questions containing copula, *do, have, stand* (be written), *be called*, and *say* addressed to Sean by mother

Age in months	Total number of questions	copula	machen	haben	stehen	heissen	sagen	included under heissen:	
								wie heisst	was heisst
17	205	177	25	3	—	—	—	—	—
18	229	198	20	9	1	1	—	1	—
19	223	191	26	5	1	—	—	—	—
20	242	203	23	14	—	1	1	—	1
21	265	187	61	12	1	3	1	3	—
22	263	118	83	22	9	27	4	27	—
23	232	107	80	20	2	20	3	20	—
24	159	50	56	10	3	20	20	18	2
25	104	43	23	10	6	9	13	8	1
26	161	70	55	10	8	13	5	11	2
27	147	48	58	9	1	14	17	10	4
28	88	28	25	5	—	14	16	12	2
29	108	37	48	8	1	9	5	8	1
30	80	29	25	7	1	15	3	14	1
31	65	29	18	2	3	8	5	7	1
32	31	8	13	3	—	4	3	3	1
Total interm.	1427	1074	238	65	12	32	6	31	1
Total	2602	1523	639	149	37	158	96	142	16

therefore are omitted completely from the analysis of *wh*-questions as a group and are classed together with "What's that called?" in a separate analysis of *what*-questions.

The circled items in *Table 2.8* are also partially or totally excluded from the analysis. In the mother's speech, the early incidental *what kind-, when-,* and *which*-questions are included in the frequency count but eliminated from consideration in the order of introduction, because their use at this time is definitely sporadic rather than systematic.[5] For child speech, however, this distinction cannot be drawn. Every spontaneous and appropriately used token of a certain type should, I believe, be considered an instance of the child's ability to apply a given piece of knowledge in a given situation. However, the two early *when*-questions, although spontaneous, are not appropriate. Contextually, both appear to be *why*-questions, and Sean still answered *when*-questions with *because* in month 29. The *which*-question is appropriate, but not spontaneous; it is a slightly modified repetition of a question asked by the mother. These three questions are therefore excluded from the analysis of both frequency and order.

A very low type-token-ratio has frequently been observed in speech to young children. In particular, Broen (1972) remarks that in her sample of ten

Table 2.9 (continued)

9B   Frequency and order in production of *what*-questions containing copula, *do, have, stand* (be written), *be called*, and *say*, Sean

Age in months	Total number of questions	copula	machen	haben	stehen	heissen	sagen	included under heissen: wie heisst	was heisst
17	—	—	—	—	—	—	—	—	—
18	—	—	—	—	—	—	—	—	—
19	—	—	—	—	—	—	—	—	—
20	—	—	—	—	—	—	—	—	—
21	—	—	—	—	—	—	—	—	—
22	—	—	—	—	—	—	—	—	—
23	2	2	—	—	—	—	—	—	—
24	4	4	—	—	—	—	—	—	—
25	10	8	2	—	—	—	—	—	—
26	92	66	22	3	1	—	—	—	—
27	136	58	50	7	4	2	15	—	2
28	200	90	60	12	5	3	30	—	3
29	106	53	23	5	1	4	20	1	3
30	141	56	42	2	2	22	17	3	19
31	131	69	19	4	22	9	8	1	8
32	112	49	12	5	31	4	11	—	4
Total	934	455	230	38	66	44	101	5	39

mothers speaking to eighteen-month-old children three verbs, *look, see,* and *put,* accounted for 20% of the total sample of sentences. The same three verbs, furthermore, accounted for 53% of the total sample of imperatives. In order to investigate whether mother-child speech indeed is not only restricted in form but also in content and furthermore, whether particular contents might be favored in particular structures, I subdivided all *what*-questions in terms of their main verb. It was found that six verbs account for 80% of the mother's and 86% of the child's *what*-questions. These verbs are the copula *machen* (to do), *haben* (to have), *stehen* (literally to stand, but used in its possible German meaning of to be written), *heissen* (to be called)[6] and *sagen* (to say). Although these verbs are also heavily favored in declaratives by both mother and child in the early data, their persistent predominance in *what*-questions is overwhelming. All *what*-questions containing these six verbs comprise the second class of questions to be analyzed. The raw data are listed in *Table 2.9.*

Two particular surface structures again must be eliminated from the analysis, since they occur only in the first four months of the corpus and then completely disappear. These are five instances of "Was wollen wir jetzt machen?" ("What do we want to do now?") and seven instances of "Was haben wir hier?" ("What have we here?"). In these instances, since the mother always immediately supplies the answer, she appears to be talking to herself at a time when a true linguistic interaction pattern has not yet been established between her and the child because his verbal ability is still very low. These questions thus fall, I believe, into the category of "adult speech overheard by the child" rather than into that of mother-child interaction.

Since some of the input studies showed an increase in different verb forms such as nonpresent tense verbs and compound verbs in mothers' speech as children grow older, those *what*-questions containing the verbs *machen, haben, stehen, heissen,* and *sagen* comprise the third class of questions to be analyzed in terms of the particular form in which the verbs appear. The copula is excluded from this class because it is syntactically not parallel to the other verbs: Its predominant past form in colloquial German is the preterite rather than the present perfect. For the other five verbs, the following different forms occur in the data: present tense singular, inflected for person; present tense plural, first and third person only, which equal the infinitive; the past participle preceded by an auxiliary, i.e., the present perfect; and the infinitive preceded by a modal auxiliary. Frequency and order of these four different verb forms are analyzed for each verb separately. The raw data for this class are listed in *Table 2.10.*

The correlation coefficients for this corpus are listed in *Table 2.11. Table 2.11A* compares the mother's frequency and order with the child's frequency and order, and *Table 2.11B* compares the mother's frequency with her own order and the child's frequency with his order. Furthermore, in order to check for possible influences of the child's frequency on the mother's, following a suggestion by Brown (1973) I calculated, in addition to the mother's total frequencies, a set of intermediate frequencies prior to the time at which the child started to use the different question types himself, i.e., through month 22 for *wh*-questions and *what*-questions and through month 24 for tensed *what*-questions. As shown in *Table 2.11C,* total and intermediate frequencies are highly correlated; the mother thus did not change her relative frequencies once the child started to use *wh*-questions.

As is the case for Savić's corpus, the mother's frequency highly correlates with the child's frequency and nearly always correlates with his order of production. That the latter correlation for *wh*-questions only approaches significance is due to the fact that the production orders for *what* and *where* are tied for the child while *what* occurs with much higher frequency than *where* in the mother's speech. If *what* is excluded, the correlation between mother's frequency and child's order of production is also significant for *wh*-questions. The mother's order of introduction also correlates with the child's order of production with the exception of *what*-questions where, I believe, the relatively late start of the recordings in month 17 resulted in a three-way tie on the mother's order of introduction.[7] For the child, again a significant correlation is found in general between his order of production and frequency of use, although, if *what* is excluded from *wh*-questions, his high frequency of *why*-questions after their relatively late emergence results in a lack of correlation for this class. Contrary to

Savić's corpus, the mother's order of introduction here correlates neither with the child's nor with her own frequency.

The combined results from Savić's data and my own[8] thus lead to rejection of the general null hypothesis that mother's input and child speech are not related. They also allow for the statement of the following particular facts:

1.   The mother's order of introduction is related to the child's order of production.

2.   The mother's modeling frequency is related to the child's order of production.

3.   The mother's modeling frequency is related to the child's frequency of use.

4.   The child's order of production is nearly always related to his frequency of use.

5.   The mother's order of introduction may or may not be related to her own frequency

6.   The mother's order of introduction may or may not be related to the child's frequency.

After establishing these facts, the causal question must be asked again. What determines these correlations? Since determination of the nature of the input by the linguistic development of the child, i.e., by his order of production and frequency of use, can be ruled out because use of certain structures by the mother may predate use of these same structures by the child by several months and as a rule mothers are not clairvoyant, the question is whether the nature of the input determines the child's production or whether any other factor could be causal in determining both independently.

One such factor, proposed by Buium, Rynders, and Turnure (1973), might be the relative frequency of different forms in the adult language. Although some of the input studies have shown that the speech of mothers to children is different from the same mothers' speech to adults, Fraser and Roberts (1975) caution that usually the situations and topics were not the same for adult-adult and mother-child speech. Thus if the language among adults were similar to mother-child speech in the same situations, this could explain the striking similarities in the speech of mother and child in that forms more frequent in the adult language are produced earlier and more frequently than forms occurring with lower frequency in the adult language by both mother and child for the sake of efficiency of communication.

In order to test this hypothesis, I analyzed in terms of frequency of different *wh*-questions a tape recording of two hours of interaction between me[9] and my adult immediate family, recorded in the same situations which occur again and again during my interactions with Sean: having dinner, talking about books or other common interests, looking at pictures. The raw data and results of this

Table 2.10

Class III: Tensed *what*-questions

10A　Frequency and order of *what*-questions containing different verb forms of *do*, *have*, *stand* (be written), *be called*, and *say* addressed to Sean by mother

Age in months	Total number of questions	M (s)	M (p)	H (s)	M (pp)	St (s)	He (s)	S (s)	S (pp)	S (p)	H (mi)	M (mi)	He (p)	H (p)	H (pp)	S (mi)
17	28	21	4	2	—	—	—	—	—	—	1	—	—	—	—	—
18	31	13	5	8	2	1	1	—	—	—	—	—	—	—	—	—
19	32	24	—	4	2	1	—	—	—	—	—	—	—	1	—	—
20	39	15	7	10	1	—	1	1	—	—	4	—	—	1	—	—
21	78	57	2	6	1	1	3	—	1	—	5	1	—	—	—	—
22	145	61	10	19	6	9	25	1	1	2	2	6	2	1	1	—
23	125	35	20	18	23	2	20	1	2	—	2	2	—	—	—	—
24	109	37	10	10	8	3	19	17	3	—	2	1	1	—	—	—
25	61	17	2	8	4	6	9	4	9	—	—	—	1	—	—	—
26	91	34	10	8	10	8	12	2	3	—	2	1	1	1	—	—
27	99	36	8	7	10	1	12	10	3	1	1	4	2	2	—	3
28	60	13	2	5	9	—	12	10	6	—	—	1	2	—	—	—
29	71	25	9	6	11	1	6	—	3	—	1	3	3	—	1	2
30	51	15	—	7	9	1	15	1	2	—	—	1	—	—	—	—
31	36	12	3	1	3	3	8	3	2	—	—	—	1	1	—	—
32	23	8	—	1	5	—	3	—	3	—	2	—	1	—	—	—
Total interm.	587	263	58	77	43	17	69	20	7	2	14	10	3	3	1	—
Total	1079	423	92	120	104	37	146	50	38	3	20	20	12	6	3	5

M machen　　St stehen　　S sagen　　p plural　　mi modal with infinitive

H haben　　He heissen　　s singular　　pp past participle

Table 2.10 (continued)

10B Frequency and order in production of *what*-questions containing different verb forms of *do, have, stand* (be written), *be called,* and *say,* Sean

Age in months	Total number of questions	M (s)	M (p)	H (s)	M (pp)	St (s)	He (s)	S (s)	S (pp)	S (p)	H (mi)	M (mi)	He (p)	H (p)	H (pp)	S (mi)
17	—	—	—	—	—	—	—	—	—	—	—	—	—	—	—	—
18	—	—	—	—	—	—	—	—	—	—	—	—	—	—	—	—
19	—	—	—	—	—	—	—	—	—	—	—	—	—	—	—	—
20	—	—	—	—	—	—	—	—	—	—	—	—	—	—	—	—
21	—	—	—	—	—	—	—	—	—	—	—	—	—	—	—	—
22	—	—	—	—	—	—	—	—	—	—	—	—	—	—	—	—
23	—	—	—	—	—	—	—	—	—	—	—	—	—	—	—	—
24	—	—	—	—	—	—	—	—	—	—	—	—	—	—	—	—
25	2	2	—	—	—	—	—	—	—	—	—	—	—	—	—	—
26	26	18	2	3	2	1	—	—	—	—	—	—	—	—	—	—
27	78	38	10	7	2	4	2	12	1	2	—	—	—	—	—	—
28	110	41	11	12	8	5	3	25	5	—	—	—	—	—	—	—
29	53	15	3	4	5	1	4	12	7	1	1	—	—	—	—	—
30	85	26	8	1	4	2	22	9	7	1	1	4	—	—	—	—
31	62	10	6	4	3	22	8	4	4	—	—	—	1	—	—	—
32	63	4	5	3	3	31	2	—	11	—	1	—	2	1	—	—
Total	479	154	45	34	27	66	41	62	35	4	3	4	3	1	—	—

M machen   St stehen   S sagen   p plural   mi modal with infinitive
H haben   He heissen   s singular   pp past participle

Table 2.11
Correlation coefficients for maternal frequency and order of
introduction and child's frequency and order of production

11A

| | Maternal frequency | | Maternal order |
	Total	Intermediate	
Child frequency			
Class I	r = .879****	r = .911****	r = .482
Class I (*what* excluded)	r = .906****	r = .933*****	r = .425
Class II	r = .981*****	r = .958****	r = .383
Class III	r = .886*****	r = .874*****	r = .469
Child order			
Class I	r = .684*	r = .701*	r = .844****
Class I (*what* excluded)	r = .865***	r = .793**	r = .843***
Class II	r = .942****	r = .934****	r = .643
Class III	r = .577**	r = .542**	r = .649****

11B

| | Frequency | |
	Total	Intermediate
Mother order		
Class I	r = .428	r = .429
Class I (*what* excluded)	r = .565	r = .481
Class II	r = .500	r = .460
Class III	r = .480	r = .476
Child order		
Class I	r = .745**	
Class I (*what* excluded)	r = .660	
Class II	r = .929****	
Class III	r = .673***	

11C

Maternal intermediate frequency	Maternal total frequency
Class I	r = .995*****
Class I (*what* excluded)	r = .982*****
Class II	r = .983*****
Class III	r = .992*****

* p < .10	**** p < .01
** p < .05	***** p < .001
*** p < .02	

analysis are presented in *Tables 2.12* and *2.13*, respectively. Different speakers' frequency of different *wh*-questions correlates very highly in adult-adult speech for *wh*-questions as a whole, not at all, however, for *what*-questions and tensed *what*-questions, where no correlation whatever was found. Since I used only two *what*-questions containing *machen, haben, heissen, stehen,* or *sagen* in my interaction with adults, only the other adults' frequencies of *what*-questions and tensed *what*-questions were compared to mother-child speech. This comparison again resulted in a complete lack of correlation for both classes.

In relative terms, adult-adult frequency of different *wh*-questions also correlates highly with frequency of different *wh*-questions in mother-child speech due to the overwhelming predominance of *what* in both adult-adult and mother-child speech. Under exclusion of *what*, however, any correlation between adult-adult speech and mother-child speech disappears, while between adults as well as between mother and child the relative frequencies of all other *wh*-questions are still highly correlated. Predominance in the adult language, therefore, cannot account for the relationship between the speech of mothers and their children.

Brown, Cazden, and Bellugi (1968) proposed that the stable mother-child frequency profile itself might direct at least the child's order of production. They argue that if frequencies are grossly unequal, the order of production may be determined by chance, since more frequent forms would have a higher probability of occurrence than less frequent ones, although all forms might have been learned at the same time. This argument, however, presupposes that the child's total number of utterances increases over time. If it remained the same, chance occurrence would scatter the less frequent forms throughout the corpus. Scattering, however, does not occur in the two corpora available. And Sean's total number of utterances, at least, does not increase during the period in which he gradually produced different *wh*-questions, since there is no correlation of his total number of utterances per sample with age, as shown in *Table 2.14*. Chance, therefore, does not determine the child's order of production.

Neither could grammatical complexity account for the relationship between the speech of mothers and their children. This has been noticed before. Gleitman (1975) showed that mothers' speech is not organized according to a measure of simplicity in terms of derivational complexity; and Brown, Cazden, and Bellugi (1968) puzzled over the differential proportions of appropriate responses by Adam, Eve, and Sarah to *where-, why-, how-,* and *when*-questions, which are "rather well matched in grammatical complexity" (p. 327).

The same phenomena hold true for my corpus. Syntactically equivalent constructions, like the adverbial *wh*-questions mentioned above or the different verbs occurring in *what*-questions, do not appear at the same time in either the mother's or the child's speech.

Furthermore, the gradual introduction and production of tensed *what*-questions (see *Table 2.10*) shows that even different verb forms are reintroduced and appear relearned over time with different verbs. Since the sole purpose of the

Table 2.12
Frequency of different *wh*-questions
in adult-adult speech

12A   *Wh*-questions

	Mother	Other adults
What	16	19
Where	3	2
Who	2	3
Why	1	—
How	7	8
What kind	2	4
When	4	2
Which	—	1

12B   *What*-questions

	Mother	Other adults
Copula	4	4
Machen	1	4
Haben	—	3
Stehen	—	—
Heissen	—	5
Sagen	1	3

12C   Tensed *what*-questions

	Mother	Other adults
Machen (singular)	—	—
Machen (plural)	—	1
Haben (singular)	—	3
Machen (past participle)	—	2
Stehen (singular)	—	—
Heissen (singular)	—	5
Sagen (singular)	—	1
Sagen (past participle)	1	2
Sagen (plural)	—	—
Heissen (modal with infinitive)	—	—
Machen (modal with infinitive)	1	1
Heissen (plural)	—	—
Haben (plural)	—	—
Haben (past participle)	—	—
Sagen (modal with infinitive)	—	—

child's LAD is presumably to help him in making grammatical generalizations, it must therefore seriously be asked why, once Sean used present plural verb inflections in *what*-questions with *machen* in month 26 and the verb *heissen* in *what*-questions in month 27, do present plurals with *heissen* occur only four months later? Even more striking is the use of modal auxiliaries. The transcription of the first Sunday in month 23 yields 29 declaratives containing modals. This

Table 2.13
Correlation coefficients for mother-adult,
mother-child, and child speech

	Frequency Mother-adults	Frequency Adults-mother
Class I		
Frequency mother-adults		r = .972*****
Total frequency mother-child	r = .866****	r = .863****
Intermediate frequency mother-child	r = .856****	r = .844****
Frequency child	r = .655*	r = .604
Order of introduction mother	r = .339	r = .354
Order of production child	r = .495	r = .483
Class I (*what* excluded)		
Frequency mother-adults		r = .829****
Total frequency mother-child	r = .021	r = .121
Intermediate frequency mother-child	r = .065	r = .073
Frequency child	r = .018	r = .232
Order of introduction mother	r = .220	r = .265
Order of production child	r = .165	r = .128
Class II		
Frequency mother-adults		r = .299
Total frequency mother-child		r = .389
Intermediate frequency mother-child		r = .305
Frequency child		r = .299
Order of introduction mother		r = .141
Order of production child		r = .121
Class III		
Frequency mother-adults		r = .138
Total frequency mother-child		r = .206
Intermediate frequency mother-child		r = .128
Frequency child		r = .075
Order of introduction mother		r = .308
Order of production child		r = .405

* p < .10   **** p < .01   ***** p < .001

month also shows the first occurrence of *what*-questions. Why did Sean wait for seven months before he produced modal auxiliaries in *what*-questions? Surely these examples are indicative of a rather severe lack of efficiency on the part of LAD.

Approaching the question from a different angle, Ingram (1972) also suggests that the acquisition of *wh*-questions is independent of grammatical development as measured in terms of MLU and syntactic knowledge as expressed in Do-Support, correct tensing, etc. For ten English-speaking children he found a pronounced implicational acquisition order for six *wh*-questions which was not related to these measures; e.g., a child might speak telegraphically but nevertheless appropriately use five different interrogative morphemes, while some other child with rather elaborate syntax might use only *what* and *where*.

Table 2.14

Correlation between Sean's age in months and Sean's total number of utterances per first two weekends in each sample

Age in months	Number of utterances
23	1339
24	1785
25	1505
26	1573
27	1783
28	1913
29	1609
30	1586
31	1714
32	1733

r = +.419, not significant

Ingram attributes the order of acquisition of different *wh*-questions to the cognitive development of the child, in other words to the same variable that Snow (1974) suggested as guiding language development in general. If Snow's contention that the mother is cued by the child nonverbally as to his cognitive development were correct, then one could assume that as a result the mother, by modeling, provides the child with the means to encode any new concept in linguistic terms. Under this assumption both the nature of the mother's and the child's speech could be accounted for.

If it is true that cognition does not equal semantics, as I contended earlier (see also note 3), then cognitive concepts must be encoded in language as semantic features. An investigation in progress into Sean's acquisition of the morpheme *what* in all its possible functions in German showed that this acquisition is determined by increasing semantic complexity independent of syntax. The features most crucial to the development of *what* are object-reference, action-reference, and event-reference. These features also crucially determine the order of introduction and production of the *what*-questions in Class II. With the copula, *haben, stehen,* and *heissen, what* carries increasingly complex object-reference; with *machen* it carries action-reference; and with *sagen* event-reference. In tensed *what*-questions, these same features interact with features independent of the morpheme *what,* i.e., reference to present, past, or immediate future.[10]

Both these sets of features appear to be ranked in terms of increasing conceptual complexity in the orders given. It must be pointed out that early child language—and Sean is no exception—generally concerns the here and now, and concrete entities rather than abstract ones. With this fact in mind, the object-concept must be a prerequisite for any action-concept, since concrete actions are not possible without concrete objects either acting or being acted upon. Similarly, both object and action concepts are prerequisites for any concept of concrete events.

Table 2.15

Interaction of semantic features in maternal order of
introduction and child's order of production of tensed *what*-questions
according to first month of use

	Haben		Machen		Sagen	
	(Object-reference)		(Action-reference)		(Event-reference)	
	Mother	Child	Mother	Child	Mother	Child
Present	17	26	17	25	20	27
Past	22	—	18	26	21	27
Future	17	29	21	30	23	—

It is more difficult to rank the tenses according to conceptual complexity. This is possible only under the assumption that for the child the concept of "now" is a prerequisite for the concept of "not now," and that personal experience is a prerequisite for abstraction from personal experience. Under these assumptions, the conceptual complexity hierarchy for tenses would be the following: present [+now, +personal experience] would be less complex than past [−now, +personal experience], which in turn would be less complex than future [−now, −personal experience].

The interaction of these two feature sets in tensed *what*-questions is shown in *Table 2.15.* Any concept higher on both the complexity hierarchies outlined above is generally not introduced by the mother nor produced by the child earlier than one lower in complexity. The obvious exception is the past tense with object-reference. Both mother and child used these questions later than questions referring to the past which contain action- or event-reference, and later than questions with object-reference referring to the future. It thus appears that either past reference to objects presents specific conceptual difficulties with *haben* or that this kind of question ranks extremely low on a hypothetical hierarchy of mutual interests of mother and child. The second exception is found in the fact that the child produced questions containing action-reference in the present tense earlier than those containing object-reference. It should be remembered, however, that the copula, because of idiosyncratic marking of the past tense, has been excluded from the questions comprising Class III. *What*-questions in the present tense containing the copula, which in the early stages always carry object-reference, were already produced by the child in month 23.

It thus appears that cumulative semantic complexity might determine the gradual introduction by the mother and the general production by the child of different syntactically equivalent surface forms. Cumulative semantic complexity, however, could not determine the child's order of production independent of input, since this kind of complexity is governed by the meaning rather than the form of sentences. Meaning, of course, has to be related to context, and context must be provided. Semantic complexity thus would have to be taught and learned anew in different contexts.

Table 2.16
Correlation coefficients between child's age
and number of questions per month

	Child's Age		
	17-22 months	23-32 months	
Number of questions	Mother	Mother	Child
Class I	r = −.595	r = −.896****	r = +.844***
Class I (where excluded)	r = +.938***	r = −.883****	r = +.848***
Class II	r = +.947***	r = −.885****	r = +.720**
Class III	r = +.849*	r = −.883****	r = +.717**

* p < .05   ** p < .02   *** p < .01   **** p < .001

Any learning process, furthermore, requires practice. And as the mother might vary her modeling frequencies relative to the degree of additional semantic complexity of every newly introduced form, so the child might vary his practicing frequencies accordingly. The assumption of a process of modeling and practicing would thus account for the stable profile of relative frequency in mother-child speech at any point in time.

Finally, this assumption would predict that the teacher's effort decreases (or perhaps shifts to other topics) as the pupil's skill increases. This prediction is borne out by the data. A significant increase in number of questions per sample on the part of the mother is found until month 22, as shown in *Table 2.16*. *Where*-questions have to be excluded from these calculations, however, since their number decreases over the entire period under discussion. This might be an indication that the mother adjusts her frequencies according to the child's comprehension rather than production, a question inviting further investigation. Beginning at month 23, when the child starts to use *wh*-questions himself, the mother's number of questions decreases significantly throughout the remainder of the corpus, while the child's number of questions significantly increases.

These findings taken together with earlier observations justify the suggestion that a model like the one outlined in *Table 2.17* might determine not only the similarities in mother-child speech but also the process of language development.

According to this model, the child's order of production should always correlate with both the mother's order of introduction and the mother's frequency of modeling, since it is determined by both. The mother's frequency of modeling should also correlate with the child's frequency of practicing, since both are directly determined by semantic complexity.

Since semantic complexity would also determine both the child's practicing frequency and his order of production, the former directly, the latter through the mother, these should also nearly always correlate.[11] However, since the child's order of production would be determined by both the mother's order of introduction and her frequency, the model would predict that the correlation

Table 2.17
Possible determinants of correlation between
mother-child speech and child speech

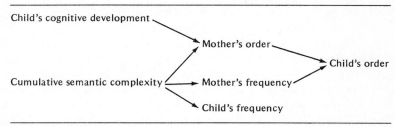

between the child's order of production and his frequency should be higher when the mother's order and frequency are related than when they are not. This prediction holds true. In the Serbo-Croatian case, in which the parents' frequency and order are related, the correlation coefficient for both children's frequency and order is significant at the .001 level. In the German case, in which no relationship is found between the mother's order of introduction and her frequency, the value of p of the child's correlation coefficients for his order and frequency varies between no significance at all for *wh*-questions, *what* excluded, and .01 for *what*-questions.

Whether the mother's order of introduction will bear a relationship to her own frequency as well as the child's frequency would be largely determined by the closeness of the match between cognitive complexity and the semantic complexity of the particular language she is teaching her child on the one hand and on different strategies on the part of the mother on the other. If in the target language cognitive complexity does not equal semantic complexity, the mother has two choices: She can either introduce particular concepts in the order in which she thinks her child is "ready" for them regardless of semantic complexity; in this case order of introduction and frequency would not be related because the order would be determined nearly exclusively by the cognitive development of the child while both the mother's and the child's frequencies would be determined by semantic complexity. Or the mother can postpone the introduction of particular concepts until the semantic prerequisites have been established; in this case semantic complexity would determine order of introduction as well as frequencies and the two should be related. If in the target language cognitive complexity largely equals semantic complexity, there would be a correlation between order of introduction and frequencies regardless of any particular strategy the mother might employ.

This model can be subjected to a rather rigorous test. Since cognitive development is independent of any particular language and should not be subject to extensive variation regardless of whether one assumes it to be maturationally determined or environmentally induced, and since furthermore the semantic differences between different *wh*-questions are probably rather similar for different languages, this model would predict that there should be a reasonably close match between the orders and frequencies of *wh*-questions in mother-child interaction in different languages. For those question types which are represented in both corpora, I therefore cross-correlated both parents and children for Savić's data and my own. Some of these correlations are highly significant, and all at least approach significance, as shown in *Table 2.18*.

Furthermore, the rank orders for the gradual emergence of six different *wh*-questions for English-speaking children has been reported by Ingram (1972). As a final test, these orders were compared with the production orders of these same questions for the three other children and with the teaching variables of the parents. These rank orders are listed in *Table 2.19*, and the resulting correlation coefficients in *Table 2.20*. With one exception, which approaches significance, all the correlations between the production orders of different children are significant. And finally, the combined teaching variables correlate with the combined relative production orders of the children at the .001 level.

This study has shown that children produce what mothers say in the same relative order and with the same relative frequency. It was further shown that neither the adult language, chance, or grammatical complexity could account for this relationship.[12] A hypothetical model of language development based on the child's cognitive development and the semantic complexity of the language he is attempting to learn, in which the mother serves a mediating function between the child and the linguistic expression of concepts, i.e., language, on the other hand, could probably provide an explanation not only for the close relationship between the speech of mothers and their children but also for the universal similarities found in language development. Furthermore, such a model would serve this explanatory function better than LAD, which fails to account for the production over time of single children as well as for the nature of the linguistic interaction between mothers and children, because the relation between input and child production at different stages of development is not statable in terms of syntax.

At least for the structures under investigation here, it was thus shown that an interaction of the variables regarded by Chomsky (1965) to be data external to language acquisition, i.e., semantic reference and the use of language in real-life situations, can account for and appears to determine "the direction that learning will take." Further investigations into the effects of differences in the immediate interaction of children with a sympathetic or nonsympathetic linguistic environment thus might at some point in the future prove the inadequacy and ultimate obsolescence of the black box which has for some length of time much too exclusively occupied the imagination of too many students of child language.

Notes

I am grateful to Amy Sheldon for first bringing the possible importance of input to language acquisition to my attention and for many subsequent fruitful discussions, to Gerald Sanders for his insightful comments on an earlier version of this paper, and to my husband Ed for his patience and the loan of his calculator.

Table 2.18
Cross-correlation coefficients, Savić—Forner

	(Total) frequency —frequency	Order—order	(Total) modeling frequency—order of production
Parents Savić—child Forner	r = .848****	r = .661*	r = .808***
Mother Forner—child Savić 1	r = .862****	r = .666*	r = .724**
Mother Forner—child Savić 2	r = .904****	r = .692*	r = .934*****
Child Savić 1—child Forner	r = .914****	r = .705*	
Child Savić 2—child Forner	r = .893****	r = .858****	

* p < .10	*** p < .02	***** p < .001
** p < .05	**** p < .01	

Table 2.19
Rank order of wh-questions investigated
in Ingram (1972) for three corpora

	Ingram's children	Jasmina	Danko	Sean	Summed ranks children	Frequency, parents Savić	Forner	Order, parents Savić	Forner	Summed ranks parents
What	1.5	1	1	1.5	5	1	1	1.5	3	6.5
Where	1.5	2	2	1.5	7	2	2	1.5	3	8.5
Who	5	3.5	3	3	14.5	3	3	4	3	13
How	3.5	3.5	4	4.5	15.5	5	5	3	3	16
Why	3.5	5	5	4.5	18	4	4	5	3	16
When	6	6	6	6	24	6	6	6	6	24

Table 2.20
Correlation coefficients for children's production order
and summed ranks of children and parents for wh-questions
investigated in Ingram (1972)

	Production order
Ingram's children—Jasmina	r = .850**
Ingram's children—Danko	r = .794*
Ingram's children—Sean	r = .818**
Jasmina—Danko	r = .985****
Jasmina—Sean	r = .940***
Danko—Sean	r = .971***
Summed ranks parents—summed ranks children	r = .982****

* p < .10	*** p < .01
** p < .05	**** p < .001

1. Brown seems to use the terms "grammatical" and "transformational" interchangeably. The term "grammatical complexity" will be used throughout this paper rather loosely to cover any purely structural properties of language.

2. Since Brown's data are not continuous, only ranks can be compared. The Spearman rank order correlation coefficient rho used by Brown will yield distorted results in the presence of ties with only a small number of pairs. The Pearson product-moment correlation coefficient r, which is not influenced by ties, under these circumstances will more accurately reflect the strength of any relationship found.

3. Not only is it necessary to make this distinction in order to accommodate the fact that children's semantic marking of lexical items may contain functional or communication features which are not conceptually determined (e.g., reference to old versus new information, Forner, 1976), but also the same concepts may be distributed differently among linguistic items in different languages (e.g., inclusive versus exclusive disjunction).

4. The comprehension or production of different *wh*-questions, at least, seems to be primarily dependent on the grasp of concepts like space (*where*), cause (*why*), manner (*how*), or time (*when*), without which different semantic marking of interrogative morphemes would not be possible.

5. Furthermore, all of these early questions were either immediately rephrased or answered by the mother herself.

6. This count does not include any instances of "How's that called?"

7. An earlier start of the recordings would probably have shown the copula to be used consistently earlier than *machen* and *haben*.

8. Psychologists might object to the results of the present study, since it is not normally accepted practice for a researcher to use himself as subject because of lack of "naïveté." Such objections could be raised under two assumptions: (1) The linguist superimposed herself on the mother, i.e., knowledge about the intricacies of the German language led to structured input. If this were the case, however, the study would still not lose its validity, because it would then have to be regarded as a controlled experiment, yielding the expected and desired results. (2) The student of language acquisition superimposed herself on the mother, i.e., knowledge of the "normal" acquisition sequence led to structured input. However, information about the acquisition order of different *what*-questions is not available for any language, and Savić's article, providing information at least about the acquisition order of different *wh*-questions in Serbo-Croatian appeared only after the crucial first eight months of the present study were already sampled.

9. This recording is over ten years old; biased frequency on my part can therefore be ruled out.

10. Only modals which refer to the future are used by both mother and child in *what*-questions. Furthermore, contextually all these questions refer to the immediate future.

11. It is not the case that the child's frequency must automatically be related to his order of production. Although it is true that a structure necessarily will have zero frequency as long as it does not appear at all, it is not true that whatever appears earlier necessarily will have higher frequencies than something appearing later because it has been used for a longer period of time. The child could, for example, produce different structures, once they appear, for the same number of times each and then discontinue their use. This would result in a linear order of production but equal frequencies for different structures.

12. Since frequently semantic complexity is reflected in grammatical complexity, in many instances grammatical complexity will doubtlessly be found to be related in mother-child interaction, i.e., grammatically less complex forms will be earlier in both the mother's and the child's speech than grammatically more complex ones. However, this would only be a corollary to semantic complexity rather than a factor which itself determines order of acquisition.

Chapter 3

Stress Acquisition: The Role of Homogeneous Rules

Thomas Roeper
Barbara Stack
Greg Carlson

The fundamental problem of language acquisition remains unsolved: how do children master the intricacies of their native tongue?[1] To answer this question we must (a) restrict the hypothesis-space available to a child, and (b) specify how a child generates hypotheses within that space. Linguistic theory approaches the first task by placing restrictions on the total range of possible hypotheses; it defines *universal grammar.* What no adult language permits, in this theory, is excluded from the range of hypotheses that a child considers. Nevertheless the range of hypotheses permitted by universal grammar is infinite. It is the special province of language acquisition research to show how a child can select the appropriate grammar for his community.

In brief, we shall argue that a child *over-restricts* his hypothesis-space in the initial phases of language acquisition. Therefore some connections that exist in the adult grammar are not seen by children. In other words, the hypothesis-generator (or language-acquisition device) systematically excludes certain rules which in fact function in adult languages. For instance a child might understand the semantics of a verb class and might understand a syntactic structure, but fail to see that the adult grammar of a particular language has a necessary link between those verbs and that syntactic structure (see Goodluck and Roeper, this volume). Our focus here falls upon stress phonology. We shall show that children may understand a morphological rule of stress and a phonological rule of stress but fail to realize that one conditions the other.

The rules of English stress assignment are unusually complex. In fact there is a great deal of current debate over how to best represent them. All of the theories recognize one fact: phonological, morphological, and syntactic information may be relevant to stress assignment. That is, information from three diverse domains in grammar must be combined in order to make consistent projections of stress for English words. In order to stress the word *object* correctly we must know if it is a noun or a verb. In order to stress *reprove* correctly we must know if there is a morphological boundary between *re* and *prove* (i.e., *re#prove* or prove again as opposed to denounce). And in order to stress *usurp* correctly one must know that the second syllable has a strong cluster.

These facts have a direct consequence for an hypothesis-generator. There is, in principle, an exponential increase in the hypothesis-space for each domain that is relevant to stress rules. If stress were exclusively phonological, the range of hypotheses would be much smaller. However, the child must multiply the set of possible phonological hypotheses by the set of possible morphological ones by the set of possible syntactic ones. There may well be some limits on the interface between grammatical levels that are established by universal grammar; it is not yet fully clear what they will be. It may well be, for instance, that only categorical information (N, V, A) will be relevant to stress, and not phrasal information (NP, VP, AP). Nevertheless the fundamental fact remains: a system which refers to several grammatical levels causes an increase in the range of grammars that an hypothesis-generator must search through.

It does not, however, follow that an acquisition device must consider all hypotheses at once.[2] It has been proposed in the past that hypotheses are completely ordered. For instance, it is claimed that in syntax hypotheses about word-order precede hypotheses about inflections. This proposal may be too strong. We propose to limit initial hypotheses by constraint:

(1)   Initial hypotheses are homogeneous

This means that a child first explores hypotheses within a domain of grammar before he explores hypotheses that entail information from two domains in one rule. This proposal presupposes the existence of formally separable domains in grammar. We have not mentioned *semantics*, but clearly semantics may also be involved in certain rules. For instance, the rules which define separable prefixes in German appear to involve both phonological and semantic information.[3]

It is not completely clear how our proposal connects with universal grammar. It may have no impact whatsoever on the statement of universal constraints on grammar. However, insofar as earlier hypotheses may affect the range of possible later hypotheses, the order in which hypotheses are generated may affect the total range of hypotheses expressible in universal grammar. (See Chomsky, 1975, p. 121.)

English Stress

A typical rule of English is the *Alternating Stress Rule* (as developed in *The Sound Pattern of English* (SPE) by N. Chomsky and M. Halle, 1968):

$$(2) \quad V \Rightarrow 1\text{str}/\underline{\quad}C_o \ (=) \ C_o VC_o V \qquad C_o]$$
$$[1\text{stress}] \qquad \text{NAV} \ (\text{NAV=noun, verb, adj})$$

This rule provides stress for words like *cóncentràte, éxtirpàte, cónvolùte*. It says, roughly, that a vowel (V) will take primary stress (1str) when it precedes a consonant (C), an optional morphological boundary (=) where parentheses mark options, a medial syllable (CVC) and a final syllable where a vowel has already received a stress. Note that the rule involves reference to grammatical category, phonology, and morphological boundaries. In principle each feature in the notation is changeable and could be different for a different language; therefore, in principle, each element of the notation could be the subject of a child's hypothesis (see Chomsky, 1967). Thus a child might need many hypotheses to confirm the numerous individual features of a single rule.

It is extremely unlikely that a child must consider every possible hypothesis. Presumably knowledge of universal constraints enables the child to preclude some hypotheses and concentrate upon others. It is also unlikely that a child can immediately fix all the parameters of a complex rule at once. Therefore we can expect that children will exhibit stages in the acquisition of stress rules. Now the question becomes what those stages are, or, put differently, what is an early approximation to a complex rule which a child exposed to the subtly variable data of English would develop? We shall suggest that the principle of homogeneous rules dictates a simple and direct approximation.

In our analysis we shall refer to a recent revision of SPE theory by Liberman and Prince.[4] Their analysis both simplifies the rules of SPE, without loss of generalization, and as we shall demonstrate, relates naturally to the grammars which we have independently developed for children. It is worth emphasis, however, that both these theories (or any other theory) pose the same question for the language acquisition device: how does a child develop a unified stress system when factors that determine stress come from different domains of grammar?

In the Liberman and Prince theory there are two important rules which assign stress to English words. They are, first, the iterative *English Stress Rule.*

$$V \Rightarrow 1\text{str}/\underline{\quad} C_o (V(C) \ )_a \ (\ \underset{[-\text{ing}]_d}{V} \ C_o \ )_b \ (\ V \underset{[+\text{str}]}{\quad} X)_c \ \#$$

conditions: ~cɔd; ~a, ~b under certain morphological and lexical conditions

This rule can reapply many times; thus it can give stress to several different vowels in a single word. It guarantees that initial syllables receive stress. These rules must be supplemented by rules which have the effect of de-stressing certain syllables in order to prevent "clashes," that is, a sequence of too many stressed syllables. Thus English maintains a generally metrical (iambic) pattern:

Destressing Rule:

$$\begin{matrix} V \\ [+\text{long}]_a \end{matrix} \Rightarrow \begin{bmatrix} -\text{stress} \\ -\text{long} \end{bmatrix} / + [\ X\ V\ ]_b\ C_o\underline{\quad}(C)\ [C_o = C_o]_c\ V$$

condition: $a \supset (b \lor c)$

The destressing rule is in an important sense defined in terms of the output of the stressing rule. These two rules must be supplemented by the *lexical category prominence rule* which, among other things, represents separately the fact that nouns and verbs receive different stress and that various special features of the lexicon (idiosyncrasies of various word classes) effect stress. We shall return to these rules when we apply them to our results.

The "Full-Entry" Theory of the Lexicon

Stress rules apply to words just as syntactic rules apply to sentences. There is an important difference however. We remember particular words in some kind of mental lexicon, while sentences are forgotten almost as soon as we say them. Recent proposals by Halle and Aronoff[5] suggest that people do not newly generate stress patterns for each word but rather remember the stress pattern for each word just as they remember the meaning of each word. The rules then describe classes in a mental lexicon and provide a means with which to assign stress patterns to new words. They are then once-only rules; as soon as a word is created and assigned meaning, phonology, and stress pattern, it is entered into the mental lexicon.

It follows that children might provide complex words, if known, with correct pronunciation although they lack the rules which form the patterns their words exhibit. This view fits simple observation: children make surprisingly few errors in stress assignment in spontaneous speech. However those errors are in the direction predictable from their developing rules. Some children will say phótogràphy and keep stress on the original word (photograph).[6] They do not apply a stress shift rule. Other forms like *póosham* (for shampoo) and *stáchemus* (for mustache) are reversals that are consistent with the generalization that nouns take initial stress.

In the experiment we report below we found further evidence consistent with this view of the lexicon. In general when we used real words, children seemed to know them and pronounce them correctly (with some interesting exceptions, see below). We assume that they had in fact learned each word as a separate lexical item.

Acquisition Rules

We return to the question: How does a child project the correct rules to organize his memory for words and enable him to stress new words? Infinite possibilities are imaginable. The child could generate a rule entirely in terms of syllables, or consonants, or the beginnings of words, or in terms of morphological boundaries, or semantics, or context. Many of these possibilities will be ruled out by universal grammar. Which remain?

There is moreover the quite real possibility that the child will deal with new words on the basis of a nongrammatical system. For instance, when one child was asked to say *cabran* she said *carbon*; for *adment* we received *admit*. This phenomenon is well known in reading. We consider this method to be *analogical* because it is based upon seeing similarities between *specific* individual words, rather than being based on a rule which operates abstractly without respect to particular phonological segments.[7] Thus a rule, but not an "analogy," can apply to *regort* and *bidimp*. If, however, a child refers to his lexicon and sees *report*, he may let it influence his pronunciation of *regort*. Adults also report that they are conscious of similar real words when they pronounce nonsense words. We attribute therefore some of the minor variability in our results to analogy.

Homogeneous Rules

How does one proceed to determine what a child's first hypothesis about stress might be? There is no a priori position from which to investigate the potentially infinite range of hypotheses. We shall derive a common sense proposal that follows from the hypothetical principle which we mentioned above: homogeneous rules.

We propose then that a child begins with separate hypotheses for each domain of grammar (which, as we shall see, relate to the Liberman and Prince set). Each hypothesis can be applied directly; each is simple to state. Each, presumably, is elaborated as far as possible within a domain before rules are hypothesized which collapse information from two domains:

(3)   A. *Syntactic*:   1. Nouns take initial stress
                    2. Verbs take final stress
        B. *Morphological*:   Words that can be analyzed into *prefix* and *stem* take
                    final stress
        C. *Phonological*:   Stress falls on vowels followed by two final consonants
        (Spelling)   (Strong Syllables)

These hypotheses apply beyond two-syllable words as stated. We have limited our current experiment to two-syllable words; we shall expand the model in the future. These generalizations should, however, be construed only with reference to two-syllable words. We shall illustrate the predictions made by the rules with nonsense words. (A) predicts that a child will know that the verb *to abtéct* has final stress while the noun *an ábtect* has initial stress. (B) predicts that *presort* will take final stress because of the prefix. (C) predicts that *pentel* will take initial stress, because it has two medial consonants.

Conflict

One might ask why these rules cannot serve as adult rules. The answer is that these rules are so broad that they often fail to make a unique decision for a given word. Adult grammars require a fairly high degree of resolution so that most words receive one and only one stress assignment. These rules often *conflict* with each other. Suppose we have a verb that has a strong cluster in initial position (to *pentel*). One rule produces final stress (the Category rule) and the other produces initial stress (the Spelling rule). The substance of our experiment deals with children's responses to conflict situations.

In our experiment we gave children nonsense words in which the set of rules will generate conflicts. This is not an unusual situation. It is presumably the existence of numerous conflict words in English which forces children to develop a more elaborate system for stress assignment. In particular, they must then consider relations of ordering, disjunction, markedness, and metrical structure in the organization of rules.

Preliminary Experiments

We shall describe two preliminary experiments in summary fashion. Then we turn to a detailed discussion of our most recent experiment. In our first experiment we held all factors constant except the fact that a given word was a noun or a verb. We used recognizable prefixes throughout and we made both syllables either strong or weak. Ten sentences were given to a group of 24 fourth graders from the University of Chicago Lab school. Here are sample sentences:

(4)   1.   we know we can drogréss/we are leaders in drógress
      2.   the óbriss is good/will he obríss the chance

The children were asked to read the sentences. The results were very clear: from a total of 215 responses, 93% of the nouns received initial stress, and 91% of the verbs received final stress (as indicated in (4.)).[8] Similar findings emerged from an experiment in German.[9]

That experiment established the claim that category alone was sufficient to trigger differential stress assignment among fairly young children. Nonetheless the children are fairly old with respect to most of language acquisition; in general stress acquisition may be somewhat delayed due to the fact that the required Latinate vocabulary does not enter the vocabulary of children until they are beyond six and seven.[10]

In the next experiment we presented a group of 20 third and fourth graders with a series of nonsense nouns with strong second syllables and real nouns. This set up a potential conflict between the Category rule (noun), which assigns stress to the initial syllable, and the Spelling rule, which assigns stress to the second syllable. On the whole the real words were stressed correctly no matter what their structure was. It is possible that on occasion they were not recognized by the children as real words; in any case, their incorrect answers were consistent with the stress rules (3):

(5)	Noun	1st syll	2d syll
	massage	8	2
	canteen	8	2
	dessert	4	6
	corral	9	1

The nonsense words all received first syllable stress except where there was a strong second syllable and a plausible analogy:

(6)	Real	1st syll	2d syll	Nonsense	1st syll	2d syll
	report	0	10	bippel	9	0
	garage	0	10	vorrage	10	0
	cement	2	8	sammige	10	0
	amount	0	10			
				regort	6	4
				bement	8	0

The real word *cement* had primarily second syllable stress while the nonsense word *bement* had first syllable stress. *Regort* may have been affected by analogy. In sum the real words generally receive correct stress even where a conflict exists between the Category rule and the Spelling rule; the nonsense words appear to follow the noun rule. All exceptions are compatible with the spelling rule. Note that the mixed responses come where there is a conflict. It is as if the children recognized that they were faced with a choice between two rules and had to choose one or the other. We shall find more evidence of mixed responses in the evidence below.

Third Experiment

We turn now to our third and most extensive experiment. Our goal was to develop tasks in which all three factors were systematically contrasted: Category, Spelling, and Morphology (hereafter Analyzability). We designed a story in which 32 nonsense words each occurred twice. The story enabled us to give categorical definition to each word and keep the children's interest: *the* signaled nouns and *to* signaled verbs. We gave the story to five groups of people to read aloud: third, fourth, fifth, and sixth graders and adults. There were ten subjects in each group. Each response was judged by two people. The set of responses was tabulated on the following Data Matrix:

Verbs:

	Nonsense	Stem	Prefix	Prefix/Stem
VCCVC (S-W)	cabran	terpel	subris	subfer
VCVC (neutral)	pratis	stamit	desab	premit
VCVCC (W-S)	tesalt	masist	prebant	presort
VCCVCC (neutral)	arbist	sabment	subrimp	absert

Nouns:

	Nonsense	Stem	Prefix	Prefix/Stem
VCCVC (S-W)	pental	balfer	adnal	adfit
VCVC (neutral)	pobet	sibel	osel	depel
VCVCC (W-S)	basant	gasist	degart	resert
VCCVCC (neutral)	sampelt	padnect	adbist	adment

S = Strong; W = Weak

We considered *de-, sub, pre, ad-* to be well-defined prefixes although it is possible that some children did not identify them as prefixes. We expected that the overall statistical preferences would outweigh the occasional lacunae in the knowledge of various children.

Performance Strategies

A rule system describes a basically deterministic model. If rules are applicable to a word's structure, then the rule must apply and it will produce a fixed array of outcomes. A number of formal constraints, however, permit percentage results. For instance, the notion of *optional* rules. The existence of optional rules means that a child (or an adult) sometimes will and sometimes will not produce a given form. Hence the form will appear in some percentage of the cases. For instance, in syntax the rule of subject-verb inversion is an optional transformation which will occur just if the speaker wants to ask a question (and a few other rhetorical conditions).

Thus the rule is not intrinsically probabilistic but probabilistic insofar as factors extraneous to grammar determine whether it shall or shall not apply. Those performance factors may include aspects of context or of the larger biology of the organism.

The question arises as to whether percentage results allow us to choose among possible formal constraints. We shall argue that they do. In particular we argue that our system of homogeneous rules, which produce conflicts, will resolve any conflicts in terms proportionate to the number of rules which potentially apply. The more rules which dictate second syllable stress, the higher the proportion of second-syllable stress. This is then a *cumulative* model of rule application. Halle has argued on independent grounds for stress rules which are cumulative.[11]

Markedness

The first feature of our results which we shall discuss is one that treats the entire set of responses as a group. We found that over 90% of the nouns received initial stress and that, in addition, over 60% of the verbs received initial stress. (Statistical analysis indicates significance of verb-noun distinction at better than the .05 level.) However, this raises the question of how to account for those numerous verbs where there is initial stress and no factor (Category, Spelling, or Analyzability) which puts the stress on the initial syllable. One possibility is that there is an *unmarked* strategy which obligatorily places the stress on the initial syllable of every two-syllable word. On independent grounds, Halle has proposed the same rule, called the "initial" stress rule (incorporated into ESR in Liberman and Prince):

(7) $\qquad V \Rightarrow 1str/ \# C_o \underline{\quad} X$

Further evidence for this unmarked rule is the fact that there were a number of children who gave exclusively first syllable stress on all words.

How then do we analyze those instances where stress falls on the second syllable? If all first syllables have stress, then second syllable stress can arise just when there is more than one rule which can place stress on the second syllable. Since some of the responses did not give second stress where *all* factors were present, we propose that none of the rules (except the unmarked rule) is obligatory. They all have the status of being *optional*. Here are the previously mentioned homogeneous rules:

(8)   Category: 1. Verb $\Rightarrow$ $1str/Syl\underline{\quad}$
                                2. Noun $\Rightarrow$ $1str/\underline{\quad}Syl$
    Analyzable: 3. V $\qquad\Rightarrow$ $1str/+\underline{\quad}$ (+ = boundary)
    Spelling: 4. V $\qquad\Rightarrow$ $1str/\underline{\quad}CCVC\#$ (1st syllable stress)
                                5. V $\qquad\Rightarrow$ $1str/VC\underline{\quad}CC\#$ (2d syllable stress)

Rules (1) and (2) show the impact of category. Rule (3) functions in terms of a boundary. Rules (4) and (5) place stress on the first syllable, if strong, or the second syllable, if strong.

First we shall show that each factor has a distinct effect. The presence of a category effect is obvious because of the difference between 93% initial stress for nouns and 61% for verbs. The effect of *analyzability* (prefix, stem, or prefix + stem) is revealed in *Figure 3.1*. The surprising fact revealed by this graph is that *stems* have little or no effect; they are equal to nonsense words in their capacity to trigger second syllable stress. In concert with that observation is the fact that *prefix + stem* is roughly equivalent to *prefix* alone. This generalization does not hold for adults where *prefix + stem* is equivalent to nonsense words. We shall recurrently find that the adult grammar does not submit to analysis in terms of cumulative homogeneous rules. The factored out effect of prefix alone and

Figure 3.1

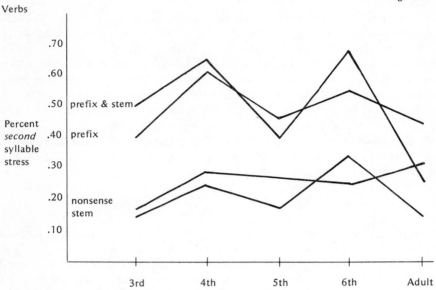

Verbs

Percent
second
syllable
stress

.70
.60
.50 | prefix & stem
.40 | prefix
.30
.20 | nonsense
stem
.10

3rd   4th   5th   6th   Adult

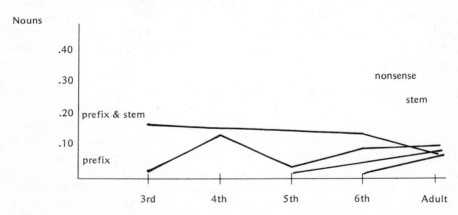

Nouns

.40
.30
.20 | prefix & stem
.10
prefix

nonsense
stem

3rd   4th   5th   6th   Adult

stem alone are revealed in *Figure 3.2.* We conclude that *analyzability* contributes to stress placement.

We turn now to the *Spelling* effect. We find that a structure of the form *weak-strong* (VCVCC) is decidedly favored to receive second-syllable stress over *strong-weak* (VCCVC). See *Figure 3.3.* The neutral cases (*W-W* and *S-S*) fall between the other two for both the nouns and the verbs. This holds, once again, for the children but not the adults. The adults show no difference in the neutral spellings and the *strong-weak.* They show, with verbs, exclusively a preference for *weak-strong* in second syllable stress. If we analyze the data entirely in terms of second syllables—*strong* or *weak*—we find the following clear spelling effects. See *Figure 3.4.* Statistical analysis shows that both first and second syllable strong

Figure 3.2

SUM: Verbs and Nouns

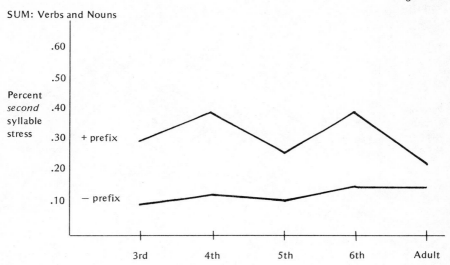

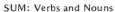

SUM: Verbs and Nouns

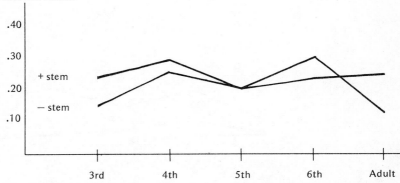

syllables are significant at the .05 level. The primary factor is nonetheless the strong second syllable. This is not surprising since the strong first syllable duplicates the effect of the unmarked rule. Nevertheless we shall show that there is value in having a rule that specifies stress on the strong first syllable.

The Cumulative Model

We shall consider a weighting system in which both first and second syllable spelling effects are considered:

(9)   Verb   = +1   Noun   = −1
        Weak-Strong   = +1   Strong-Weak   = −1
        Prefix   = +1   Nonsense   = −1

        Weak-weak and Strong-strong = 0

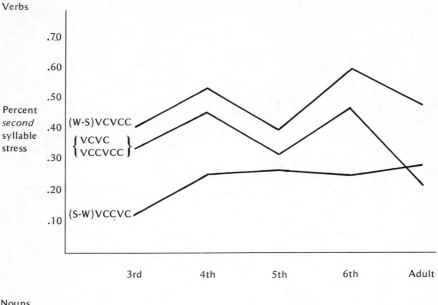

Figure 3.3

We find an even progression (of 20%) among the children with the addition of each factor above zero. There is a jump for the adults between zero and one, and then a fairly constant percentage thereafter. This fits, as we shall show, a rule system for adults in which two rules are collapsed.

This system reveals the following progression in our data:

(10)		−3	−2	−1	0	+1	+2	+3
Child		0	0	06	10	30	50	68
Adult		0	0	14	02	39	32	47

(All figures represent percentages)

We find an even progression (of 20%) among the children with the addition of each factor above zero. There is a jump for the adults between zero and one, and then a fairly constant percentage thereafter. This fits, as we shall show, a rule system for adults in which two rules are collapsed.

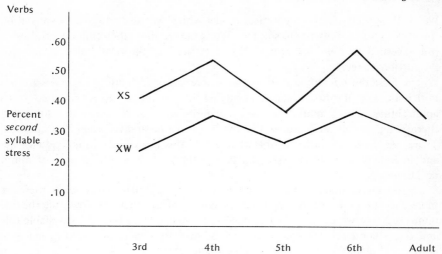

Figure 3.4

Verbs

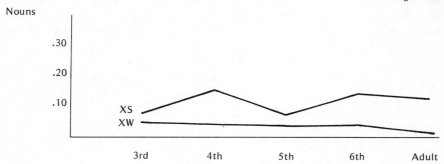

Figure 3.5

Nouns

Data Grouping

We have chosen to analyze the children as a group rather than by each grade. This is a consequence of the fact that we found surprisingly little shift between third and sixth grade and that we found a dip among fifth graders. This does not mean that we believe that there are no developmental shifts. The primary developmental differences may occur before third grade and after sixth grade when the bulk of the Latinate vocabulary is assimilated.[12] We think however that our failure to find developmental trends between grades lies in the fact that grades (and age) are not the appropriate criteria. Children show substantial differences in their linguistic maturity and in their ability to read. Some other linguistic criterion might be preferable as a guide to earlier and later phases of acquisition.

Theoretical Discussion

We shall now clarify the theoretical model which we advocate as an explanation for the results presented so far. We assume that the children follow a rule-governed system in which the presence of optional rules allows for proportionate results.

First the *unmarked rule* applies to every word. Therefore every word has initial stress on the first syllable. Then each of the rules in (8) is examined for its applicability. If it is applicable, then it *may* be applied. We chose to assume that there is an overall 50% probability that a given rule applies when it is optional. There are doubtless other factors that affect this probability in individual rules and in individual children. We take these other factors as the source of minor deviations.

In the cumulative model there will be second-syllable stress when there are more than two rules which favor second syllable stress; they then overrule the one unmarked rule which gives first syllable stress. When there is one first syllable rule and one second syllable rule that applies, then we expect the child to make an arbitrary choice: 50% will fall on each syllable.[13]

We shall now do a kind of "performance derivation" for two similar words: *degart* and *resert*. These are both *nouns*; they have an identifiable prefix, hence they are *analyzable,* and they have a *strong* second syllable. They thus have two features which cause first syllable stress (the unmarked rule and the noun rule) and two which cause second syllable stress. We shall consider all the alternatives that each of the optional choices allows:

(11)	*degart*	*1st syllable*	*2d syllable*
A.	Unm: = +1	100%	
B.	Unm + N = +2	100%	
C.	Unm − Sp = 0	50%	50%
D.	Unm − A = 0	50%	50%
E.	Unm + N − A = +1	100%	
F.	Unm + N − Sp = +1	100%	
G.	Unm − Sp − A = −1		100%
H.	Unm + N − Sp − A = 0	50%	50%
		550%	250% 250/800 = 32%

Unm	=	unmarked
Sp	=	spelling
A	=	analyzability
N	=	noun rule

Under this analysis every combination of possible optional rules is chosen once. (For other words only two or three rules are possible.) The notion that most rules are optional during certain phases of language acquisition has independent support in numerous studies.[14] The results here suggest that *degart* and *resert* should

Figure 3.6

Verbs	Predicted	Actual	Verbs	Predicted	Actual
cabran terpel	.06	.21	subris subfer	.31	.26
stamit pratis	.12	.15	desab premit	.50	.63
tesalt masist	.31	.30	prebant presort	.69	.68
abrist sabment	.12	.36	subrimp absert	.50	.54

Nouns	Predicted	Actual	Nouns	Predicted	Actual
pental-balfer	.00	.00	adnal adfit	.06	.02
pobet sibel	.00	.00	osel depel	.06	.11
basant gasist	.06	.00	degart resert	.32	.32
sampelt padnect	.00	.01	adbist adment	.06	.05

receive second syllable stress 32% of the time. In *Figure 3.6* we show how all the different nouns and verbs fared under this analysis. There were only two counterexamples to the analysis and they appear in boxes. We conclude that our model has made correct predictions in both an overall analysis and an analysis in terms of individual words.

Mispronunciation and Stress

We found, not surprisingly, that children mispronounced a fair number of real words. This one might consider to be random breakdown in a performance system that had not reached full development. We found, however, that there was a high degree of regularity in the children's errors and that an overwhelming number of those errors favored the stress patterns predicted by our rules. There were the following kinds of transformations:

(12) $\quad VC_1C_2VCC \Rightarrow VC_1C_2C_3VC \quad$ or $\quad VC_1C_2VC_3C_4 \Rightarrow VC_1C_2VC_3$

The effect is to transform a *Strong-strong* sequence into a *strong-weak* sequence with stress on the first syllable:

(13)
sampelt	$\Rightarrow$	sámplet	33 instances
masist	$\Rightarrow$	más(s)it	19 instances
gasist	$\Rightarrow$	gás(s)it	25 instances

There were a total of 85 instances of metathesis that favored stress. There were 58 instances of deletion that favored stress. Four instances were contrary to stress and one case was neutral. There were a few others which were wildly inaccurate mispronunciations and as we mentioned before, there were instances where real words were substituted for the nonsense words. There were also occasional instances of children adding a completely new segment to a word. Here is a selection of the errors:

(14)   *1st Syllable*   *2d Syllable*

     pratis =⇒ pártis
     sabment =⇒ sábmet   desab =⇒ desérp
     stamit =⇒ stámpit
     presort =⇒ préstor   absert =⇒ abérst
     osel =⇒ óslo
     degart =⇒ dérgat   adment =⇒ amént
     padnect =⇒ pádnet
     basant =⇒ bánset
     desab =⇒ déstab

We find for instance that *desab* is shifted to *déstab* for first syllable stress and to *desérp* for second syllable stress. In each case the metathesis works to favor stress. One of the few counterexamples is a case like *balfer* → *bláfer* where the strong medial cluster is dissolved. These "errors" reveal how linguistic rules work in concert to eliminate conflict where possible. This is just what one would expect if we assume that conflict is psychologically real.

Tensing

We asked if tensing attracts stress. Consider those cases where we find tensed first syllable vowels together with a stressed second syllable. We computed the ratio of second-syllable stress to first-syllable stress among those cases where tensing occurs and to cases where tensing does not occur. We found that tensing has no consistent effect on the placement of stress.

Adult Data

First it is important to mention special factors that affect the adult data. Baker and Smith found that adults often regarded nonsense words as somehow "foreign."[15] This could invoke special rules that are used to deal with subsets of foreign words in English. Second, many adults reported that they found themselves consciously searching for real-word analogies. It is not clear how these factors may have affected the adult responses.

    Our results clearly show that both children and adults have a Category rule: there is a noun/verb distinction in the stress rules of adult language. The point requires emphasis because there have been proposals that the noun/verb distinction might be illusory. In particular, under the full-entry theory one could mark each word for the stress rule it undergoes without reference to syntactic category. However, this argument does not apply when one uses nonsense words. If the noun/verb distinction were unreal, then we would expect to see no consistent pattern of difference in adult responses to nonsense words. The distinction is captured, however, in the Lexical Category Prominence Rule advocated by Liberman and Prince. Our evidence provides further support for that distinction within their system.

We have argued that it is a property of the acquisition device, at an early stage, to seek homogeneous rules. We expect, in contrast, that adults reveal nonhomogeneity in their application of rules. We have evidence for this claim. We shall look at the effects of Analyzability and Spelling (see *Figures 3.7* and *3.8*). We shall concentrate upon the verbs, but the argument holds for the nouns as well. If we look (*Figure 3.7*) at the adult matrix for verbs we find that they give 63%, 65% and 66% first-syllable stress when either Spelling or Analyzability or both are a factor. For the children we find that there is a sharp decrease from 67% and 55% to 38% when both factors are present. In the latter case there is a

Figure 3.7

CHILDREN GRADES 3-6: Percent first syllable stress

	VERBS				NOUNS		
	−Prefix	+Prefix	Ave.		−Prefix	+Prefix	Ave.
XW	121/147	81/146			156/156	144/155	
	.82	.55	.69		1.00	.93	.96
XS	91/135	55/145			111/112	122/148	
	.67	.38	.52		.99	.82	.90
	.75	.47	.61		1.00	.88	.93

ADULTS

	−Prefix	+Prefix	Ave.		−Prefix	+Prefix	Ave.
XW	39/39	25/40			40/40	38/39	
	.82	.63	.72		1.00	.97	.99
XS	25/38	24/37			30/33	36/40	
	1.00	.65	.65		.91	.90	.90
	.74	.64	.69		.96	.94	.95

Percent First Syllable Stress   Figure 3.8

VERBS

	−Prefix	+Prefix	
3rd XW	31/36 .86	23/35 .66	.76
3rd XS	25/33 .76	14/34 .41	.58
	.81	.54	.67
4th XW	28/36 .78	17/34 .50	.64
4th XS	22/32 .69	11/38 .29	.46
	.74	.39	.56
5th XW	30/37 .81	24/38 .63	.72
5th XS	25/35 .71	17/35 .49	.60
	.76	.57	.66
6th XW	32/38 .84	17/39 .44	.64
6th XS	19/35 .54	13/38 .34	.44
	.70	.39	.54
Adult XW	32/39 .82	25/40 .63	.72
Adult XS	25/38 .66	24/37 .65	.65
	.74	.64	.69

NOUNS

	−Prefix	+Prefix	
3rd XW	38/38 1.00	36/39 .92	.96
3rd XS	25/25 1.00	31/34 .91	.95
	1.00	.92	.94
4th XW	40/40 1.00	36/39 .92	.96
4th XS	29/29 1.00	28/38 .74	.85
	1.00	.83	.91
5th XW	38/38 1.00	37/40 .93	.96
5th XS	29/29 1.00	31/39 .84	.91
	1.00	.88	.94
6th XW	40/40 1.00	35/37 .95	.97
6th XS	28/29 .97	32/39 .82	.88
	.98	.88	.93
Adult XW	40/40 1.00	38/39 .97	.99
Adult XS	30/33 .91	36/40 .90	.90
	.96	.94	.95

cumulative effect; in the former, adult, case we find no evidence for cumulative rules whatsoever. The effects are very clear across all the grades (see *Figure 3.9*). These results are precisely what one would predict for adults if the Analyzability rule and the Spelling rule were in fact collapsed into one rule. In effect there is a disjunctive choice:

(15)

$$V \implies 1str \ / \ \begin{bmatrix} +\underline{} \\ \\ \underline{} CC\# \end{bmatrix}$$

Only one environment needs to apply and the presence of the other becomes irrelevant. Both spelling and morphology, two different domains of grammar, are referred to in a single stress rule.

These facts are expressed in SPE (with slight modifications in Liberman and Prince) through a subpart of the Destressing rule (above), which mentions the morphological boundary:

The Prefix Rule

$$\begin{matrix} V \\ [m \ stress] \end{matrix} \implies \begin{bmatrix} -str \\ -long \end{bmatrix} \ / \ \#C_o\underline{}C_o = C_o \begin{matrix} V \\ [n \ stress] \end{matrix}$$

Condition: m is weaker than n

The prefix is automatically destressed if the second syllable receives stress. Thus the two rules are interdefined. Where the second syllable does not receive greater stress, the destressing of the prefix does not occur. How does this differ from the children's rule? Our evidence is consistent with the hypothesis that the children first acquire a prefix rule that is separate from other stress rules before it revises that rule to operate in terms of other stress rules. This claim seems very natural to us. It states, in effect, that the first observation a child makes, faced with the surface of English words, is that stress follows prefixes. Therefore he makes a post-prefix stress rule. He makes a parallel observation that stress falls on strong syllables. Later he revises these rules to make them operate in terms of each other. The situation is not unlike what one finds in the acquisition of questions by children. At one stage they either perform *wh-movement* (Where John can go) or *subject-verb inversion* (Can John go) but not both.[16]

Acquisition Theory

We must now ask how our results fit into a plausible model of language acquisition. First, do the differences between the adult model and the child model violate linguistic universals? They do not. Our notion of *homogeneity* is defined with reference to grammatical levels that are features of universal grammar. The restriction to homogeneous rules increases the number of rules that a child applies to a given word. However, the structural description of each rule is extremely simple. We should, therefore, suggest that it is the complexity of structural descriptions in adult grammar and not the number of rules which poses a challenge to the child.

The fact that rules are cumulative does not necessarily entail their having additive effects. In SPE rules which apply 1stress cannot increase 1stress. However, Halle has recently proposed on independent grounds that stress assignment should function cumulatively and that a special rule of destressing would take effect in terms of the number of 1stresses a syllable receives. In Liberman and Prince the interaction with metrical structure is more complex. In general our putative child grammar is not at odds with universal grammar.

How does our model suggest an improvement in the learnability of grammars? We suggested earlier that the hypothesis of homogeneous rules limits the set of possible hypotheses at the first phase of stress acquisition. It is worth note that the adult rules which replace the homogeneous rules may not involve a radical reanalysis of those rules. The operation is primarily one of collapsing the existing rules into a set of interdefined rules. Or, as in our analysis, there is a shift of a rule from a stress rule to a destress rule. It is conceivable that the child loses hypothesis-power during the latter phases of acquisition, namely the power to project the initial stress rules. This view would preclude a radical reanalysis of stress rules in terms of new information at the later stages of acquisition. It is possible that an acquisition device ought to keep this power: a new phonological feature might entail a reanalysis that involved every aspect of a hypothesis-generator. However, the opposite possibility would improve learnability. If some hypothesis-powers decayed as other powers matured, then at each phase of acquisition the child would have a different range of potential hypotheses, but at each phase the range would be significantly smaller than if a child had to consider all hypotheses at each stage. There would, in fact, be an exponential decrease in possible grammars if the hypothesis-power changed but did not increase. Far more data is needed before we can decide upon either of these possibilities.

A good deal of current work in language acquisition has shown that it is important to verify claims through several methodologies.[17] This work is meant to fit into a larger study of how children acquire multisyllabic stress systems. All of our hypotheses must remain tentative until further work is done.

Notes

1. We would especially like to thank Charles Clifton for a great deal of helpful advice and good discussion on many aspects of this paper. We would also like to thank the members of the Summer Acquisition Research Group at Amherst, and Anke de Rooij, Alan Prince, and Barbara Skladanek of the University of Chicago, who carried out the initial experimental work. This work was supported by a grant from the University of Chicago and NIH grant HD09647-02S1 to S. J. Keyser and T. Roeper.

2. This is the issue of the "instantaneous" model. This model assumes the power of Universal grammar applies at once to a sufficient body of data to produce English. The claim is obviously false, but the assumption that universal grammar is honored throughout language acquisition may not be.

3. See Roeper (1974) for discussion of the acquisition of prefixes in German.

4. Liberman and Prince (1977).

5. Halle (1973) and Aronoff (1976).

6. See Roeper *op cit* for discussion of children's tendency to stress roots and not affixes.

7. See Smith and Baker (1976).

8. Smith and Baker *op cit* also found these results.

9. See Roeper *op cit*. We found that the first syllable was stressed in *Missbrauch* and the second syllable was stressed in the verb *missbrauchen*. Occasionally the noun was given second syllable stress, but it was never the case that the verb received first syllable stress.

10. See Myerson (1976).

11. Halle (1973).

12. See Myerson *op cit* for evidence that children do control some of the Latinate shifts by this age.

13. There could, of course, be variation among individuals and among individual rules that would cause deviations from 50%. We expected these deviations to disappear across the data. In fact, the estimate of 50% appears to have been surprisingly accurate insofar as the predicted and actual stress preferences were very close. We do not, of course, know which of the rule combinations a child has chosen when he stresses a given word. Therefore, it is impossible to see directly whether 50% is accurate as the breakdown of stress preferences where an equal number of rules applied to both first and second syllable stress.

In general, there could be a wide range of factors which cause certain optional rules to interact and thus be more likely or less likely combinations. As long as their interaction is not a formal aspect of the grammar, we would expect these differences to average out. This is just what our results suggest.

14. Brown (1973) and Miller (1973).

15. Smith and Baker (1976).

16. Jessica Wirth has suggested to us that the restriction may be stronger than a limitation to homogeneous rules in the initial phase. It could be that there are no collapsed rules (therefore, no parentheses) in use by the children. This seems plausible to us and a possible subject of further investigation.

17. Maratsos (1974a), Myerson (1975).

Chapter 4

The Acquisition
of Perception
Verb Complements

Helen Goodluck
Thomas Roeper

There is a relationship between the syntactic behavior of some words and their semantic properties.[1] In this paper we examine how children learn this kind of relationship. Our results suggest that the child's early syntactic hypotheses for the constructions we tested are independent of semantic restrictions.

The Adult Grammar of Participial Phrases

Consider the contrast between sentences containing the main verb *see* and sentences with the verb *hit*,

(1)　　John saw Bill sitting on the bench.

(2)　　John hit Bill sitting on the bench.

Sentence (1) is ambiguous. It can mean that either *John* or *Bill* is the subject of the verb *sitting.* We will refer to the reading in which *John* (the subject NP of the main verb) is the subject of *sitting* as the *subject controlled reading*, and to the reading in which *Bill* (the object of the main verb) is the subject of *sitting* as the *object controlled reading.*[2] In adult grammar, the object controlled reading of sentences such as (1) is the preferred reading. Sentence (2), however, excludes the reading in which *Bill* is the subject of *sitting*; the subject of *sitting* must be *John.* There is a semantic basis for object control: all perception verbs (*watch, look at, hear*, etc.) allow it. Nonperception verbs (*hit, kick,* etc.) do not permit object control.[3] As we have seen, both perception and nonperception verbs allow subject control.

Some speakers report an object controlled reading for nonperception verbs, particularly when the semantics of the sentence make a subject controlled reading highly implausible, as in *John hit Fido having puppies.* Other readers find such sentences totally anomalous, since their grammar requires that *John* be the subject of *have puppies.* In this paper we will be concerned with the acquisition of the grammar of these latter speakers. As we will see below, some of the older children in our experiment strictly held to the block on object control for nonperception verbs.

Our analysis of the distinction between perception and nonperception verbs with respect to object control is based in part on the work of Akmajian (1977) and Williams (1975).[4]

Participial gerunds such as those in (1) and (2) can be analyzed as instances of VP; they have all the properties of verb phrases plus an *-ing* affix on the verb. We propose to generate such participial verb phrases directly in the base in two positions: as sentence modifiers or VP complements. The phrase structure rules in (3) will permit sentence (1) to have two structures, (4) and (5).

(3) S → NP Aux VP (VP)
     VP → V (NP) (PP) (VP)

(We leave open the presence of an adverb node dominating a participial VP attached to the S node.)

(4)

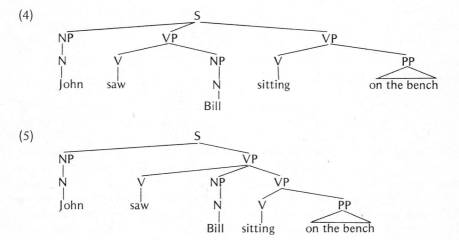

(5)

Our claim is that the structure in (4) corresponds to the subject controlled reading of sentence (1), and the structure in (5) corresponds to the object controlled reading.

Control in these constructions can therefore be defined in terms of phrase structure trees: S-node attachment entails subject control, and attachment to the VP entails object control. In effect this says that the verb of a participial complement phrase is controlled by the nearest NP (in terms of the number of intervening phrase nodes) on the phrase structure tree. Control by the nearest NP is not a universal, although it is the general case for English. Violations of this principle in English, such as the control of the infinitival complement of *promise*, are exceptions (in *John promised Bill to go, John* is the subject of *go*, not *Bill*). Edwin Williams (1975:256) has observed that a verb in English can never be controlled by an NP that is lower on the phrase structure tree (where *lower* is defined in terms of a hierarchy of nodes dominating the controller and the subjectless verb; the VP node, and hence all nodes it dominates, is lower on the hierarchy than the matrix S node). We will assume this restriction to be a language universal.

The object controlled reading of sentences like (2), in which the main verb is not a verb of perception, can be excluded in a straightforward way. The device of verb subcategorization (Chomsky, 1965) permits restrictions to be placed on the phrasal nodes that can be sister to a given verb. A phrase node may not occur in the VP unless the verb that heads the verb phrase is subcategorized for that node. In order to permit structures like (5) for sentences like (1), perception verbs must be subcategorized to allow optional recursion of VP within the verb phrase. *See*, for example, will have the subcategorization frame (6) as part of its lexical entry,

(6)   *see* [_____ NP (VP)]$_{VP}$

If the subcategorization frame for nonperception verbs like *hit* does not include an optional VP,

(7)   *hit* [_____ NP]$_{VP}$

then such verbs will be blocked from being inserted into a phrase structure tree like (5). Given our assumption that object control requires VP attachment of the participial phrase, object control will be excluded in sentences like (2) if nonperception verbs have the subcategorization frame in (7).[5] Subject control will be permitted, however; subcategorization restricts only the occurrence of nodes in the VP, and nonperception as well as perception verbs may be freely inserted into structures like (4), in which the adverbial VP is attached to the S node. As we have seen, both sentence (1) and sentence (2) have a subject controlled reading.

Notice that the structural distinction we use as the basis for subject and object control has independent syntactic support. If the participial phrase is preposed,

(8)   Sitting on the grass, John saw Bill.

only the subject controlled reading is possible. This follows under the analysis we adopt, given that the preposing rule moves only phrases that are immediate constituents of the S node.

The Acquisition of Participial Phrases

The work of Chomsky (1969) and Tavakolian (1975, 1977) lead us to make some predictions concerning the acquisition of participial phrases in sentences like (1) and (2).

Tavakolian (1975, 1977) has shown that at a very early stage of syntactic development (3-4 years) children interpret missing subjects in complex sentences as co-referential with the subject of the first verb they have processed. In conjoined sentences such as (9) and *in order to* clauses in sentences like (10), this strategy for interpreting subject will lead to a correct (adult) response,

(9)   John saw Bill and $\triangle$ picked up the box.

(10)   The lion jumped over the pig $\triangle$ to stand on the horse.

($\triangle$ indicates the empty subject position in conjoined and complement clauses; for example, (9) has the structure, $[_S[_S NP\ VP]$ and $[_S[_{NP} \triangle]\ VP]]$.) In other constructions, such as the infinitival complements of verbs such as *tell* (11) and some types of relative clauses (12),

(11)   John told Bill $\triangle$ to go.

(12)   John kicked the man that $\triangle$ hit Bill.

the subject control strategy results in an incorrect response: *John* is chosen as the subject of the embedded verb in (11) and (12) by children in Tavakolian's experiments. Overgeneralization of subject control in relative clauses was also found by Sheldon (1974).

Tavakolian's discovery of this early stage in which the first subject controls all embedded verbs was an important and surprising result, since it had been widely assumed on the basis of the word of Carol Chomsky that the first principle used by children for interpreting missing subjects was one in which the matrix object is the controller. Control by the matrix object was in fact found to be the second stage in Tavakolian's results.

On the basis of Tavakolian's work, we predicted that very young children would interpret the subject of a participial phrase in sentences such as (1) and (2) as co-referential with the subject of the main verb. As in the case of conjoined sentences such as (9) and *in order to* clauses like (10), this would be a correct adult response. However, a child who showed only subject control for the participial complements of both perception and nonperception verbs would not have a fully adult grammar, since object control is also a possible, and indeed the preferred, reading for participial complements of perception verbs among adults.

Assuming that the child knows that a subjectless verb may not be controlled by an NP lower on the phrase structure tree, control of a participial complement by the matrix subject in all cases will follow if the child's grammar permits participial phrases to be attached only to the matrix S node, and not within the VP.[6]

Regardless of whether our initial prediction is correct, we must consider how children will acquire object control. In order to acquire an adult grammar of object control in participial phrases a child must do two things. First, he must add a participial VP option to his phrase structure rule for VP. Second, he must subcategorize the correct verbs (verbs of perception) for this option. We made two hypotheses about the way in which a child might acquire object control of participials.

Hypothesis A: Semantically Bounded Innovation

Under this hypothesis, the child observes object control in sentences like (1). He changes his phrase structure rule to permit a participial VP option in the verb phrase, and subcategorizes *see* for this option. As he encounters more verbs with object controlled participial complements, he adds a participial VP option to each of their subcategorizations. At some point, he observes the semantic basis for object control, and changes the subcategorization of all perception verbs to include a participial VP.

This hypothesis makes the crucial assumption that the child only changes his grammar on the basis of positive evidence of object control. The only generalization he makes is the correct semantic one. Under Hypothesis A, the child never makes any mistakes; he never allows object control in participial phrases in the complement of nonperception verbs.

Hypothesis A leaves open the question of whether the child's initial addition of subcategorizations for a participial complement is semantically based (i.e., whether he at first adds a VP option to subcategorization frames on a verb-by-verb basis, given that the verb meets some semantic criterion, such as being in the class "perception"). However, under Hypothesis A the child must grasp the semantic basis for subcategorization before making a generalization with respect to VP attachment of a participial phrase.

Hypothesis B: Structural Innovation

As under Hypothesis A, the child observes the possibility of object control and changes his phrase structure rule to permit a participial VP within the verb phrase. However, the child also makes an incorrect generalization, and subcategorizes all verbs for this option.

At this stage, object control of participial phrases will be possible for all verbs, including nonperception verbs. Only at a later stage will the child realize the semantic restriction on object control, and eliminate the subcategorization for a participial phrase from nonperception verbs.

The structural hypothesis is a plausible one in view of the considerable body of evidence that there is a stage in which object control becomes the predominant response. Chomsky (1969) found that the missing subject in the complement of *promise* in sentences like (13) is invariably interpreted by five year olds as co-referential with the matrix object,

(13)   John promised Bill △ to go.

Object control of the infinitival complement of *promise* can be seen as an incorrect generalization from the interpretation of complement subjects of verbs like *tell*. For *tell* verbs, the complement subject and the matrix object are co-referential, and sentences with such verbs were correctly interpreted by Chomsky's five year old subjects,

(14)   John told Bill △ to go.

Chomsky proposed that children at this stage interpret the missing subject of complement verbs by use of the Minimal Distance Principle. The MDP as used by Chomsky claims that the missing subject of a complement verb is interpreted as co-referential with the nearest NP to its left. *Bill* and not *John* will be the subject of *go* in both (13) and (14) by this principle.

The term MDP is open to two interpretations. It may refer to a linear surface interpretation of the notion "nearest." This is the way in which Chomsky used the term. Or the MDP may define "nearest" in terms of the number of intervening nodes on the phrase structure tree. This is the sense in which we will use the term (and in which Rosenbaum (1967) originally formulated it as the basis for a syntactic rule of co-referential NP deletion).

It is not clear from Chomsky's results, however, that overgeneralization of object control to the complement of *promise* is based purely on the overuse of a structural principle (the MDP). The basis for the overgeneralization could be semantic. E. Clark (1973:97-98) suggests that verbs may be grouped by young children into general semantic classes on which a uniform syntactic analysis is imposed. Clark's hypothesis could be used to account for the overgeneralization of object control to *promise*. *Promise* is an illocutionary verb, and could plausibly be grouped by the child with verbs like *say* and *tell*, which require object control, by virtue of belonging to the same general semantic class. Chomsky's results are compatible with a theory of acquisition, therefore, in which structural over-generalization only takes place when the child can identify some semantic basis for the application of the structural principle.[7]

Our research was designed to determine the degree of independence from semantic restrictions of the child's capacity to make syntactic generalizations. If Hypothesis B is confirmed, then we have evidence that the child is insensitive to the semantic basis for permitting object control. Confirmation of the structural hypothesis would thus support a theory of acquisition in which very general hypotheses about structure play a role in the child's linguistic development.

Experimental Evidence

We designed an experiment to test our hypotheses about the acquisition of the grammar of perception verb complements.

Materials and Design

Subjects acted out with dolls sentences like (15) and (16).

(15)   Bozo saw her carrying the basket.

(16)   Bozo kissed her wearing the watch.

The appropriate dolls (for (15) and (16) a clown doll and a girl doll) and props (a basket, a watch) were laid out before the subject, who acted out the sentence as soon as the experimenter had read it to him. Subject or object control of the participial phrase was determined by which doll was made to carry the basket/wear the watch.

The test for the presence of a subcategorization for a participial phrase for a verb in adult grammar is object control of that phrase. If a child made the object of the main verb in sentences like (15) and (16) carry the basket/wear the watch, then we had evidence that the matrix verb was subcategorized for a participial phrase in the verb phrase. However, failure to make the matrix object the subject of the participial phrase does not, for any one sentence, constitute evidence that the matrix verb was *not* subcategorized for a participial phrase. The child may subcategorize the verb for a participial phrase but have chosen to attach the participial phrase to the S node (with consequent subject control of the participial phrase) in acting out the sentence. For this reason, more than one presentation of each verb tested had to be made before a lack of object control could be asserted. Each verb tested was presented five times to each subject. Failure to respond with object control of the participial phrase for all five presentations of the verb was taken to establish lack of subcategorization of a verb for a participial phrase in the VP.

Subjects responded to sentences containing the perception verbs *see* and *watch* and the nonperception verbs *kick* and *kiss*. Five presentations of each test verb gave a total of 20 test sentences. The object of the main clause was always pronominal (as in (15) and (16)). Since the pronoun object referred to a doll previously identified in the experimental situation, a restrictive relative reading was excluded (see footnote 5 above). The sentences were read with a neutral intonation contour. The complete set of test materials is given in *Appendix 1*. The test sentences were presented to each child individually in four groups of five sentences. Each group of five sentences was acted out using a different pair of dolls. Each verb *(see, watch, kick, kiss)* was contained once in three of the four groups of sentences and twice in one of the four groups. Two questionnaires were used (each being presented to half the total number of subjects). Each questionnaire contained a different random order of sentences within each group of five sentences, with the constraint that the same doll was never subject of more than two consecutive sentences. The matrix subject and object were reversed in the two questionnaires. These measures were designed to identify carry-over effects from one sentence to the next, and unpredicted effects of plausibility of the different dolls as subject or object of a matrix verb or participial phrase. A comparison of the results of the two questionnaires showed no systematic differences.

Before beginning the experiment, the subject was taught the name and sex of all the dolls, and the name of all the props used in the experiment. The experimenter then showed the subject how to act out sentences. The examples used were conjoined sentences in which dolls in the first five sentences presented used the props and were at the same time actor or recipient of the action of the verb in the first sentence (e.g., *Bill hits Jane and he carries the basket*; *Jane hits Bill and he wears the watch*). These example sentences, and the division of the materials into four sets, were intended to guard against the subject adopting a strategy in terms of one doll for the interpretation of the missing subject. Thirty-two subjects between the ages of 3.4 and 6.7 were tested.

Results

Each child responded to sentences containing each of the four test verbs (*kiss, kick, watch, see*) five times. The following classifications were used in our analysis of the data for each subject.

1.   S: Subject Control.
Subject control of the participial phrase for all five presentations of a verb.
2.   O: Object Control.
Object control of the participial phrase for all five presentations of a verb.
3.   PS: Preference for Subject Control.
Subject control for four out of five presentations of a verb.
4.   PO: Preference for Object Control.
Object control for four out of five presentations of a verb.
5.   NoP: No Preference for Subject or Object Control.
Subject control in two or three of the five presentations of a verb.

Three examples of this classification of subjects' responses are given in *Table 4.1*. The subjects were grouped into four classes on the basis of this classification of their responses.

1.   Subject-oriented grammar.
Children in this category have an S, PS or NoP response pattern for all verbs (perception and nonperception), and have at least two S or PS responses. Subject No. 13 in *Table 4.1* is an example of a subject-oriented grammar.

Table 4.1

Subject No. 13

Verb type	Nonperception				Perception			
Verb	kick		kiss		watch		see	
Control	Sub.	Obj.	Sub.	Obj.	Sub.	Obj.	Sub.	Obj.
Number of responses	2	3	4	1	5	0	4	1
Response type	NoP		PS		S		PS	

Subject No. 16

Verb type	Nonperception				Perception			
Verb	kick		kiss		watch		see	
Control	Sub.	Obj.	Sub.	Obj.	Sub.	Obj.	Sub.	Obj.
Number of responses	0	5	1	4	3	2	2	3
Response type	O		PO		NoP		NoP	

Subject No. 21

Verb type	Nonperception				Perception			
Verb	kick		kiss		watch		see	
Control	Sub.	Obj.	Sub.	Obj.	Sub.	Obj.	Sub.	Obj.
Number of responses	5	0	4	1	0	5	1	4
Response type	S		PS		O		PO	

S	Subject Control (5/5 responses)
O	Object Control (5/5 responses)
PS	Preference for Subject Control (4/5 responses)
PO	Preference for Object Control (4/5 responses)
NoP	No Preference for Subject or Object Control (2, 3/5 subject control)

2.   Object-oriented grammar.
Children in this category have an O, PO, or NoP response pattern for all verbs (perception and nonperception), and have at least two O or PO responses. Subject No. 16 in *Table 4.1* is an example of an object-oriented grammar.

3.   Mixed grammar.
These children have NoP responses for all verbs except one, for which the response is either PS or PO.

4.   Adult grammar.
Children in this category have an S or PS response pattern for nonperception verbs, and an O or PO response pattern for perception verbs. Subject No. 21 in *Table 4.1* is an example. This classification includes children whose grammar is strictly nonadult, since a PS response for nonperception verbs includes one object controlled response, which is ungrammatical for nonperception verbs in adult grammar. However, the overall response pattern is adult, in that a distinction is made between the two verb classes with respect to the possibility of object control.

Table 4.2

Verb type				Age		
Nonperception		Perception		3.4	4.4	5.4
kick	kiss	watch	see	4.3	5.3	6.7
1. Subject-oriented grammar						
S	S	S	S	X	X	
S	S	S	NoP			X
PS	S	PS	S		X	
NoP	PS	S	PS		X	
2. Object-oriented grammar						
O	O	O	O	X	X	X
O	O	O	PO		X	
O	O	NoP	O		X	
O	PO	O	O	X		X
PO	O	PO	O			X
PO	O	O	NoP		X	
O	PO	NoP	NoP		X	
O	NoP	PO	NoP	X		
NoP	PO	O	O		X	
NoP	PO	O	PO		X	
PO	NoP	PO	O			X
NoP	PO	PO	NoP	X		
NoP	NoP	O	O			X
3. Mixed grammar						
PS	NoP	NoP	NoP		X	
NoP	PS	NoP	NoP			X
NoP	NoP	NoP	PS		X	
NoP	NoP	PS	NoP	X		
NoP	NoP	NoP	PO	X		
4. Adult grammar						
S	S	O	O			X
S	S	O	PO			X(2)
S	PS	O	PO			X
PS	PS	PO	O			X

X   one subject with response pattern
X(2)   two subjects with response pattern

The complete range of response patterns within these categories and the distribution of the categories by age is given in *Table 4.2.* The largest category of responses is object controlled grammar (16/32 children). There are five children in each of the three remaining response categories.[8]

Table 4.2 shows one very clear correlation between age and the child's grammar. The adult grammar of participial phrases does not appear before five years (the youngest subject in the adult grammar category in *Table 4.2* is 5.5). No correlation between subject or object controlled grammar and age emerges from our data; children with subject and object oriented grammars are found across the complete age range of our subjects (the average ages of children with subject and object oriented grammars was 57.80 and 57.06 months respectively).

Discussion

Our initial hypothesis was not supported by our results: although we did find that most of the subjects who had not yet mastered the adult grammar of participial phrases showed an overall preference for either subject control or object control, we did not find that children who favor a subject controlled reading of participial phrases were younger than children who favor an object controlled reading.

There are two ways of looking at our inconclusive results with respect to the ordering of subject and object controlled grammars. First, it may be that the subject controlled grammar is an earlier stage than the object controlled stage (as it is in Tavakolian's work with infinitival complements), but that our data is not extensive enough to tap this ordering of stages by the measure of average age of subjects in each group. Age is not always a good diagnostic of grammatical ability. It may be that older children with subject-oriented grammar in our results are late in entering an object-oriented stage, and younger children with object-oriented grammar have entered this stage earlier than usual.

Alternatively, it may be that children do not pass through the same subject and object controlled stages for participial constructions as they do for infinitival complements. The individual child may adopt a subject-oriented grammar for participial phrases that he uses until he refines his grammar to permit object control only for perception verbs. Or he may have a grammar in which object control is the predominant response.

The children with object-oriented grammar form the largest group of subjects. Of the two hypotheses we made concerning the grammar of children who do not restrict control of a participial phrase to the subject NP, Hypothesis B rather than Hypothesis A is supported with respect to the data from these children. All the subjects with object-oriented grammar in *Table 4.2* (together with all the subjects with mixed grammar and two of the children with subject-oriented grammar) showed overgeneralization of object control to participial phrases in sentences with nonperception verbs. Primacy of object control for some subjects in our sample provides support for the importance of semantically unrestricted hypotheses in the child's early grammar of control relationships.[9] Our work thus supports Chomsky's interpretation of the overgeneralization of object control to the complement of *promise* as the result of overapplication of a nonsemantic principle (the MDP).

At this point, let us sketch the grammars of the children in our sample who have not yet acquired the adult grammar of perception verbs. For each stage we will propose a grammar that is consistent with the principle that a controller is never lower on the phrase structure tree than the subjectless verb.

For the children with subject-oriented grammars (I, *Table 4.2*), a participial phrase must be generated as sister to the matrix NP and VP (as in (4)). Two children with subject-oriented grammar permit only subject control; we can account for this by excluding a participial phrase from the VP in their grammars. Object control will thus be excluded by the block on control by a lower NP. The remaining subject-oriented children allow some object control; a participial phrase is permitted within the VP for at least some verbs, but its occurrence is not governed by the distinction between perception and nonperception.

Three children with object-oriented grammar permit only object control of a participial phrase. We can account for the grammar of these children by generating a participial phrase within the VP, but not as sister to the matrix NP and VP. All the verbs we tested will have the subcategorization frame for a participial phrase; the complement subject will be interpreted by the MDP. The remaining children with object-oriented grammar permit subject control for some verbs. For example, one child with object-oriented grammar had the response pattern in (17),

(17)   *Nonperception*   *Perception*

     kick   kiss   watch   see
     PO   O   O   NoP

In this child's grammar, evidence for subject control was found only for *kick* and *see*. This type of grammar can be accounted for in one of two ways. We could assume that complements attach only to the VP, and that the subject may be interpreted as co-referential with any higher NP; at this stage, the MDP will determine the preferred interpretation. Alternatively, both VP and S node attachment of the complement may be permitted, and the complement always interpreted by the MDP; the predominance of object control would result from VP attachment being the preferred structural analysis.

With the exception of the last child with object-oriented grammar in *Table 4.2*, none of the object-oriented children correlate the possibility of subject control with the semantic distinction between perception and nonperception verbs. Notice that this exceptional child, whose grammar we repeat here,

(18)   *Nonperception*   *Perception*

     kick   kiss   watch   see
     NoP   NoP   O   O

is in our oldest age group. His grammar is adult, except that he does not favor subject control for nonperception verbs.

The children in *Table 4.2* with mixed grammar may be at various transition stages: for example, the first and second child in this class, who show a preference for subject control for one nonperception verb, may be at a stage immediately prior to adult grammar.

Conclusions

In our experiment, we found that the restriction of object control by verb class semantics does not appear before age five years. Children under five understand complement sentences, and they understand both perception and nonperception verbs, but they do not make a connection between these two aspects of their linguistic ability. They may restrict subject or object control, but they do not do so in terms of the semantic class of the matrix verb, at least for the small sample of verbs we tested. We must now ask the question: assuming that our results will hold for a wider range of verbs than those in our experiment, how do our results affect the theory of language acquisition?

Part of the goal of linguistic theory is to identify the common properties of all human languages, and to specify the devices that may be used by a grammar. These general properties of grammars constitute universal grammar (UG). Two possibilities for language acquisition can be considered: (1) It could be the case that every device of UG is reflected in the child's early syntactic hypotheses, or (2) it could be the case that only some of the devices found in adult grammars are reflected in the child's earliest syntactic hypotheses.

We assume the following to be part of UG,

A. A verb is never controlled by an NP lower on the phrase structure tree. (= Williams' principle, p. 68, above).

(A) constrains the form of any rule of control in a language: to the extent that a language has control rules, the rules must be subject to (A). This type of universal is discussed by Chomsky in his treatment of language acquisition (Chomsky, 1975:29).

On a rather different level, UG will also specify powers that may be used in human languages, although a given language may fail to do so. (B) is such a device,

B. Subcategorization frames may (but need not) be governed by semantic restrictions.

(B) is part of UG in the sense that it must be included in an account of the characteristics of a possible human language. (Thus it is analogous to a given member of the set of distinctive features specified in UG for the sound system of languages, members of which may or may not be utilized in a particular language.)

Let us first observe our account of children's grammar in the pre-adult grammar stages in our experiment never violates (A). This is consistent with an innateness hypothesis of language acquisition in which children never violate universal constraints (Chomsky, 1975:34). Chomsky expressed this claim in his assumption that learning is "instantaneous." The principle feature of this model is that adult universals limit the child's principles of hypothesis projection from the outset.

A second feature of the "instantaneous" hypothesis is the suggestion that children acquire the entire grammar at once.[10] As Chomsky observes (p. 119) this is clearly false: children do pass through a sequence of stages in their linguistic development. Our work begins to look at the question of identifying the properties of adult grammar that do not enter the child's earliest hypotheses about grammar. We found that children before age 5 showed no evidence that they have the power to project a relationship between semantic verb classes and syntactic rules (subcategorization frames). This preliminary work suggests that the observed stages in the child's syntactic development may result in part from the relatively late entry of optional devices of human language (such as (B) above) into the child's hypothesis formation.

Our claims require support from other experiments and other languages.[11] Nevertheless we can tentatively conclude that, during the early stages, certain grammatical powers are not used by the child. Does this simplify or complicate the "problem of acquisition"? We take the fundamental question for a theory of acquisition to be the determination of how a child selects one from among infinitely many possible grammars. Both the requirement that the child obeys obligatory principles of UG (such as (A)) and that the child initially does not explore possibilities resulting from optional devices of UG (such as (B)) serve to restrict the range of possible grammars during the early phases of syntactic development, and thus to reduce the number of initial hypotheses the child may consider.

Appendix 1.   Materials

A.   *See*
1.   Pluto see him wearing the watch (Donald Duck)
2.   Bill see her wearing the watch (Jane)
3.   Bill see her carrying the red basket (Jane)
4.   Bozo see her wearing the white beads (Jane)
5.   Bozo see her carrying the red basket (Nancy)

B.   *Watch*
1.   Pluto watch him carrying the yellow basket (Donald Duck)
2.   Pluto watch him wearing the blue beads (Donald Duck)
3.   Bill watch her wearing the blue beads (Jane)
4.   Bozo watch her carrying the red basket (Jane)
5.   Bozo watch her wearing the white beads (Nancy)

C.   *Kick*
1.   Pluto kick him wearing the watch (Donald Duck)
2.   Bill kick her carrying the green basket (Jane)
3.   Bill kick her wearing the blue beads (Jane)
4.   Bozo kick her wearing the watch (Nancy)
5.   Bozo kick her carrying the yellow basket (Nancy)

D.   *Kiss*
1.   Pluto kiss him wearing the white beads (Donald Duck)
2.   Bill kiss her carrying the yellow basket (Jane)
3.   Bozo kiss her wearing the watch (Jane)

4. Bozo kiss her carrying the green basket (Jane)
5. Bozo kiss her wearing the blue beads (Nancy)

All sentences were read in the frame "Can you make _____." Names in parentheses indicate the doll used as object NP in acting out the sentence. Each pair of dolls occurs once with three of the four verbs, and twice with one verb.

Notes

1. We would like to thank Edwin Williams for suggesting the relevance of the grammar of perception verbs to the issues in this paper, and for his help in the planning stages of our experimental work. Our thanks are also due to the members of the Research Seminar in Language Acquisition at the University of Massachusetts at Amherst in the summer of 1976, S. J. Keyser, E. Matthei, G. Carlson, L. Solan, and S. Tavakolian, for much valuable discussion of this research topic. Susan Tavakolian and Jane Perlmutter also contributed time and expertise in the design of our experiment. In addition, we wish to gratefully acknowledge Charles Clifton and Barbara Partee for comments on an earlier draft of this paper. All errors are the authors' responsibility. This research was supported by NIH grant No. HD 09647 to S. J. Keyser and T. Roeper.

Our experimental work was made possible by the generous help of the staff and children of The Living and Learning School, Amherst, Ma., South Hadley Child Care Association, South Hadley, Ma., The Little Red Schoolhouse, Amherst, Ma., and the Bement School, Deerfield, Ma.

2. Perception verbs also allow bare infinitival complements with object control,

i) John saw Bill sit on the bench.

In our experimental work, we chose to test the acquisition of perception verb complements with *-ing* complementizers because there are exactly parallel control sentences with nonperception verbs (i.e., (1) contrasts with (2); for *John saw Bill sit on the bench* there is no grammatical equivalent **John hit Bill sit on the bench*).

3. Examples like

i) John disliked Bill sitting on the bench

would appear to suggest that "perception" is too narrow a characterization of the class of verbs taking object control. Note, however, that the syntax of sentences like (i) differs from that of sentences like (1), as a comparison of the passive forms shows,

1)' John was seen by Bill sitting on the bench

i)' **John was disliked by Bill sitting on the bench

These facts will be accounted for if *Bill* is not the direct object of the verb *dislike*; rather the whole complement sentence is the object of *dislike*,

ii) John disliked $[_{NP}[_{S}$Bill sitting on the bench$_S]_{NP}]$

4. The use of verb subcategorization to account for the selection of gerundive complements by perception verbs and the analysis of *-ing* participials as instances of VP is derived from Akmajian. Our analysis of the principles governing control and the structural position of modifiers is based on Wlliams. Akmajian's account of the grammar of perception verb complements differs somewhat from that presented here. Specifically, Akmajian claims that gerundial complements of perception verbs are dominated by NP in deep structure, and that the structure (5) is a derived structure, the result of (vacuous) extraposition of a VP complement from NP. The question of whether (4) is a base structure for gerundial perception verb complements or only derived by extraposition from NP does not crucially affect the developmental issues discussed in this paper, although how and when the child learns that gerundial complements to perception verbs may behave like NP constituents is an interesting issue that our research leaves unexplored. See Gee (1977) for a detailed critique of Akmajian's analysis. In Akmajian's analysis, the subject controlled reading of sentences like

(1) is correlated with the result of extraposition from the VP complement of a subject noun phrase, i.e., (1) will be derived from

    1) [$_{NP}$ John, sitting on the grass] saw Bill.

While surface structures like (1) may result from extraposition, note that the preposing facts, (8), suggest that (5) should be an independently derived deep structure, since extraposed complements do not prepose,

    i) a.   A review of a book about China will soon appear.
       b.   A review will soon appear of a book about China.
       c.   *Of a book about China, a review will soon appear.

5. The object controlled structure for participial phrases is distinct from that for both restrictive and nonrestrictive relatives. For example, neither type of relative can have a pronominal head,

    i) a.   *They all hate him, who ran away.
       b.   *They all hate him who ran away.

Sentences such as the following, although somewhat archaic sounding, appear to be counterexamples to the block on pronominal heads of restrictive relatives,

    ii) He who runs away is guilty!

Notice, however, that the pronoun head of such constructions may not be referential,

    iii) a.   John$_i$ enjoys jogging.   *He$_i$ who runs is healthy.
        b.   John$_i$ enjoys jogging.   I saw him$_i$ running today.

In (iiia), *he* must refer to a general class; the second sentence in (iiia) is ungrammatical on a reading in which *he* refers exclusively to John. In (iiib), *he* can refer to John.

    See Akmajian (1977) for a number of further arguments that the object controlled reading for perception verb complements must be distinguished from both restrictive and nonrestrictive relatives. Akmajian also presents evidence that participial complements of perception verbs must be distinguished from true gerunds (with possessive marking on the head NP), and may not be derived from (reduced) *while/when* clauses.

    The object controlled reading that some speakers report for nonperception verb sentences (p. 87 above) may be the result of a relaxation by these speakers of the restriction that the head of a participial relative may not be a proper noun or a pronoun.

    6. Tavakolian (1977) proposes an analysis of overuse of subject control in which complement clauses are analyzed as conjoined sentences; Sheldon (1974) suggests that the child's rules for interpreting missing subjects refer to functional relations such as *subject* and *object*. At this point, these differing approaches do not appear to bear significantly on the issues in this paper.

    7. An interpretation of Chomsky's results based on the child's semantic classification of *promise* with *say* and *tell* as members of a general class of "illocutionary" verbs involves assuming a less developed understanding of the semantics of *promise* on the part of the child who overgeneralizes than that assumed by Chomsky. Chomsky (1969:11-14) points out that illocutionary verbs like *tell, order, require,* and *command* have the force of commands, and all have object control of infinitival complements. *Promise* does not share the property of being a command, and has subject control of infinitival complements. Thus the exceptional control properties of *promise* in adult grammar do have a semantic correlate. Support for this observation comes from verbs like *ask* and *beg,* that are semantically intermediate, according to Chomsky, between a request and a command, and can take either subject or object control of an infinitival complement (compare, *The child asked the teacher (for permission) to leave the room,* and *The teacher asked the child to leave the room*). If the children in Chomsky's experiment did fully understand the meaning of *promise,* it would be possible to say that they are making a structural generalization that ignores a semantic distinction that restricts the syntax of *promise* in adult grammar. Clark (1971) has pointed out, however, that Chomsky's claim that her subjects fully understand the meaning of *promise* is not necessarily borne out by the evidence that she presents for this understanding, based on the subjects' responses to questioning about *promise.* Chomsky established only that the child understood the

obligation involved in a first person promise (*I promise that . . .*), but does not, as Clark observes, establish that the child understood that in third person promises (*Bozo promises Bill to . . .*) the subject of the matrix must perform the action of the embedded sentence.

8. An inspection of *Table 4.2* shows that there is no correlation between response pattern and the individual verbs within the perception and nonperception classes (for example, it was not the case that *kick*, but not *kiss*, received object control at a particular stage for a number of children).

Only one of our 32 subjects responded in a way that does not fit one of the four response categories. This subject gave the following responses:

Subject No. 8 (age 4.2)

Nonperception		Perception	
kick	kiss	watch	see
S	O	PO	NoP

It appears that this subject may have a lexically governed grammar of control, in which individual verbs are specified for exclusively subject, exclusively object, or either subject or object control of a participial phrase.

9. Notice that our argument will hold even if it were to be argued that the child with the object-oriented grammar is attaching the participial phrase to the object NP rather than directly to the VP node.

10. See Roeper (1977) for a fuller discussion of the "instantaneous" model.

11. Slobin (1973:205-206) reports that Gvozdev and that Slovoyeva have found the acquisition of distinct accusative case endings for animate and inanimate masculine nouns in Russian was a relatively late development. At first children use a single accusative form for all nouns. This late acquisition of a semantically governed syntactic distinction is in accordance with our findings. However, Slobin also reports (p. 207) that Kernan found a choice of articles in Samoan, based on the distinction [$\pm$human], is acquired very early (in the two-word stage). It may be that this early semantic-syntactic correlation is based on the child learning the article-noun as a unit. (We have not yet been able to consult Kernan's work.) We expect that the interaction of semantic and syntactic factors in acquisition will be very complex; future research must be directed at finding principles that govern the possibility of an early syntactic-semantic correlation such as that found by Kernan, and which will distinguish a case of this type from the evidence presented in this paper.

Chapter 5

The Acquisition of Tough Movement

Lawrence Solan

In recent transformational literature, there has been considerable controversy as to whether (1) is derived by movement or deletion.

(1)   John is easy to please.

The movement hypothesis (see Postal, 1971) claims that the surface structure subject *John* is actually the deep structure object of *please*, and is moved to the front of the sentence by a transformation generally called *tough movement*. The deletion hypothesis, introduced by Lasnik and Fiengo (1974), makes the claim that (1) is derived by deleting a second occurrence of *John* from the complement object position.

It will be argued in this paper that certain facts about the acquisition of these sentences are crucial in deciding between the movement hypothesis and the deletion hypothesis, and that these facts support the movement hypothesis. In section 2, we will elaborate on the two theories, and discuss the predictions each theory makes regarding language acquisition. In section 3, an experiment involving children between the ages of three and five will be presented, and the results discussed. Section 4 will offer an alternative explanation and present further experimentation showing this explanation to be incorrect. Section 5 is a conclusion containing a brief discussion of the role of acquisition data in linguistic argument.

Movement vs. Deletion for *Tough* Sentences

The basic claim of the movement hypothesis is that (1) is derived from (2) transformationally.

(2)   It is easy to please John.

The transformation replaces the *it* (or an empty node) with the complement object.

In their paper, Lasnik and Fiengo (1974) raise a number of objections to this analysis, most of which involve circumstances under which sentences like (2) are not adequate sources for sentences like (1). Consider the following pairs of sentences:

(3)   A.   John is being easy to please.
       B.   *It is being easy to please John.

(4)   A.   John is intentionally easy to please.
       B.   *It is intentionally easy to please John.

At first glance, the fact that the (B) sentences are not grammatical sources for the (A) sentences might appear to present a serious problem for the movement hypothesis. Note that the deletion hypothesis is not in any trouble since (3A) would be derived from (5), and (3B) would have no possible source.[1]

(5)   John is being easy [to please John]

As Jackendoff (1975) points out, however, these claims depend on the assumption that constraints on the progressive aspect and adverb placement occur in the deep structure. He presents evidence demonstrating that this assumption is not well-founded. Consider first the progressive. If there is such a thing as the passive transformation, then (6B) is derived from (6A) Jackendoff's (15).

(6)   A.   John is finding out that crime doesn't pay.
       B.   ??It is being found out by John that crime doesn't pay.

Both sentences in the corresponding pair without the progressive aspect are grammatical.

(7)   A.   John found out that crime doesn't pay.
       B.   It was found out by John that crime doesn't pay.

Because of sentences like (6B), restrictions on the progressive cannot be stated in deep structure, so the sentences in (3) no longer present evidence in favor of the deletion hypothesis.

Similarly, as Jackendoff demonstrates, (4) does not prove to be an argument against the movement hypothesis. Consider (8).

(8)   A.   The police carelessly have arrested Fred.
       B.   Fred carelessly has been arrested by the police.

The adverb *carelessly* in (8) (and other subject-oriented adverbs) is interpreted as describing the actions of the surface structure, not the deep structure subject.[2] Thus (4B) is not necessarily an ill-formed deep structure. That it is not a good surface structure can be explained on the grounds that one cannot credit an entire clause (the subject, semantically) with being careless. As a semantically anomalous string, it is ruled out.

Several other arguments are presented by Lasnik and Fiengo. Jackendoff attacks them on similar grounds, and we will not reproduce the arguments and counterarguments here. Lasnik and Fiengo also cite examples of sentences in which deletion and not movement must have occurred.

(9)   A.   Mary is pretty to look at.
       B.   Frogs' legs are tasty to eat.
       C.   Martha is nice enough to talk to.

Note that there are no corresponding grammatical sentences in (10).

(10)   A.   *It is pretty to look at Mary.
       B.   *It is tasty to eat frogs' legs.
       C.   *It is nice enough to talk to Martha.

In both the movement and the deletion hypotheses, the sentences in (9) will be generated by a deletion (or corresponding semantic) rule. Thus the movement hypothesis makes the claim that (1) is derived from (2) transformationally, and that (9) is derived from (11) by a deletion rule.

(11)   Mary is pretty [to look at Mary]

The deletion hypothesis makes the claim that both (1) and (9) are derived by means of the same deletion rule from the same type of underlying structure, i.e., (11).

The above discussion leads us to the conclusion that the correct derivational history of (1) has not yet been determined. Other linguistic literature, such as Postal and Ross (1971) and Akmajian (1972), also leaves the question open.

Let us now look at the predictions that each of the two theories under discussion makes for language acquisition. First, we shall consider the movement hypothesis. If it is the case that children learn to understand sentences such as (1) and (9) at different times, we shall consider that evidence, *ceteris paribus*, that the children are learning two different constructions. (This will be further discussed in sections 3 and 4.) That is, the process used to interpret one type of sentence is not sufficient to supply the child with the correct interpretation for the other type. This would be consistent with the movement hypothesis which claims that (1) is derived from one construction with a movement rule, while (9) is derived from another with a deletion rule. We shall elaborate on this statement below. If, on the other hand, the child has equal difficulty in interpreting (1) and (9), then this would be consistent with the deletion hypothesis, which derives both sentences from a single construction with a single deletion rule.

These claims we make about language acquisition data are strong ones, and must be examined more closely. A possible problem is that the results of an experiment may be biased by a child having more exposure to predicates of one type than to predicates of the other type. In order to differentiate between predicates such as *pretty* and *easy*, not only must one learn both syntactic structures (according to the movement hypothesis), but one must also learn which predicates fit into each syntactic paradigm. Since these are not necessarily the same process, a child may know both syntactic structures, but not be able to accurately classify predicates as to which syntactic structures they belong in. Similarly, if the deletion hypothesis is correct, lexical bias may play a role. The sentences chosen for the experiments described below were carefully chosen to eliminate the problem of lexical bias, to whatever extent possible.[3] Furthermore, the experiment described in section 4 indicates that at least one lexically-based explanation of the order of acquisition is inferior to the syntactic one which we propose here.

Another consideration must be noted. If a child demonstrates that he has acquired (1) and (9) virtually simultaneously, this cannot be considered empirical evidence against the movement hypothesis. We cannot eliminate the possibility that two different constructions are learned by the child at the same time. That is, it is possible that there is a point at which a child learns all object interpretation rules, regardless of the variety of constructions involved.

Let us now review the possibilities for the implications that language acquisition might have in choosing between the movement hypothesis and the deletion hypothesis.

(12)   A.   If children have equal difficulty understanding sentences with the predicate *easy* (1) and *pretty* (9), then the results are inconclusive. Either the child learns two constructions at about the same time, which is consistent with the movement hypothesis, or he learns a single construction, which is consistent with the deletion hypothesis.

B.   If children have more difficulty understanding sentences with *pretty* than sentences with *easy*, then the results support the movement hypothesis. The results also indicate that the movement rule is learned earlier than the deletion rule.

C.   If children have more difficulty with predicates such as *easy* than with predicates such as *pretty*, then the results support the movement hypothesis. Furthermore, the results indicate that the deletion rule is learned earlier than the movement rule.

Of the three possible experimental results, only (12B) and (12C) provide us with any real measure of choosing between the two hypotheses. In the experiments to be described below, it will be seen that (12B) is actually consistent with the order in which children learn these sentences.

Experiment I

Subjects

The subjects for Experiment I were children who attended the Living and Learning School in Amherst, Massachusetts, and the Greenfield Child Care Center in Greenfield, Massachusetts. All of the subjects were between the ages of three and five years, and most were of college-educated parents.

Procedure

The subject and the experimenter sat across a small table. The subject was then asked to place a small hand puppet of a tiger on one hand, and a small hand puppet of a monkey on the other.[4] To make the child comfortable with the puppets, a small amount of play was encouraged in which the subject generally made the puppets bite each other and the experimenter. Following this, the child was asked to play a special game in which the experimenter would read a list of sentences, and the subject would act out the sentences using the puppets. A small number of practice sentences was read until it was clear that the child understood, and felt comfortable with the task. Then a list of sentences was read (fourteen in Experiment I), and the subject's responses recorded. When, either because of the nature of the action in the sentence, or an ambiguity of the movement of the puppets by the child, the subject's response was unclear, he was further questioned. Such questioning took the form, "Who hit who?" or "Who is looking at who?" All responses which had been at one point unclear, were disambiguated by such questioning.

A number of children who began the test lost interest in it before it was over, and dropped out of the experiment. The data discussed below are for only those children who actually finished the questionnaires. All of these children showed complete cooperation, and a strong interest in completing the task to the best of their ability.

Results

Of the sentences in each questionnaire for Experiment I, the first group of eleven were of the form in (13).

(13)   A.   Mary is eager to please.
      B.   Mary is easy to please.
      C.   Mary is pretty to look at.

In sentences with *eager*, the subject of the main clause is also interpreted as the subject of the complement clause. For *easy* and *pretty* it is the complement object which gets the interpretation of the matrix subject. The *easy* and *pretty* predicates were differentiated according to whether sentences containing them have corresponding sentences, "It is *predicate* to . . ." Sentences with these predicates will now be referred to as *eager sentences, easy sentences,* and *pretty sentences,* respectively.

Three examples of *eager* sentences, and four each of *easy* and *pretty* sentences were presented to each subject. They were presented in random order, and are listed below.

Eager Sentences

1. The monkey is eager to bite.
2. The tiger is anxious to kiss.
3. The monkey is willing to kiss.

Easy Sentences

4. The monkey is easy to kiss.
5. The tiger is nice to jump over.
6. The monkey is fun to bite.
7. The tiger is hard to jump over.

Pretty Sentences

8. The tiger is pretty to look at.
9. The monkey is delicious to bite.
10. The tiger is nice enough to talk to.
11. The monkey is too tall to jump over.

If a child correctly interpreted two out of three or three out of four of the examples for a given sentence type, then the child was considered able to understand the sentence type. The data then indicate that children can be grouped as being in one of three stages. Four of the seventeen children, whose responses are presented in *Table 5.1,* understood the *eager* sentences, but misinterpreted both the *easy* sentences and the *pretty* sentences. We will refer to these children as being in stage one.

Five of the subjects, who were in stage two, correctly interpreted the *eager* and the *easy* sentences, missing only the *pretty* sentences. The data for these subjects are presented in *Table 5.2.* The remaining eight subjects (aged 4.6-5.11) had adult interpretations for all three of the sentence types. These children are in stage three.

Table 5.1
Incorrect responses for each subject in stage one

| | Subject's age | | | |
	3.11	4.0	4.5	5.7
Sentence				
Eager	(0)	(0)	(0)	(1)
(1)				
(2)				X
(3)				
Easy	(4)	(3)	(2)	(2)
(4)	X	X	X	X
(5)	X	X	X	X
(6)	X	X		
(7)	X			
Pretty	(4)	(3)	(3)	(4)
(8)	X	X	X	X
(9)	X			X
(10)	X	X	X	X
(11)	X	X	X	X

The following generalizations can be drawn from the data: Every child who was able to correctly interpret *pretty* sentences was also able to correctly interpret *easy* sentences, but not conversely. These results are consistent with the movement hypothesis, as indicated in (12B) above. That is, for at least this sample, *easy* sentences are learned before *pretty* sentences.[5]

As was pointed out above, it is possible to argue that the results presented in *Tables 5.1* and *5.2* reflect only that certain lexical items are learned earlier than others, independent of the number of syntactic structures involved. But the data presented here appear to be too strong to permit such an evaluation. First, the lexical items associated with *pretty* sentences were *pretty, delicious, nice,* and *tall.* The *easy* predicates were *easy, fun, nice,* and *hard.* There is no evidence that *pretty* and *delicious* are acquired later than *easy* and *fun.* Neither is there any evidence that *hard* is acquired before *tall.* To the contrary, having examined several "basic vocabulary" lists, I found that the *pretty* predicates were each at least as common as any of the *eager* or *easy* predicates.[6] While this does not constitute evidence that these children learned *pretty* first, it should indicate that children normally learn this lexical item at a relatively early age. Since most of the children correctly interpreted the sentence with *delicious,* it hardly seems necessary to argue about the time of that word's acquisition.

Furthermore, the predicate *nice* appeared in both the context of an *easy* sentence (5.) and a *pretty* sentence (10.). Although only six subjects misinter-

Table 5.2
Incorrect responses for each subject in stage two

			Subject's age		
	4.9	5.3	5.3'	5.4	5.8
Sentence					
Eager	(0)	(0)	(1)	(0)	(0)
(1)					
(2)			X		
(3)					
Easy	(0)	(0)	(0)	(1)	(1)
(4)					
(5)				X	X
(6)					
(7)					
Pretty	(2)	(3)	(3)	(3)	(2)
(8)		X	X	X	
(9)					
(10)	X	X	X	X	X
(11)	X	X	X	X	X

preted (5.) (see Tables 5.1 and 5.2), twelve subjects misinterpreted (10.). In addition, there were no children who got (10.) correct, but missed (5.). The difficulty of (10.), then, may be attributed to the syntactic structure, and not to the children's familiarity with that word. It thus seems inappropriate to argue that the subjects' having an easier time with *easy* sentences than with *pretty* sentences was caused by lexical bias of this sort, and we can still consider (12B) to be a reasonable explanation of the data displayed in Tables 5.1 and 5.2.

The remaining three sentences on the questionnaire are listed below.

12. It is eager to hit the monkey.
13. It is easy to bite the tiger.
14. It is delicious to bite the monkey.

Note that of these three sentences, only (13.) is grammatical. However, all three of them are interpretable, with the one specified NP in each sentence being interpreted as the complement object. To avoid confusing the subjects, these were all placed at the end of the questionnaire.

Of the seventeen subjects who finished the experiment, none missed any of the three sentences listed above. That is, of 51 responses, there were 51 correct responses, interpreting the only mentioned NP as the complement object. In the next section, we correlate the results of the two sections of the experiment, indicating which strategies children might have used to interpret the various sentences the way they did. A preliminary explanation for why movement rules might be acquired before deletion rules will also be offered.

Discussion of the Acquisition Data

Having found support for hypothesis (12B), let us now return to our discussion of the order in which children acquire these structures. We will deal with each of the three stages in turn.

The child who is in stage one corresponds to the children discussed by Chomsky (1969) who misinterpret the sentence, "The doll is easy to see." Looking at a blindfolded doll, children are asked whether it is easy to see or hard to see. Generally, the younger children answered that the doll was hard to see. These results are corroborated by a puppet-manipulating experiment done by Richard Cromer (1970). Both Cromer and Chomsky interpret a child's being in stage one as an indication that he has a single rule for interpreting sentences of this type which makes the correct predictions for *eager* sentences only. This explanation seems perfectly reasonable. The rule (referred to by Cromer as the "primitive rule") might be stated as follows:

(14)   A sequence of N V is interpreted as subject-verb.

Note that this strategy applies at the surface structure level.

The strategy proposed in (14) adequately accounts for the results of the stage one children in *Table 5.1*. Furthermore, it has been proposed elsewhere that such a strategy has a far more general role in the perception of language (see Bever, 1970). Similar conclusions were drawn by Legum (1975) in his discussion of strategies children use to interpret relative clauses. In a strategy of this sort, only surface structure word order is crucial in determining who the actor is and who the object is.

The children in stage two show more complicated linguistic behavior. A simple surface structure strategy such as (14) is not sufficient to explain the experimental results. We remember that the deep structures of *easy* and *pretty* sentences take the forms of (15A) and (15B), respectively.

(15)   A.   It is easy to bite the monkey.
        B.   The tiger is pretty [to look at the tiger].

Let us assume that at a certain point the child realizes that the strategy (14) is not adequate to handle all of the sentences he encounters. We hypothesize that what the child learns first is that the surface structure subject is really the deep structure object, for some cases. It is then incumbent on the child to learn which predicates have surface structure subjects which are also deep objects. This task should be much easier with *easy* sentences than with *pretty* sentences, since for the former, the deep structure corresponds to a surface structure with which he is familiar, namely, the sentence corresponding to (15A).

There are two kinds of evidence which we will present here to support this hypothesis. First, let us consider the last three test questions, 12-14. That none of the children missed any of these sentences indicates that they certainly have a strategy for interpreting (15A) in their control at an early age. Thus the task is a matter of associating a surface structure tree which the child already has as part of his grammar (observe the results in *eager* sentences) with a deep structure tree which the child also has as part of his grammar. That is, no new structures must be learned by the child to enable him to interpret correctly *easy* sentences.

The children's correct responses for sentences 12-14 indicate that they have the following strategy:

(16)   Interpret a V N sequence as verb-object.

The existence of such strategies is confirmed also by evidence presented in Bever (1970), Legum (1975) and Echeverria (1975). We can now restate our claim by saying that when the child learns to correctly interpret *easy* sentences, he learns to apply strategy (16) at a deep structure level instead of strategy (14) at a surface structure level. Of course, this explanation makes sense only if we adopt the movement hypothesis. If the deletion hypothesis were correct, we could not correlate the results of sentences 12-14 with the acquisition of *easy* sentences independent of the acquisition of *pretty* sentences.

A second piece of evidence is found in Austin (1976) and Gruber (1967). In an experiment involving the acquisition of passive constructions, Austin found that children interpret the surface structure subject of the passive sentence as the deep structure object at a very young age. If we look at such data as providing evidence that leftward movement rules are acquired at an early age, then the deep-surface structure pairing that occurs for *easy* sentences is simply a part of a more general process that is affecting the development of the linguistic competence of the child. This fact is even more striking if Chomsky's (1973, 1975) suggestion that transformations such as passive and tough movement might actually be parts of the same generalized rule proves to be true. Topicalization, discussed by Gruber (1967), is also a leftward movement rule which is learned very early. Perhaps this also may be looked at as a part of a more general process.

The analysis of children's acquisition of *easy* sentences presented here, then, takes the following form. The data in *Tables 5.1* and *5.2* indicate that children acquire *easy* sentences before they acquire *pretty* sentences. By adopting the movement hypothesis, which makes the claim that the two sentence types have different structures and different derivational histories, we can explain this fact. Once we have adopted the movement hypothesis, we see that certain other facts, namely the early acquisition of the passive construction and of topicaliza-tion fit into the larger strategical change of rejecting (14) as the appropriate surface structure strategy and replacing it with the strategy (16) at the deep structure level.

Finally, there are two anomalies in the data presented which should be explained. First, even though many of the subjects were unable to interpret correctly a majority of the *pretty* sentences, only two (*Table 5.1*: 3.11, 5.7) misunderstood the sentence with *delicious*.

9. The monkey is delicious to bite.

While it seems that the children in stage one and stage two have not yet acquired the knowledge necessary in interpreting *pretty* sentences, they still have no trouble with this sentence. One possible explanation for this is that for children, at least, *delicious* is actually an *easy* predicate. Sentences such as (17A), while marginal, seem much better to me than sentences like (17B).

(17)   A.   It is delicious to eat ice cream in the summer.
       B.   *It is pretty to look at Mary in the afternoon.

If it is the case that children classify *delicious* as an *easy* predicate, it would help to account for this anomaly.

The second peculiarity in the data involves the relative difficulty of the various *pretty* sentences. Of the three sentences not containing *delicious*, the one with *too tall* is the most difficult, then the one with *nice enough*, and finally the sentence with *pretty* is the easiest of the three. Even some children with otherwise adult interpretations miss one or the other of (10) and (11). It is not surprising that some children get only some of these right. Both Cromer (1970) and Chomsky (1969) report stages in the acquisition of a particular construction in which the child gives inconsistent responses. But the fact that specific sentences are obviously more difficult than others does require some explanation.

When *too* is used in the context of sentence (11), it often produces an ambiguous sentence.

11. The monkey is too tall to jump over.

If we were to substitute *hit* for *jump over*, we would have such a context. In the revised (11), the subject can either be the antecedent for the missing subject or for the missing object. Since children have strategies for correctly interpreting the subject reading of the sentence (note that they all interpret *eager* sentences correctly), it would follow that they might learn the subject reading with *too* and *enough* before they ever are able to interpret *pretty* sentences at all. Thus, when they finally learn the *pretty* construction, they reject *too* and *enough* as possible *pretty* predicates, since they have already classified them as *eager* predicates. In keeping with the results of Cromer (1970), then, there is a stage during which children try to ascertain which predicates fit into a syntactic structure which they have just learned.

An Alternative Hypothesis

Most of this paper thus far has been devoted to arguing that the movement hypothesis is consistent with a plausible theory of language acquisition for these particular constructions. But by no means have we argued that the movement hypothesis is necessary. In this section we will consider another theory of the acquisition of these sentences which adequately accounts for the data. We will then provide further experimental evidence which indicates that the movement hypothesis is preferable.

First, let us consider the following sentences:

(18)   A.   ?Harry is easy.
       B.   ?Harry is hard.

(19)   A.   Harry is too tall.
       B.   Harry is pretty.

In simple sentences, the *easy* predicates in (18) do not readily allow individuals as subjects. They require abstract subjects. On the other hand, as (19) indicates, individuals can be the subjects of *pretty* predicates. We can now paint the following picture of the acquisition process.[7]

Children learn *eager* predicates early. In addition, they learn *pretty* predicates in simple constructions, such as (19). Note that children cannot learn *easy* constructions which correspond to (19), since they do not exist. The child must discover that *easy* predicates take abstract subjects. Having done this, an understanding of *easy* sentences should follow. In order to learn *easy* as a predicate of English one must learn its appearance in this more complicated construction.

The situation with *pretty* predicates is not as complicated. Having learned sentences such as (19), the child feels that he has learned the predicate. Thus, he does not learn to understand these predicates with complement constructions until later.

This theory is consistent with both the acquisition data and the deletion hypothesis. We can assume here that both *pretty* and *easy* sentences have the same syntactic structure. What makes *pretty* sentences more difficult is that the child goes through a stage during which he ignores complement clauses, having classified the predicates syntactically already. Quite often this will not present the child with communication problems. In many *pretty* sentences the meaning comes across without the complement. Knowing that Mary is pretty, for example, gives the child sufficient information to process (9A).

Experiment II was designed to test the validity of this theory against the one which we are proposing. The first part of the experiment tests the claim that children ignore the complement of *pretty* sentences. If this were true, then children in stages one and two should not be able to correctly interpret *pretty* sentences which have no missing noun phrases. The subjects were ten of the seventeen subjects who participated in Experiment I. They were given the tiger puppet and a crumpled paper bag, and asked:

15. Is the bag too big for the tiger to pick it up?

Note that both the subject (*the tiger*) and the object (*it*) are present in the complement clause. All ten of the subjects understood this sentence. Nine answered "no" and manipulated the tiger so that it actually picked up the bag. One subject said "yes" and manipulated the tiger to indicate that it was unable to lift the bag. Thus the claim that the children fail to associate *pretty* predicates with complement clauses is incorrect. This supports the claim that children misunderstand *pretty* sentences because of their unfamiliarity with a particular syntactic structure.

A second possibility for distinguishing between the two theories involves the predicate *ready*. Semantically, *ready* behaves as an *easy* predicate, but syntactically, it behaves as a *pretty* predicate. It does not allow the "it is . . ." construction. Furthermore, sentences with *ready* are ambiguous.

(20)   The car is ready to pull.

The two meanings of this sentence involve either the car pulling something, or something pulling the car. According to the movement hypothesis, only stage three children should be able to get the object reading of this sentence, since syntactically, it is a *pretty* sentence. The alternative deletion hypothesis, however, predicts that both stage two and stage three children should be able to get the object reading. We tested these predictions.

The subject was presented with a car hooked up to a truck. Both vehicles were facing in the same direction, and a barrier stood behind the car. The subject was then asked test sentence 16.

16. Is the car ready to pull?

Because of the barrier, the only simple action was to make the truck pull the car (which corresponds to the reading with the missing object). Of the ten subjects, five answered no, indicating that they understood the sentence to mean that the car is ready to pull the truck (subject reading). Two children answered "yes," but made the car pull the truck through the barrier. Actually, only two subjects (4.0, 5.2) demonstrated knowledge of the missing object reading. The younger of these subjects was in stage one, and the older in stage three. One stage two subject was uncertain of his answer.

The experiment described above fails to disconfirm the movement hypothesis. None of the subjects in stage two got the object reading. We look at the one correct answer from a stage one subject as an anomaly, and both hypotheses predict that some stage three children should get this reading. But note that this experiment does not strongly support the movement hypothesis. It is always possible that the subjects simply prefer one reading over the other. This kind of test does not prove conclusively that these children are not able to understand the object reading, only that they do not. The only support that the experiment gives to the movement hypothesis is in that so many of the subjects failed to see the object reading in spite of such heavy semantic bias in favor of it.

The two parts of Experiment II were designed to compare the movement hypothesis to another plausible hypothesis. Both parts indicate that it is preferable, and we therefore reassert the claim that the difference between the acquisition of *easy* sentences and *pretty* sentences is caused by differences between the syntactic structures for each sentence type.

Conclusion

Throughout this paper we have assumed the following premise to be valid:

(21)   Given two weakly equivalent grammars, G_1 and G_2, which differ only with respect to a particular rule (or rule schemata) X, then whichever of G_1 and G_2 presents a more psychologically plausible account of X is the more highly preferred grammar.

In our case, it is possible to construct two grammars which differ only in that one incorporates the deletion hypothesis, and the other incorporates the movement hypothesis. On the basis of (21) we have chosen the movement hypothesis as belonging to the more highly preferred grammar. This is not to say that within its grammar, the deletion hypothesis does not adequately account for the generation of all and only grammatical sentences within its domain. But we are now adding psychological plausibility as a criterion for choosing between weakly equivalent grammars.[8]

The principle described in (21) has as its basis some of the goals implicit in linguistic research. For example, Bach (1974) assesses the basic (Chomskyan) puzzle as being in two parts (p. 157):

A.   What is the class of grammars G from which the acquirer of a human language selects the grammar for his/her language?
B.   How does the acquirer find *the* right grammar (=descriptively adequate grammar) or *a* right grammar for his/her language?

The work described in this paper is directed toward the second of these two questions, which Peters (1972) has also called the "projection problem."[9]

We have attempted to present a reasonable account of the acquisition of *easy* sentences. Our proposal is only as strong as the weaker of the two questions posed in Bach's question B. We certainly cannot claim that the grammar which includes the movement hypothesis is *the* right grammar, and (21) makes no such claim. But if the notion of *a* right grammar is to be tied in with the acquirer of that grammar, then the psychology (and perhaps physiology) of that acquirer must be taken into account. A "right grammar" could never be one which is inconsistent with the acquisition of language, for the simple reason that there is empirical evidence that it wasn't acquired. Thus, taking seriously Bach's assessment of the goals of linguistic theory, psychological plausibility seems to be a necessary criterion (along with strong generative capacity) for "a right grammar."

Notes

I wish to thank Tim Austin, Emmon Bach, Carol Chomsky, Ed Matthei, Tom Roeper and Edwin Williams for their valuable discussions and suggestions. I also wish to express my gratitude to the staffs and children at the Bement School, Deerfield, Mass., the Living and Learning School, Amherst, Mass., the Lemberg Children's Center, Waltham, Mass., and the Greenfield Child Care Center, Greenfield, Mass.

1. According to the deletion hypothesis, only some predicates subcategorize to take the "it is *adj* to . . ." construction. While *easy* is such a predicate, (3B) is ungrammatical in that the verb *be* does not subcategorize to take the progressive aspect, at least in this context.

2. Actually, the interpretation occurs at the end of the cycle, and not in surface structure. See Jackendoff (1975) and Perlmutter (1971) for discussion of this matter.

3. Another potential problem of lexical bias might be considered. Fodor, Garrett and Bever (1968) point out that some verbs are more complex than others. In an experiment, subjects were given pieces of paper with words which had to be unscrambled to form grammatical sentences. The sentences could later be analyzed as pairs, with one member of the pair having a verb which could be used only transitively, and the other member having a verb which was being used transitively, but which could also be used in a complement construction. (i), their (1), is a typical example.

(i) The man whom the child $\begin{array}{l}\text{(a) met}\\\text{(b) knew}\end{array}$ carried a box.

The results of the experiment support the claim that sentences whose verbs have the complement subcategorization are more difficult to unscramble than sentences with simple transitive verbs.

Since all of the sentences discussed here contain complement constructions, it is not possible to use this particular measure of complexity in any meaningful way. But it should be noted that if such a measure were to be found, it would undoubtedly be relevant to studies of this kind.

4. The design of this experiment is essentially the same as the design of Cromer (1970). The only substantial difference is in the focus of the sentences in the questionnaire.

5. In a pilot study conducted at the Lemberg Children's Center in Waltham, Mass., one subject was found to be in stage one, three subjects were in stage two, and two subjects were in stage three. Once again there were no subjects getting *pretty* sentences correct, but misinterpreting *easy* sentences. This study differed from the one described in the text only in that it did not include sentences (7) and (11).

6. See, for example, Carroll, Davies and Richman (1971).

7. This possibility was pointed out to me by Edwin Williams.

8. See Peters and Ritchie (1973) for a discussion of equivalence between transformational grammars.

9. Works such as Emonds (1970), Chomsky (1973) and many others are directed at the first of these two questions.

Chapter 6

Children's Interpretation of Reflexive Pronouns in English

Charles Read
Victoria Chou Hare

Co-reference is by its very nature fundamental to the nature of language. This in itself makes it of the utmost importance for linguistic theory. But this property of sentences becomes even more significant as a testing ground for linguistic principles and theories when it is realized that co-referential elements involve a host of special restrictions and properties.
Paul Postal (1971, p. 6)

We tested 266 subjects of various ages on their interpretation of two types of English sentences containing reflexive pronouns. The first type of sentence, "type A," requires knowing a clause-mate constraint for its correct interpretation; the second type of sentence, "type B," does not. Our results reveal that even some of the youngest children, mean age 6;9, obey the clause-mate constraint in type A sentences consistently. Children up to a mean age of 12;3 give essentially the same interpretations, with none of the age groups performing as consistently as adults. In type·B sentences, adults consistently choose the main-clause subject instead of the nearer noun as the referent of the reflexive pronoun. While younger children randomly choose either noun as the referent, older children begin to approximate the adult strategy. Learning the clause-mate constraint on type A sentences appears to precede learning the strategy for interpreting type B sentences. We look upon these results as supporting Carol Chomsky's hypothesis that regular constraints are learned at an earlier age than strategies for dealing with exceptions. However, our results tend to disconfirm C. Chomsky's speculation that a regular constraint is learned at a relatively uniform age.

Theoretical Background

Carol Chomsky (1969) showed that children systematically misunderstand certain syntactic structures at age five and beyond, because these structures involve exceptions, structural or lexical, to otherwise general principles. She thus demonstrated that these grammatical principles play a role in children's sentence comprehension. The hypothesis of Chomsky's which our study examines most directly is that a structural restriction on a grammatical operation is learned relatively late. In Chomsky's research, the instance of such a restriction was the constraint on backward pronominalization, which requires that a pronoun may occur to the left of its referent only if the pronoun is in a subordinate clause. This constraint applies to sentences such as (1A) and (1B) below.

(1) A. When he was tired, John usually took a nap.
     B. He knew that John was going to win the race.

In terms of the listener's task, the constraint determines that in (1A), "he" may refer to John, but that in (1B), "he" must refer to someone else. Confirming her hypothesis, Chomsky found that children at age five regularly interpret sentences like (1B) to mean that John knew that he, John, was going to win.

We propose that the conditions on reflexivization in English involve a comparable constraint which may also be learned late. The relevant condition on reflexivization is the so-called clause-mate constraint, which requires, roughly, that the referent of a reflexive pronoun must be a member of the same minimal clause as the reflexive itself. This constraint applies to sentences such as (2A) and (2B).

(2) A. Bill knew that John had hurt himself.
     B. *Harry wished that Mabel would respect himself.

Again from the listener's point of view, in (2A) the constraint determines that "himself" must refer to John, not to Bill, and in (2B), in the same way, the constraint determines that the only possible referent for "himself" is Mabel—thus the sentence is ill-formed. The real significance of such constraints is that they exemplify the "projection problem": the problem of how children manage to infer that sentences like (2B) are actually ruled out, rather than being merely one of the (millions of) English sentences which they have not yet heard.

In fact, the constraint must be stated somewhat more precisely; the clause-mate relation must hold at a particular point in the derivation of the sentence, namely the point at which reflexives are formed. Because clause memberships may change during a derivation, the reflexive and its referent need not be clause-mates at other points in the derivation, including both the deep and surface syntactic structures. Furthermore, the clause-mate condition itself must be defined in a precise way. For an introductory but careful formulation, the reader may wish to consult Keyser and Postal (1976), chapters 3, 5, and 6, especially definition (8) on page 45 and rule (1G) on page 55. Keyser and Postal show that the principles can be stated in a reasonably simple manner, although we should note that reflexivization in English has been the subject of considerable discussion (Postal, 1971; Jackendoff, 1972, chap. 4). Whatever the precise formulation, there is general agreement among linguists that the clause-mate constraint on reflexivization is a valid principle of English syntax. We submit that it is, in Chomsky's terms, "a restriction on a grammatical operation which applies under certain [structural] conditions only." Accordingly, we hypothesize that children will acquire this bit of grammatical knowledge relatively late, after age six. We shall put forth other hypotheses below.

Relation to Other Studies

A considerable number of other investigators has reviewed, replicated, and extended Chomsky's original research. Three of the reviews are by S. W. Stearns (1973), E. V. Clark (1971), and J. McNamara (1970); the replications and extensions are tabulated below according to the construction(s) in Chomsky's original study that they have dealt with.

> *Easy to see*:   Chomsky, 1971; Cromer, 1970, 1972; Kelleher, 1973; Kessel, 1970; Roeper, 1972, 1976; Solan, 1976.
> *Tell vs. promise*:   Chomsky, 1971; Kelleher, 1973; Maratsos, 1974b; Ramig, 1974.
> *Tell vs. ask*:   Chomsky, 1971; Kelleher, 1973; Kessel, 1970; Kramer, Koff, and Luria, 1972; Olds, 1968; Ramig, 1974; Sanders, 1971.
> *Pronominalization*:   (not replicated)

Despite extensive attention to the other three constructions, Chomsky's research on backward pronominalization has not been replicated or extended to comparable constructions, to the best of our knowledge.

Besides demonstrating unexpectedly late acquisition, Carol Chomsky made a further tantalizing observation: in her study, children appeared to master the constraint on backward pronominalization at a uniform age. With few exceptions, those younger than six years failed in their interpretation of sentences like (1B), while those older than age six succeeded. This regularity contrasted strikingly with the wide variability in the age at which children mastered the other three constructions that she studied, all of which involved exceptional lexical items. Chomsky speculated that this difference in age might prove to be general.

> *The rules for pronominal reference are qualitatively different [from the three cases involving* easy to see, promise, tell, *and* ask]. *They pertain to no specific word or class of words, but derive from principles which apply to whole [sentences], very generally, on the basis of their structure. In order to learn them the child must deal with a general principle, rather than with lexical exceptions. We may speculate that perhaps it is this difference which accounts for their more regularized acquisition. Since a*

> *basic principle of the language is involved, rather than a fact related to a specific lexical item or class of items, the child may acquire it at a certain maturational level.* (pp. 109-110)

Because of the relative inattention to this aspect of Chomsky's work, this interesting proposal remains to be substantiated. Chomsky herself clearly identified it as speculative, since she had only one construction on which to base it. Thus the second hypothesis that we wish to test is that children exhibit a mastery of the clause-mate constraint beginning at a relatively uniform age.

Two Types of Sentences

The clause-mate constraint requires that a reflexive pronoun refer to a noun in the same minimal clause as the pronoun; this requirement can be used as a comprehension principle when there are two nouns to which the reflexive might refer but only one of them occurs in the proper clause. In (3), for example,

(3)   Bert told Ernie to choose a shirt for himself.

himself might refer to either *Bert* or *Ernie* on the basis of gender and number, but only *Ernie* occurs in the same clause as *himself* (at the point at which the reflexive is formed). Accordingly, we predict that a listener who knows the clause-mate constraint will select Ernie as the one whom the shirt is for, while listeners who do not know the constraint will select either Bert or Ernie in near-chance proportions.

The essential characteristic of sentences such as (2) and (3) is that they have one and only one noun in the same clause as the reflexive, to which the reflexives can refer, although they have another semantically possible referent outside that clause. It is because of this structure that the clause-mate constraint can guide a listener's interpretation of the reflexive. In this article, we shall refer to such sentences as "type A" sentences.

There are, however, well-formed sentences in English with more than one possible referent for a reflexive pronoun, which the clause-mate constraint cannot resolve. These are of two basic types: those with *more* than one possible referent in the same clause as the reflexive (nothing in the clause-mate constraint rules out this possibility) and sentences which, because of an exceptional structure, contain *no* possible referent in the same clause as the reflexive. These two subtypes are illustrated in (4A) and (4B) below:

(4)   A.   Big Bird told Oscar a story about himself.
        B.   Cookie Monster told Bert that a picture of himself was on the wall.

Sentence (4A) is generally assumed to have just one clause at both deep and surface levels, so, of course, both *Big Bird* and *Oscar* occur in the same clause as *himself*. On the other hand, (4B) has two clauses, with the clause boundary coming before *that,* so both *Cookie Monster* and *Bert* appear outside the clause in which the reflexive occurs. Sentences of this variety occur only with constructions like *picture of Xself,* in which a small class of nouns behave like *picture,* in allowing a reflexive with no clause-mate referent. Various grammatical descriptions have been proposed for these so-called picture noun constructions and their apparent exceptionality; see Ross (1968:82-88), who points out other ways in which these constructions are exceptional; N. Chomsky (1970), who proposes a deep structure which does not assume that these are reduced relative clauses; and Jackendoff (1972, chap. 4), who discusses these cases in some detail, following Chomsky's proposed structure. Despite differences among these descriptions, all agree on two facts which are relevant to our investigation, namely, that both *Cookie Monster* and *Bert* occur in a different clause from *himself* and that if either occurs with *himself* at the point at which the reflexive is formed, it is impossible to say from the surface structure which noun it is. Therefore, the clause-mate constraint can be no guide to interpretation, and we predict that adults will find such sentences potentially ambiguous, although, of course, they may resolve the ambiguity on the basis of some other consideration, such as context. Keyser and Postal (1976), for example, specifically cite a sentence parallel to our example (4A) as being ambiguous. Concerning their example (10 i, p. 63),

Jack spoke to Larry about himself.

they note, "*Himself* can be co-referential to either *Jack* or *Larry,* and must be co-referential with one of them." Sentences like either (4A) and (4B), to which the clause-mate constraint does not apply, will be called "type B" sentences in this article.

The nature of the clause-mate constraint. Increasingly in recent years, the question has been raised whether the principles which govern linguistic performance are syntactic or semantic in nature. Maratsos (1974b) effectively raised this question with respect to a surface-structure interpretive principle which Carol Chomsky proposed. In many instances, this question cannot be answered, for we still have no clear general distinction between syntactic and semantic processes. In this instance, however, one can ask whether the children and adults in our experiment might choose referents for the reflexive pronouns on the basis of grammatical function or semantic role, rather than on the basis of the clause-mate constraint, a structural principle. Certainly people might use such an approach in choosing a referent in the type B sentences, where the clause-mate constraint does not apply, but what about type A sentences? In these cases, the predicted referent is always a grammatical subject and semantically an *agent*—but so is the *other* possible referent. The predicted referent is always the subject and the agent of the *embedded* clause, while the other possible referent has the same function and role in the *main* clause. Selection by semantic role would do nothing for the listener unless it were coupled with a syntactic principle, and the syntactic principle alone would suffice. Thus our sentences of type A appear to provide a test of whether listeners are able to use syntactic information, as opposed to purely semantic information, in interpreting reflexive pronouns. It is not the case, incidentally, that the referents of reflexives are always subjects and agents (or sources) in English. In (5)

(5)   The book gave Bert ideas about himself.

it is the semantic *goal* which is the referent of the reflexive.

There is a second alternative strategy, however, which it is impossible for us to rule out, given our design. It is possible to choose simply the *nearest* possible referent for the reflexive pronoun; with the type A sentences we used, such a strategy would give the same results as choosing the noun in the same minimal clause as the reflexive. One could determine which strategy listeners used by introducing sentences which had undergone rearrangements, such as passives; for example, in

(6)   Oscar was made by Cookie Monster to wash himself.

the nearest noun (Cookie Monster) is not the one which belongs to the same clause as the reflexive. We avoided such sentences in order not to introduce additional complexity (of unknown magnitude) and an additional variable into this initial study of the reflexive construction. We will, however, be able to determine whether children or adults apply a "near-noun" strategy in interpreting type B sentences, where that strategy cannot be confused with a clause-mate strategy, since the latter does not apply.

In fact, the question of whether listeners choose the nearest noun in type B sentences is of some interest in itself. Carol Chomsky used Rosenbaum's (1967) notion of the Minimal Distance Principle to describe a strategy for assigning subjects to the verbs of complement clauses. One might ask what is the status of the MDP as an interpretive principle? Is it limited to the assignment of complement subjects, or is it applied to other cases of inexplicit reference, including the pronominal variety, when structural cues are not available? Maratsos (1974b) suggests that children do not really use a Minimal Distance Principle in interpreting complement clauses; in fact, one of the most interesting conclusions of his study is that children use semantic role as a basis for complement-subject assignment. Still, it is possible that surface-structure distance is a factor in the interpretation of type B (ambiguous) sentences.

In sum, the clause-mate principle governs the use of English reflexives, so that in certain cases it can guide the listener. It is a syntactic constraint which applies to most sentences containing reflexives, not a lexical exception. In this respect, we are predicting that listeners' interpretation of type A sentences is structure-dependent; this supposition is supported by the studies of C. Chomsky (1969); Frederick, Golub, and Johnson (1970); and D. T. Chai (1967), in which aspects of the interpretation of personal and relative pronouns were shown to depend on structure, rather than on, say, lexical or situational context.

Hypotheses

With all the foregoing considerations in mind, but specifically on the basis of Carol Chomsky's research, we put forth the following hypotheses:

A.   With respect to type A sentences:

1.   Children learn the clause-mate constraint on reflexive pronouns relatively late; i.e., after age six. They will exhibit this knowledge, when they acquire it, by consistently choosing the clause-mate as the referent of the reflexive in type A sentences. Before they learn the constraint, they will choose either possible referent, at chance levels overall.

2.   Children learn the clause-mate constraint within a narrow age range, i.e., the change from chance to consistent performance on type A sentences will occur within, say, one year of age rather than across six years of age. We cannot be certain what the age range for learning is, but on the basis of Carol Chomsky's results with the constraint on backward pronominalization, we predict that the learning will take place closer to age six than to age ten (Chomsky, 1969:108-109).

B.   With respect to type B sentences, it is less clear what one should predict, since the clause-mate constraint simply does not apply. In the absence of studies of adults' or children's interpretation of these constructions, we predict:

3.   That adults regard type B sentences as potentially ambiguous and will choose either possible referent for the reflexive, at chance levels overall.

4.   With no previous evidence to rely on, and consequently, with no great confidence, we suppose that children may apply an analog of the Minimal Distance Principle, so we predict that in type B sentences, younger children will choose the nearer noun as the referent of the reflexive, to a greater degree than chance alone would predict.

5.   Since type A sentences obey a general constraint, to which type B sentences constitute exceptions, we predict that children will exhibit consistent interpretations of type A sentences at an earlier age than they do so for type B sentences, if they interpret type B sentences consistently at any age. That is, we predict that children learn the clause-mate constraint before they learn any general principle for dealing with the exceptions, if indeed they ever acquire such a principle.

Method

Subjects. Children in grades one through six, whose ages ranged from 6;3 to 12;11, participated in the study. All students attended Waterloo Elementary School in Waterloo, Wisconsin. Thirty-six undergraduates from two University of Wisconsin reading methods classes made up the adult sample. All subjects were native English speakers, without any discernible aural, visual, or linguistic disorders.

Materials. For the experiment, we wrote sixteen reflexivization sentences, eight of type A, where the clause-mate constraint applies, and eight of type B, where the constraint does not apply. All sentences were of the form N . . . N . . . reflexive . . . , where semantically the reflexive could refer to either noun. We tried to select words commonly in the listening vocabularies of most children. Mean length of sentences in both Sets A and B was 9.0 words. Sentences are listed below, along with test questions which were constructed so as not to suggest either answer:

Set A

1.   Bert said that Ernie spilled some paint on himself today.
Who got paint all over himself?
2.   Cookie Monster made Oscar wash himself.
Who was washed?
3.   Big Bird made Bert pat himself on the head.
Who was patted on the head?
4.   Ernie was sorry Cookie Monster hurt himself.
Who was hurt?
5.   Oscar made Big Bird look at himself in the mirror.
Who would be reflected in the mirror?
6.   Ernie let Big Bird choose a new red shirt for himself.
Who was the shirt for?
7.   Oscar wanted Bert to write a short story about himself.
Who would the story be about?
8.   Cookie Monster made Ernie draw a picture of himself.
Who would the picture be of?

Set B

1.   Big Bird told Oscar a story about himself.
Who was the story about?
2.   Oscar gave Cookie Monster a book about himself.
Who was the book about?
3.   Bert gave Big Bird a picture of himself.
Who was the picture of?
4.   Cookie Monster talked to Ernie about himself.
Who was talked about?
5.   Oscar showed Big Bird a drawing of himself.
Who was the drawing of?
6.   Cookie Monster told Bert a picture of himself was on the wall.
Whose picture was on the wall?

7.   Big Bird told Ernie a painting of himself was for sale.
Whose picture was for sale?
8.   Bert told Oscar a show about himself was on television.
Whose show was on television?

All sentences from Sets A and B were randomly ordered together. To minimize any order-of-presentation effect, we then rotated the resulting list of sentences to form three different sequences.

For the interview, we used five finger puppets which represented the Sesame Street characters Ernie, Bert, Cookie Monster, Big Bird, and Oscar the Grouch. We wrote five sentences in addition to the two sets of test questions, to use as a check on whether children recognized these familiar Sesame Street characters and also as a warm-up. We asked children to manipulate the appropriate puppets, as follows:

1.   Bert likes to walk fast. Make him do it.
2.   Cookie Monster likes to eat tables. Make him do it.
3.   Oscar would like to sit in your lap. Make him do it.
4.   Ernie wants to jump up and down. Make him do it.
5.   Big Bird feels like hiding. Make him do it.

Procedure. Each class of children was introduced by its teacher to the interviewer (VCH). In turn, the interviewer told the children why their help was needed; at this point, she exhibited and named the puppets for the first time.

The experimenter interviewed children one at a time in a quiet location. An average interview lasted from fifteen to twenty minutes. The interviewer first asked each child to identify the five puppets and then asked him as many warm-up questions as necessary to confirm that he recognized each of the characters. Once the child appeared at ease, the interviewer instructed him that he would be playing a game. In this game, there would be no right or wrong answers; the interviewer was only interested in finding out what the child thought about various sentences. The child could ask for a sentence to be repeated.

For each question, the interviewer displayed only the appropriate pair of puppets. Each child demonstrated his preferred answer by touching a desired puppet and by saying the name of the puppet aloud. The interviewer gave the child praise and encouragement throughout the interview, no matter how he or she answered.

The interviewer tested the adults later in two group sessions. At each session, she read the entire list orally to one of the adult groups. Adults wrote down their own answers.

Results and Discussion

For analyzing the results, we divided the children into nine groups by age at eight-month intervals. We extended the intervals at the lower and upper extremes to 11 and 14 months, in order to achieve approximately equal group sizes. The distribution of the nine groups is presented in *Table 6.1.*

Table 6.1
Sample size, mean age, standard deviations and
ranges of ages in nine groups used in analysis

Group	n	Mean age (mos.)	s.d.	Range (mos.)
1	21	80.6	2.8	75-85
2	25	89.6	2.2	86-93
3	27	98.3	1.9	94-101
4	27	105.6	2.1	102-109
5	32	113.7	1.9	110-117
6	19	120.9	2.6	118-125
7	23	129.3	2.2	126-133
8	25	138.6	2.2	134-141
9	31	147.3	3.5	142-155

Type A Sentences

Our first and second hypotheses concern children's interpretations of type A sentences. We predicted that such sentences, to which the clause-mate constraint applies, would be correctly interpreted relatively late, i.e., after age six. The solid line in *Figure 6.1* shows the mean A-score, or number of clause-mate responses, by age group. Every group fared better than chance. This difference is significant for group 1, t (20) = 5.2, $p < .0001$, and for the group with the smallest mean, group 2, t (24) = 4.009, $p = .005$. Group 9, the oldest group of children, responded with significantly fewer appropriate responses than did adults, t (47) = -3.6, $p = .0007$; however, this particular result must be interpreted cautiously. The memory and patience requirements of the sixteen-question task may have influenced children's performance more than that of adults, accounting in part for the children's lower scores. Also, the adults' task was slightly different from the children's, in that adults wrote down their own answers; however, we expected that this difference would increase the relative difficulty of the adults' task, if anything.

Hypothesis 1 is therefore disconfirmed. All of the age groups, even the youngest ones, performed better than chance. We cannot say at what age learning of the clause-mate constraint begins, but it is evidently before age six.

With regard to Hypothesis 2, a one-way analysis of variance testing for age effects showed no significant learning of the clause-mate constraint across the age groups, F (8, 221) = 1.60, $F_{crit.}$ at .05 = 1.98. However, a comparison of means, as in the t-tests and the analysis of variance, can be misleading, especially when we wish to study rule-governed, i.e., consistent, behavior. In such a case, we are most concerned with the proportion of individuals who consistently choose the correct referent, because it is these who can be said to be following a rule. We defined consistency as seven or more clause-mate choices, because the probability of making seven or eight consistent choices on eight independent trials by guessing alone is .035. The solid line in *Figure 6.2* shows the percentage of individuals at each age group who consistently chose the clause-mate as referent. At each age the

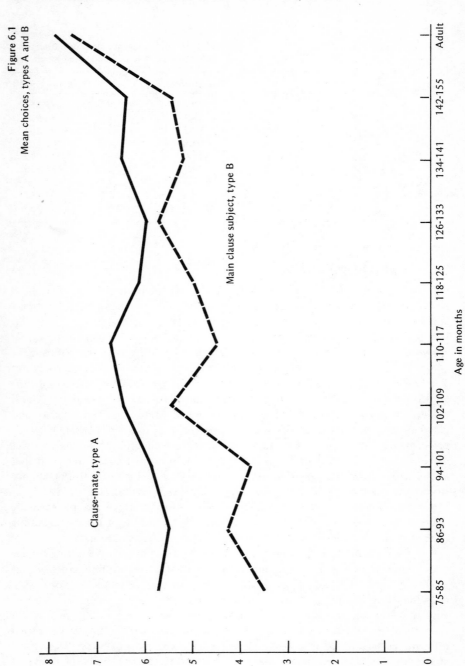

Figure 6.1
Mean choices, types A and B

Figure 6.2

Percent consistent choices, types A and B

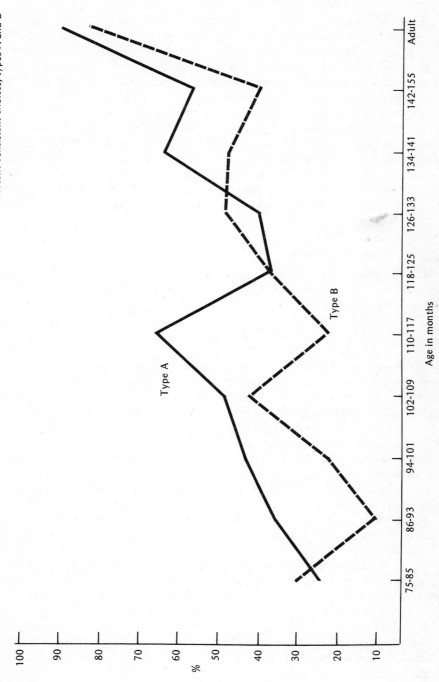

Type A

Type B

% 100 90 80 70 60 50 40 30 20 10

Age in months

75-85 86-93 94-101 102-109 110-117 118-125 126-133 134-141 142-155 Adult

percentage is substantially greater than chance would predict (3.5%: the dotted line). We applied a test for the equality of the proportions of children who were consistent at the nine age groups; this test uses a normally-distributed transform of the proportion, and the resulting statistic is distributed as Chi-square with degrees of freedom equal to the number of groups minus one. The test indicates that there is significant change across the age groups, $\chi^2 (8) = 16.96, p < .05$. This change is not monotonic, but is rather erratic in the older groups.

Hypothesis two, therefore, is also rejected. With increasing age there is an increase in the number of children who answer consistently, but this increase is not confined to a narrow range. In fact, the youngest child who chose the clause-mate consistently (in the above sense) was 6;5, while the oldest who failed to choose even five out of eight clause-mates was 12;4. This evidence argues against Carol Chomsky's proposal that a regular constraint is learned at a comparatively uniform age.

Type B Sentences

Our third hypothesis concerned adults' interpretations of type B sentences. It was based on the standard observation in discussion of reflexives in English, that sentences such as:

Jack spoke to Larry about himself.

are ambiguous, with respect to whether the speaking was about Jack or Larry. Our own judgments agree with this observation; we find all of our type B sentences potentially ambiguous in this same way. Consequently, our third hypothesis was that adults would choose one referent or the other at chance levels overall.

The facts quite definitely disconfirm this hypothesis. Twenty-nine out of 36 adults, or 81%, chose the noun *farther* from the reflexive, the subject of the main clause, on 7 or 8 out of 8 trials. Indeed, of the remaining 7 adults, 5 chose the farther noun on 6 of 8 trials, and 2 chose it on 5 of 8 trials; no one chose the nearer noun even 4 times, which we had expected to be the overall mean number of choices. In fact, adults were nearly as consistent in choosing the farther noun as the referent in type B sentences, as they were in choosing the clause-mate, the nearer noun, in type A sentences; the mean choices (out of 8) are 7.36 and 7.58, respectively.

We continue to believe, along with others who have commented on the syntax of English reflexives, that sentences of type B are *potentially* ambiguous. We believe that in appropriate contexts, either interpretation of such sentences can be brought out and will seem acceptable to adult speakers of English. In fact, it is a common observation that listeners interpret potentially ambiguous sentences as having only one reading unless the existence of two readings is brought to their attention in some way; what is striking in this case is that one particular reading predominates, even though the context is neutral. We believe that our results reveal the type of behavior which has become known as an "interpretive strategy" in recent discussions of sentence processing and language acquisition (e.g., Bever, 1970). A strategy, in this sense, is a general principle of interpretation which listeners apply, usually without being aware of it, which is not necessary to sentence understanding and which may even be at variance with the grammar of the language in some exceptional cases. Listeners use such strategies, apparently, as shortcuts to sentence understanding, based on the inductive observation that *in most cases* a certain relationship holds. In this case, the principle seems to be that when the clause-mate constraint fails to apply, and when the context is neutral, one should interpret a reflexive as referring to the subject of the main clause. Indeed, listeners may apply this principle to other anaphoric pronouns, not only to reflexives.

In fact, the sharp contrast between adults' interpretations of type A and type B sentences serves to confirm the importance of the clause-mate constraint; in these two types of sentences, it is *only* where the clause-mate constraint applies that adults choose the nearer noun as the referent of a reflexive. Our hypothesis about adults' interpretations of type B sentences was wrong, but our assumption that types A and B are structurally different has been strongly confirmed. With respect to children's interpretations of type B sentences, the question now becomes not only what do children do when the clause-mate constraint fails to apply, but also when and in what way do they come to approximate the consistent behavior of adults?

This question is rendered all the more interesting by the observation that the adult interpretations are not only opposite, but are governed by principles of different types. The clause-mate constraint is a structural principle which determines the meaning and even the grammaticality of English sentences, as in example (2B). The subject-of-main-clause interpretive strategy, on the other hand, is a listener's rule of thumb; it does not absolutely constrain the formation or interpretation of any sentence. For example, sentence (7) below violates the strategy in the same way that (2B) violates the clause-mate constraint, but (7), unlike (2B), is not rendered ungrammatical.

(7)   Harry told Mabel a story about herself.

These considerations, then, bring us to our fourth hypothesis, which concerns how children interpret type B sentences. In the absence of any published evidence, we speculated that children might select the nearer noun as the referent of the reflexive. The dashed line in *Figure 6.1* represents the mean number of far-noun choices on type B sentences by age group, showing that once again we were wrong. Children in the youngest group chose a mean of 4.6 near-nouns out of 8; children in the oldest group chose only 2.6 near-nouns on the average, so the development is from near-chance performance to a preference which resembles, but does not equal, that of adults. At no point do children appear to have a clear preference for the nearer noun.

Statistical tests confirm the graphic evidence. The choices of the youngest group are not distinguishable from chance, $t(20) = -.865$, $p = .40$, and with their mean of 3.8 near-noun choices, the second-youngest group is also choosing at chance levels. The oldest group, by contrast, is unlikely to be choosing at random, t (30) = 3.4, p = .002, but their choices are still statistically distinct from those of adults, t (65) = -4.2, p = .0001. Such a comparison between our children and our adults should be viewed with some caution, however, since the two groups are not strictly comparable. The children were a random sample from an elementary school in a small suburban/rural Wisconsin community; the adults were a sample of undergraduates taking a course in reading at the University of Wisconsin. Consequently, the adult population was subject to a special selection process, University admission. Nonetheless, we feel that our adult sample provides a useful view of the ultimate interpretation of these sentences by some people, at least.

A one-way analysis of variance, applied to the number of choices of farther nouns (main-clause subjects) across the nine age groups of children, shows significant change across the groups, F (8,221) = 2.7, $p < .01$. This result contrasts with the lack of significant change in children's interpretation of type A sentences, as measured by the analysis of variance, although the actual difference in the rate of change is fairly modest. (See *Figure 6.1*.) Furthermore, the change in interpretation of type B sentences is quite gradual; Scheffe multiple comparisons, applied to the scores of each adjacent pair of age groups, show that there is no single age at which we can say that the change is significant. There is, moreover, nonsignificant change between the first three age groups and the last six, or the first three and the next three, or the middle three groups and the last three. Only across a wide age range is the change significant: between the first age group and the last, or indeed the first group and the seventh.

Our conclusion is that while children may change significantly during the elementary school years, choosing the main-clause subject in sentences of type B with increasing frequency, the change is gradual and is not associated with any particular age group. (The youngest child who chose main-clause subjects consistently was 6;3, while the oldest who failed to choose more than four such subjects was 12;6.) This conclusion is, in fact, what one might expect, when one considers that the strategy of choosing the main clause subject applies only to the (exceptional) type B sentences and only when context does not indicate a referent; when context governs, the strategy itself is subject to exceptions, as sentence (7) shows, for example. Therefore, the gradual acquisition of this exceptional and variable strategy is consistent with Carol Chomsky's results concerning lexical exceptions, and with the general observation that acquisition of irregular forms is gradual and variable (e.g., Dale, 1976:34-35). We suppose that learning to interpret type B sentences depends more on a child's particular and somewhat happenstance linguistic experience than on age-related maturation.

As we indicated in our discussion of type A sentences, a simple comparison of mean scores, as in the t-tests and the analysis of variance, can be misleading. It is the children who choose a particular referent consistently who demonstrate that they are applying a strategy. Again, let us use seven or eight choices of main-clause subject as our criterion for consistency. The dashed line in *Figure 6.2* shows the percentage of such children across the age groups. The percentage predicted by the binomial distribution if the children were truly choosing randomly is 3.5% at each age group (dotted line). There appears to be gradual but real change across age in the degree to which children apply a consistent strategy to type B sentences. Our test for equality of proportions confirms that there is significant change, χ^2 (8) = 19.96, $p < .02$.

The earlier observation that children in the age range we studied do not change significantly in their interpretation of type A sentences, together with the present observation that they do change, albeit gradually and somewhat erratically, in interpreting type B sentences, brings us to our fifth hypothesis, a comparison of the development on these two sentence types. We predicted that children would follow the constraint on type A sentences at an earlier age than they followed any consistent pattern on type B sentences, a prediction which is made all the more relevant by the observation that children do indeed come to choose referents in a reasonably consistent manner on type B.

This time the evidence from every point of view supports our hypothesis. One way to look at the question is to consider mean choices by age group. In *Figure 6.1* compare the number of clause-mate choices for type A (solid line) with the number of main-clause subject choices for type B (dashed line). At no age group, including adults, do these lines cross; that is, the mean number of choices in the predicted direction, or in the direction of adults, is always greater for type A than for type B.

Again, though, it is the proportion of children who choose consistently which may give the better indication of applying a principle or strategy. *Figure 6.2* presents this percentage across the age groups for both sentence types, again defining "consistent" as seven or more choices in the adult direction. Here we see that at six of the nine age groups the proportion for type A exceeds that for type B. In the three exceptions, the discrepancy is quite small.

Another way to evaluate the relative periods of acquisition is to consider the number of children "passing" type A (choosing the clause-mate seven or eight times) while "failing" type B (choosing the main-clause subject fewer than seven times), as compared with the opposite situation—failing type A while passing type B. If children learn the clause-mate constraint before they learn the exceptional strategy, the former case should predominate. *Table 6.2* lists these figures, along with the numbers of children passing both types and failing both types. In every age group, there are some children who are consistent on type B but not on type A; therefore, the earlier learning of the constraint on type A is by no means absolute. However, in most age groups the number of children passing type A and failing type B exceeds the converse, sometimes to a significant degree, while in the three exceptions the difference is only 0 or 1. By an exact binomial test, the differences for age groups 2 and 5 are significant, with $p = .03$ and $p = .0007$, respectively. The totals in "pass A, fail B" versus "pass B, fail A" are significantly different from a random distribution, χ^2 (1) = 11.27, $p < .001$.

Consequently, whether one considers mean number of choices or proportion of children choosing consistently, the evidence generally supports our hypothesis that children choose referents consistently in type A, according to the

Table 6.2

Numbers of children and adults choosing referents
of reflexives consistently in accord with constraints
("passing") on two types of constructions

	1	2	3	4	5	6	7	8	9	Adult	Total
Pass both	0	0	1	6	5	1	4	6	6	26	55
Pass A, Fail B	5	9	11	7	16	6	5	10	12	6	87
Fail A, Pass B	6	2	5	5	2	6	7	6	6	3	48
Fail both	10	14	10	9	9	6	7	3	7	1	76
Total	21	25	27	27	32	19	23	25	31	36	266

clause-mate constraint, at an earlier age than they follow a consistent pattern in
type B—in short, that children learn a regular constraint at an earlier age than
they learn a somewhat variable principle for interpreting exceptional cases.

Other Analyses

We assumed that within each sentence type, children would treat the eight
examples essentially alike. We tested that assumption in an analysis of the
interpretations of individual items in set A and set B. We found significant
variation among the items of set A and some variation, generally not statistically
significant, among the items of type B. This result is somewhat surprising, since it
was type B which contained two structurally distinct subtypes, as in examples
(4A) and (4B). Upon closer inspection, it turned out that there was indeed a
difference between the two-clause and the one-clause type B items, with reflexives
in the latter being more often interpreted as referring to the main-clause subject.
Among the type A items, it was those with the shortest distance (fewest words)
between the reflexive and the nearer noun (embedded clause subject) in which the
reflexive was most often interpreted as referring to that noun. This variation may
reflect nothing more than the memory requirement which is a part of this task;
that is, it may be that children sometimes become confused when the distance
between the reflexive and the target noun is too great.

We also found a significant effect of order of presentation (for children
only) after the effect of age group is taken into account. For type A, F (2,203) =
3.76, p = .025; for type B, F (2,203) = 5.25, p < .01. This order-of-presentation
effect took the following form: children did "better" (i.e., more like adults) on
type A with the orders which began with type A sentences, and better on type B
with the order which began with a type B sentence. We suspect, then, that
children tended to continue the type of response which they gave to the first
sentence with which they were presented. This suggests that the eight trials for
each type were not truly independent; accordingly, none of the statistical tests
which we have applied has required that the trials be independent. Also, we note
that these order-of-presentation effects, though significant, were quite small: in

the analyses of variance, the net reduction in the residual mean square from taking order of presentation into account after age group is 2.4% for type A and 3.6% for type B.

Having observed significant variation by individual items and by order-of-presentation, we should note that when both of these factors are eliminated, the large difference between sentence types A and B remains. To show this, we consider just every child's *first* item. (Because two of the three orders began with type A, about two-thirds of these first tries are with type A.) The difference between types A and B remains great; χ^2 (2) = 55.3, $p < .001$.

Finally, we considered the relation between performance on these tasks and on standardized school tests. For each child in grades three through six, with three exceptions, we had composite and subtest scores from the Iowa Test of Basic Skills (1971), which had been administered by the school system two months before the interviews in this study. These achievement scores correlate with scores on our sentence-interpretation tasks at a statistically significant but, for practical purposes, negligible level. Even the largest coefficient, .26, between total (A + B) score and the reading subtest, indicates that only about 7% of the variance in total score is explained by the reading test. This result is to be expected, since the constructions we tested were selected for their relationship to a developing theory of language acquisition; there is no reason to believe that they have any special role in school performance. The absence of a strong relationship between the interpretation of reflexives and the standardized test scores underlines the importance of not using such language acquisition measures as predictors of school performance.

Limitations and Conclusions

In the light of the fact that even our youngest subjects performed better than chance on the type A sentences, we now think that the principal limitation in our study is the absence of younger subjects from our sample. It would be interesting to study younger children's interpretation of the same sets of sentences. Finally, the effects of individual items in type A and order-of-presentation must also be included among the limitations of our study.

We have had the pleasure of having our results prove us wrong more often than they have proved us right. This experience is always a distinct possibility in empirical investigations, of course. We do not yet know at what age children begin to follow the clause-mate constraint in interpreting sentences of type A, but we do know that even those in our youngest group, of mean age 6;9, did so to a substantial degree. Moreover, children's judgments of these sentences remained relatively constant over the age range that we studied, up to a mean age of approximately 12;3, although these oldest children were still less consistent than adults in their judgments. As for sentences to which the clause-mate constraint does not apply, we found that in the absence of contextual cues, adults choose the main-clause subject, rather than the nearer noun, as the referent of the reflexive pronoun. Nor did children choose the nearer noun; instead, the youngest children chose one noun or the other at chance levels, while older children began to adopt the adult strategy. Finally, it is quite clear that children begin to choose referents in accord with the clause-mate constraint at an earlier age than they apply any consistent strategy to the exceptional (type B) sentences. This evidence supports the growing conviction, initiated by Chomsky (1969) and extended by Maratsos (1974b), that structurally regular constraints are acquired earlier than principles for dealing with exceptions.

Chapter 7

The Acquisition of Ask and Tell Structures by Arabic-Speaking Children

Wayne K. Aller
Sonia K. Aller
Lina Malouf-Saad

To determine the general principles underlying language acquisition and to gain insight into strategies utilized by children in language processing, it is necessary to investigate child language acquisition in diverse languages. This paper is a contribution to this endeavor.

Carol Chomsky (1969) was among the first to demonstrate that there are some seemingly fairly simple syntactic structures that many English-speaking children do not comprehend even by the age of ten. Among these structures are those with verbs requiring sentential complements. This paper will report the results of an investigation of the comprehension of two such structures, those involving Ask and Tell, by three age groups of monolingual Lebanese Arabic-speaking children.

In Chomsky's study an Ask/Tell imperative was given to one child who was to execute it by verbalizing to another child. For example:

(1)   Ask Paul what to feed the baby.

(2)   Tell Paul what to feed the baby.

It is apparent that (1) and (2) have identical surface structures, namely a main VP, *Ask/Tell Paul,* plus a question word, *what,* and an infinitival complement, *to feed the baby.* Where they differ is in the assignment of the logical subject of the infinitival verb. In (2) it is *Paul* who is to do the feeding, whereas in (1) it is *you,* unexpressed in the surface of the English imperative.

A linguistic analysis describing this phenomenon proposed by Rosenbaum (1967) is as follows—for structures of the form:

(NP_1) Tell NP_2 wh- to inf VP

the general rule is to assign the NP closest to the complement verb as its subject, in this case NP_2. Thus in (2) it is Paul who is to feed the baby since *Paul*, NP_2, is closer to the complement verb *feed* than (*you*), NP_1. This principle, the *Minimal Distance Principle* (MDP), applies to a large number of verbs in English which use sentential complements, e.g., *tell, permit, persuade, want, expect*, etc. In the latter two verbs, when there is no NP_2, e.g., *John wanted to leave*, application of the MDP assigns the correct subject to the complement verb. In contrast, in (1) it is (*you*), NP_1, who is to do the feeding. Thus, in the case of sentences of the form:

(NP_1) Ask NP_2 wh- to inf VP

with the main verb *ask*, the rule is to assign the NP further from the complement verb, NP_1, as its subject, thus violating the MDP.

Since the vast majority of NP_1 *V* NP_2 *wh- to inf VP* constructions in English conform to the MDP, Chomsky reasoned that children should internalize this principle and thus correctly comprehend sentences where it applies before they learn exceptions to it. Having learned to apply the MDP, children would be expected to initially overextend it to those cases where it does not apply. Thus the Ask structures she studied should be more often misinterpreted than the Tell structures. Young children should thus respond to (1) *Ask Paul what to feed the baby* with *What should you feed the baby?* Of course there is another type of Ask construction in English which conforms to the MDP, namely that involving *ask* meaning *request*, as in *Ask John to get the tickets*. It is possible that this dual meaning of *ask* might make the child's task of learning to violate the MDP in the *ask*-as-question cases even more difficult.

Chomsky set out to test her MDP-based predictions of child language acquisition, but at an early stage in her research found that her 5- and 6-year-old children were *telling* irrespective of whether they had been instructed to *ask* or *tell*. Furthermore, when questioned as to whether they had asked or told, the children would insist that they had asked when in fact they had told. She concluded that children at a certain stage simply were not differentiating between the two words, and thus she proceeded "to explore the Ask/Tell distinction more generally, considering the MDP question in the context of Ask/Tell processing in general" (p. 46). She accomplished this by testing children with Ask/Tell structures which varied in the syntactic complexity of their complement clauses.

Table 7.1 shows the Ask/Tell sentences which Chomsky used in her study. The following summary focuses on the Ask constructions, since these caused the most difficulty for her children.

Case 1 sentences are the simplest in that the complement clause, e.g., *what color this is* in (1A), contains in its surface form all the information necessary for

Table 7.1
Constructions used in the Ask/Tell interview,
listed in order of increasing complexity
(adapted from Chomsky, p. 47)

Case 1	wh-clause, subject supplied

A.	Ask/Tell Laura what color this is.
B.	Ask/Tell Laura what you/she should feed the doll.
C.	Ask/Tell Laura how many pencils there are here.
D.	Ask/Tell Laura who this is.

Case 2	noun phrase

A.	Ask/Tell Laura her/your last name.
B.	Ask/Tell Laura the color of this book.
C.	Ask/Tell Laura her/your teacher's name.

Case 3	wh- clause, subject omitted

A.	Ask/Tell Laura what to feed the doll.
B.	Ask/Tell Laura which food to put in the box.
C.	Ask/Tell Laura what to put back next.
D.	Ask/Tell Laura what color to make the square.

the correct assignment of verb-subject relationships. What the child must do to carry out the Ask instruction is to invert the copula (*is/are*) with the demonstrative pronoun (*this/there*). Thus, in:

(3)   Ask Laura what color this is.   →   What color is this?
       (complement clause)   (resulting question)

It should be pointed out, however, that sentence (1B) does not fit the pattern of the other three examples. We will return to this point shortly.

Case 2 sentences are next in complexity, since both the question word (*what*) and the copula (*is*) are omitted from the complement clause. Thus the child has to provide the two missing elements in their proper order to succeed in interpreting the Ask instruction. In addition, the child must change the personal pronoun from *her* to *your* for a correct response, as in:

(4)   Ask Laura her last name.   →   What's your last name?
       (complement clause)   (resulting question)

Case 3 sentences are the most complex since, not only is the subject of the complement clause missing, but there is also no surface clue as to which NP should be assigned as subject of the complement clause. Thus to interpret the Ask construction correctly the child has to assign the missing pronoun (*you*) as the subject of the complement verb, and to respond correctly s/he has to change this to *I* and provide the appropriate auxiliary.

(5)   Ask Laura what to feed the doll. → What should I feed the doll?
       (complement clause)   (resulting question)

Hence, Case 3 provides a direct test of the child's knowledge of the MDP, for in Tell imperatives it must be applied, while in Ask imperatives it must be violated if the sentence is to be correctly responded to.

Arabic, like English, has a sizable group of verbs which take sentential complements. Furthermore, the MDP seems also to assign the proper NP as the subject of the complement verb. Among these verbs are *?aal* (tell), *samah* (allow), *jabar* (force), *raad* (want), etc. Interestingly enough, *?as?al* (ask) is one verb in Arabic which takes a sentential complement but violates the MDP. Since Arabic, like most languages, uses two different words, *?as?əl* and *?ətlob*, to convey the *ask* (question) versus *ask* (request) meanings, children must learn a consistent violation of the MDP in Ask constructions.

The specific Ask/Tell structures used to test our Arabic-speaking children's comprehension are presented below along with a rationale for their inclusion in the study. *Table 7.2* shows all construction types used, with example sentences.

Case A1:   Ask/Tell Sonia wh- NP

(6)   ?as?aliy-ya la Sonia shou ?əsm   ?əm-ma.   →
       Ask (to) Sonia what (her) mother's name (is).   →

       Shou   ?əsm   ?əmmaik?
       What (your) mother's name (is)?

(7)   ?oulɪ-la la Sonia shou   ?əsm   ?əmmaik. → Rita.
       Tell (to) Sonia what (your) mother's name (is). →   Rita.

This corresponds to Chomsky's simplest, Case 1, structures, i.e., excluding her (1B) type. In Arabic, however, the embedded question and its corresponding question response, unlike English, do not differ in word order, i.e., the question in Arabic does not require the auxiliary/pronoun inversion. The only change necessary is the person-marking suffix on the last word of the sentence. However, in a pilot study investigating these structures we found that our Arabic-speaking children were, in general, *asking* when instructed to *tell*, the converse of what Chomsky observed in her English-speaking children. For example, when (7) was given, the children tended to respond with *Shou ?əsm ?əmmaik?* (What (your) mother's name (is)?) It was hypothesized that this confusion might be due to the fact that the word order in the wh-clause in the Arabic Tell instruction (*shou ?əsm ?əmmaik*) is identical to that of a question. This being the case the children might have been interpreting the instruction as being in the direct report mode, i.e., as containing a direct quotation of a question, thus yielding, *Say to Sonia, 'What (your) mother's name (is)?'* We will return to this later.

Case A2:   Ask/Tell Sonia NP

(8)   ?əs?aliy-ya la Sonia ?əsm   ?əm-ma. → Shou   ?əsm   ?əmmaik?
        Ask (to) Sonia (her) mother's name. → What your mother's name (is)?

(9)   ?oulı-la la Sonia   ?əsm   ?əmmaik. → Rita.
        Tell (to) Sonia your mother's name.   → Rita.

This type of structure is the same as Chomsky's Case 2. Note that the complement is an NP without the wh- question word. Based on the observations from our pilot study, this construction was expected to influence responses to *ask* and *tell* differently. In the Tell instruction the child is spared the potentially misleading wh- word which, when present, may cause the child to misinterpret the instruction as containing a direct quotation. In the Ask instruction, however, the wh- question word is missing and has to be supplied by the child. Thus, we would predict the following performance comparisons: Ask A1 > Ask A2, but Tell A2 > Tell A1.

Case B: Tell/Ask Sonia wh- modal pro VP

As previously mentioned, Chomsky's sentence (B) in her Case 1 seems to differ substantially in structure from the other sentences in that Case. It does not fit the pattern of Tell/Ask wh-clause with a copular VP, e.g., *Tell/Ask Laura what color this is*, but rather contains a full sentential complement which requires a differential interpretation of the personal pronoun depending on whether the instruction is to *tell* or *ask*. For example:

(10)   Ask Laura what *you* should feed the doll.   → What should *I* feed the doll?

(11)   Tell Laura what *she* should feed the doll. → *You* should feed the doll eggs.

This differential requirement for correct interpretation is not entailed by the demonstrative pronouns in the rest of her Case 1 sentences. Since Chomsky did not analyze responses to such structures individually, by particular sentence, it is impossible to determine how the children performed on this particular structure compared to her other structures of Case 1. In the present study this major discrepancy among Case 1 sentences was rectified by inclusion of the two structures as different Cases, our A1 and B. Thus, for Case B structures

(12)   ?əs?aliy-ya la Sonia shou lazaim ?ənti taʕti l-ləʕbai.   →
         Ask (to) Sonia what should *you* give the doll.   →

         Shou lazaim (?ana) ?aʕti l-ləʕbai?
         What should *I* give the doll?

Table 7.2
Types of Arabic Ask/Tell constructions used

Constructions		Example instructions	Example responses
Case A1	Ask	?es?aliy-ya la Sonia shou ?əsm ?əm-ma. Ask - her to Sonia what name mother-her. *Ask (to) Sonia what (her) mother's name (is).	Shou ?əsm ?əm - maik? What name mother-your? What (your) mother's name is?
	Tell	?oult-la la Sonia shou ?əsm ?əm-maik. Tell - her to Sonia what name mother-your. Tell (to) Sonia what (your) mother's name (is).	Rita. Rita.
Case A2	Ask	?es?aliy-ya la Sonia ?əsm ?əm-ma. Ask - her to Sonia name mother-her. Ask (to) Sonia (her) mother's name.	Shou ?əsm ?əm-maik? What name mother-your? What (your) mother's name (is)?
	Tell	?oult-la la Sonia ?əsm ?əm-maik. Tell - her to Sonia name mother-your. Tell (to) Sonia (your) mother's name.	Rita. Rita.
Case B	Ask	?es?aliy-ya la Sonia shou lazaim ?ənti taʕti l-ləʕbai. Ask - her to Sonia what should you give the-doll. Ask (to) Sonia what should you give the doll.	Shou lazaim (?ana) ?-aʕti l-ləʕbai? What should (I) I-give the-doll? What should I give the doll?
	Tell	?oult-la la Sonia shou lazaim hiyya taʕti l-ləʕbai. Tell - her to Sonia what should she give the-doll. Tell (to) Sonia what should she give the doll.	(ʕatha) bayd-a (Give-her) egg - an (Give her) an egg

Table 7.2 (continued)

Constructions		Example instructions	Example responses
Case C	Ask	ʔəsʔaliy-ya la Sonia shou lazaim t-aʕti l-ləʕbai.	Shou lazaim (ʔana) ʔ-aʕti l-ləʕbai?
		Ask - her to Sonia what should { you / she } -give the-doll.	What should (I) I-give the-doll?
		Ask (to) Sonia what should give the doll.	What should give the doll?
	Tell	ʔouli-la la Sonia shou lazaim t-aʕti l-ləʕbai.	(ati-ha) bayd-a
		Tell - her to Sonia what should { you / she } -give the-doll.	(Give-her) egg - an
		Tell (to) Sonia what should give the doll.	(Give her) an egg.

*The second of each translation is the one used in the text.

(13)   ?oulɪ-la la Sonia shou lazaim hiyya taʕtɪ l-ləʕbai.   ⟶   (ʕatɪha) bayd-a.
        Tell (to) Sonia what should *she* give the doll.   ⟶   (give her) an egg.

it was expected that children would make more errors on these than on Case A structures. (Note that the auxiliary *should* (lazaim) precedes the pronoun in both the Ask and Tell instructions and in the correct response to *ask*.) The specific predictions were therefore: Ask A1 > Ask B, Ask A2 > Ask B, Tell A1 >Tell B, and Tell A2 >Tell B.

Case C: Ask/Tell Sonia wh-modal VP

It will be observed that in the Case B structures just discussed the subject of the complement verb, *give*, is provided as a surface pronoun after the wh- word. So the application of the MDP will result in correct interpretation of both Ask and Tell Case B structures. In order to directly test children's knowledge of the MDP, the following Case C structures, where the subject of the complement verb is omitted, were used. These are identical to Chomsky's Case 3 structures.

(14)   ?əs?aliy-ya la Sonia shou lazaim t-aʕti l-ləʕbai. ⟶

        Ask (to) Sonia what should $\begin{Bmatrix} you \\ she \end{Bmatrix}$ give the doll.   ⟶

        Shou lazaim (?ana) ?-aʕti l-ləʕbai?
        What should (I) give the doll?

(15)   ?oulɪ-la la Sonia shou lazaim t-aʕti l-ləʕbai.   ⟶   Bayd-a.

        Tell (to) Sonia what should $\begin{Bmatrix} you \\ she \end{Bmatrix}$ give the doll. ⟶ An egg.

Since these Tell and Ask Case C sentences have identical surface structures, to interpret them correctly a child must know that *tell* requires the application of the MDP and *ask* requires its violation. Thus we would predict that performance would be better on Tell C than on Ask C.

In comparing Ask B with Ask C, and Tell B with Tell C it is obvious that the child might more easily comprehend both the B structures because of the presence of the subject (pronoun) in the complement clause. However, the advantage of the Ask B over the Ask C structure is expected to be much greater than the advantage of the Tell B over the Tell C because in both Tell constructions the application of the MDP will result in correct comprehension. In the case of Tell B the presence of an explicit pronoun in the surface of the complement clause may be of some help, but in the case of Ask B the presence of the surface pronoun should be of tremendous help in correctly interpreting the sentence compared to Ask C. In Ask C, where the MDP is violated, the child, if s/he doesn't know it is violated, assigns NP_2 as the subject of the complement verb, resulting in an incorrect interpretation. But applying the MDP results in correct interpretation of the sentence in Ask B where the subject of the complement clause appears in the surface. Our predictions are then: Tell C $>$ Ask C, Ask B $>$ Ask C, and Tell B $>$ Tell C.

In order to construct Case C, subject omitted, sentences, a problem inherent in Arabic had to be overcome. The problem is that Arabic verbs are marked initially and/or terminally for gender and person of their subjects. For example, suppose we were to choose the verb *daras* (study). When the instruction's addressee is a male, as in sentences (16) and (17) below, there is no problem because the initial and terminal gender/person markings on the verb are identical in *tell* and *ask*, yielding *tədros*, and thus do not give away the subject of the complement verb.

(16)   ʔəsʔal-a la Sonia shou lazaim tədros.
       Ask (masculine) her to Sonia what should you (masculine) study.

(17)   ʔəlla la Sonia shou lazaim tədros.
       Tell (masculine) her to Sonia what should she study.

Therefore, to assign the correct subject of the complement verb one must have in her/his grammar the knowledge that the MDP is to be applied for Tell but violated for Ask constructions. However, in the case of (18), where the instruction's addressee is a female, the terminal /ɪ/ on the complement verb marks its subject for second person feminine, thus making the sentence in fact a Case B, subject supplied, sentence. (The initial marker /t/ in (16), (17), and (18) marks the subject as second person masculine, or feminine, or third person feminine.)

(18)   ʔəsʔaliy-ya la Sonia shou lazaim tədrəsɪ.
       Ask (feminine) her to Sonia what should you (feminine) study.

To eliminate this problem we selected verbs such as taʕtɪ (give), and taʕmɪ (feed) with initial /t/ and terminal /ɪ/ phonemes for all combinations of female experimenters, male and female child addressees. Only if one knows that the MDP holds for *tell* but must be violated for *ask* does the terminal ending read *you* in the Ask structures but *she* in the Tell structures.

Since our pilot study with Arabic-speaking children indicated that they were asking when instructed to tell, even in the simplest cases, several other conditions were added to test the possibility that factors other than "linguistic knowledge" might be influencing their performance. They involved (1) the influence of the cognitive load which linguistic tasks impose on the child, i.e., whether the child had to make a choice before s/he could respond, and whether the response could be retrieved from short term store or must be retrieved from long term store, and (2) the difference between linguistic comprehension and linguistic production. The technique employed here was to use Show constructions paralleling the four Tell construction types. Promise and its non-MDP-violating Tell counterparts were also investigated. Only 8 of the 17 sentence construction types actually used will be discussed in this paper.

Experimental Design and Procedure

Each of the sentence structure types used was represented by four sentences. From each structure type two sentences were chosen at random and assigned to Form A, the other two being assigned to Form B. Within each Form all sentences were randomized and typed, 12 sentences per page. The pages were then randomized. Each child was tested on two different days within the same week. Half received Form A first, and half Form B first.

The subjects of the experiment were 48 Lebanese monolingual Arabic-speaking children from three private elementary schools in Beirut, each of slightly above average (for Lebanon) socio-economic standard. There were 8 boys and 8 girls in each of three age groups. The mean age for each group was 6; 4, 8; 5, and 10; 4 (years; months) with a range of from 8 to 9 months around each mean.

The experimenters (E's) were two adult female speakers of Arabic, the one giving the sentences to the children in the experiment ($E1$) having a Beirut accent. The Es both spent several days at each school getting to know the children, interacting with them at recesses, etc., prior to the beginning of the experiment. Each child was tested individually in a quiet room with $E1$ giving the instructions to the child while $E2$ served as a conversation partner for the child. A variety of toys, including dolls, dolls' clothing, a cat, a horse, two cars, boxes, and plastic food items were used to create the concrete situations necessary for each instruction given by $E1$ to the child. At the outset of the first session $E1$ acquainted the child with all the toys to be used by asking the child to name each one individually. Next $E1$ acquainted the child with the task by engaging her (him) in conversation with $E2$ using instructions similar to those to be used in the experiment. Several example sentences were used to emphasize to the child that sometimes s/he would have to *ask* a question and other times s/he would have to *tell*, and that s/he should listen carefully to each instruction. We particularly emphasized that the Tell instruction was not to be interpreted as a *repeat* or *say to* ... instruction. On approximately one-third of the trials where a child interpreted *ask* as *tell* or *tell* as *ask* s/he was asked *Now did you just ASK, or did you just TELL?* This was done to keep the child attending to the two instruction words. After insuring a child's understanding of the task, the first session started. $E1$ repeated each instruction twice. A slightly abbreviated orientation procedure was used prior to the beginning of second sessions.

Results and Discussion

An Age by Construction Type ANOVA with repeated measures on Construction Type was carried out on the correct response data. Both Age and Construction Type were found to be statistically significant: $F(2,45)=3.395$, $p=.0426$ and $F(16,720)=48.04$, $p < 1 \times 10^{-7}$, respectively. There was no interaction between Age and Construction Type. A priori t tests between 6- vs. 8-, and 8- vs. 10-year-olds collapsed across all eight constructions revealed that both pairwise comparisons were significant beyond the .01 level. Thus, performance on these structures taken as a whole does improve with age.

Preplanned comparisons were conducted to test for the significance of differences between the pairs of constructions shown in *Table 7.3*. This table also summarizes the direction of the predictions, their theoretical bases, and the results of the statistical tests.

As can be seen from *Table 7.3*, relatively few errors were made on Ask and Tell A1 and A2 sentences. Our predictions of children's performance based on syntactic complexity of the complement clause were not substantiated. Recall that we reasoned that Ask A1, *Ask (to) Sonia what (her) mother's name (is)*, would be easier than Ask A2, *Ask (to) Sonia (her) mother's name*, because in the former the question word, which is required for a correct response, is provided in the instruction, while in the latter it is not. There was a very small (but insignificant) difference in the predicted direction. In the Tell instructions we reasoned that Tell A2, *Tell (to) Sonia (your) mother's name*, would be easier than Tell A1, *Tell (to) Sonia what (your) mother's name (is)*, because in the former the child is spared the presence of the potentially misleading question word. The differences observed were in the predicted direction, but failed to reach significance (p=.061). It would appear that since all four of these constructions were so easy, a ceiling effect may have reduced the possibility of obtaining statistically significant differences.

Let us now look at Case A1 and A2 versus Case B constructions. We claimed that Chomsky's Case 1-B construction was more complex than the rest of her Case 1 constructions, and that it presented even more complex problems for children than her Case 2 constructions. Our data bear out these claims. All our B constructions are, as *Table 7.3* shows, much more difficult than the A1 and A2 constructions ($p <$ .001 for all Ask and Tell comparisons). It is perhaps worth noting that Kessel (1970) chose Chomsky's Case 1-B, her one-of-a-kind construction, as the model for the complement clauses of all his "Case 1" sentences, and

Table 7.3
Predictions and results of preplanned comparisons of
various Ask and Tell constructions

Theory	Predictions	Percent correct at three ages			Statistical Conclusions
		6	8	10	
MDP not violated vs. violated	Tell C $>$ Ask C	55/9	59/8	66/16	$p <$ .0001
	Ask B $>$ Ask C	44/9	62/8	66/16	$p <$ .0001
Syntactic complexity of complement clause	Tell B $>$ Tell C	45/55	50/59	55/66	p = n.s.
	Ask A1 $>$ Ask B	81/44	97/62	94/66	$p <$ .001
	Ask A2 $>$ Ask B	78/44	97/62	94/66	$p <$ .001
	Tell A1 $>$ Tell B	77/45	80/50	83/55	$p <$ .001
	Tell A2 $>$ Tell B	83/45	91/50	91/55	$p <$ .001
	Ask A1 $>$ Ask A2	81/78	97/97	94/92	p = n.s.
	Tell A2 $>$ Tell A1	83/77	91/80	91/83	p = .061

then went on to compare his results using three Ask and three Tell sentences of this kind with Chomsky's Case 1 (pp. 48, 55). This comparison is unfortunate since, as we have demonstrated, the sentences are not at all comparable.

It is clear that, contrary to Carol Chomsky's contention, complement clause complexity (defined as the number of grammatical elements missing) does not determine comprehension difficulty. Not only are A1 constructions, with no missing elements, not significantly easier for children to comprehend than A2 constructions, where the subject of the complement clause is missing, but B constructions, with no missing elements, are significantly harder for children than the A2's.

An analysis of the B and C constructions likewise leads to the conclusion that complement clause complexity defined by missing elements does not determine comprehension difficulty. Recall that we predicted that Tell B would be easier than Tell C because the former provided the complement clause subject in surface structure. But notice that Tell B is *not* easier to comprehend than Tell C.

The two predictions based on the MDP were both strongly supported. Performance on Tell C constructions, where the MDP applies, was much better than performance on Ask C constructions, where the MDP is violated. Second, performance on Ask B constructions was significantly better than that on Ask C constructions. Recall, however, that this second outcome was predicted by two factors: (1) Application of the MDP leads to correct comprehension of Ask B, but not Ask C constructions; and (2) Ask B contains an explicit subject of the complement clause, whereas in Ask C this subject has been deleted, thereby making it more complex and harder to comprehend. But notice that these two factors are confounded in the Ask B versus Ask C comparison, i.e., the only reason the MDP predicts that the wrong NP will be taken as the subject of the complement verb in Ask C is because the deep subject has been deleted. However, we infer from the fact that TELL C, with its NP deletion, was not harder to comprehend than TELL B that complement clause complexity (deletions from surface) does not play a role in the poorer comprehension of Ask C compared to Ask B either—but that it is the MDP application which makes Ask B easier than Ask C.

The unexpected Tell B/C result focuses our attention on the structure of the B Cases, both Ask and Tell, and the pattern of errors children made on these structures. Let us examine these errors. Considering Ask C first (see *Table 7.4*) we observe that over half of all RESPONSES were errors which MAY be attributed to the misapplication of (failure to violate) the MDP, resulting in the response, *What should YOU give the doll?* Notice, however, that this same response constitutes almost half of the ERRORS in the Ask B case also. But in the Ask B case we cannot attribute this response to the misapplication of the MDP, since application of the MDP would result in the correct response, *What should I give the doll?* Thus, we propose that in the case of Ask B, at least, children who responded with *What should YOU give the doll?* were interpreting the instruction as being in the

Table 7.4
Percentage of different types of responses out of
total responses which are errors on Ask and Tell A and B
constructions by three age groups

Construction	Type of error	Age 6	Age 8	Age 10
Ask B: e.g., Ask (to) Sonia what should you give the doll?	Ask, as if wh- clause were direct report: e.g., What should you give the doll?	20.3%	20.3%	17.2%
	Tell, with Sonia as subject: e.g., Give the doll eggs.	12.5%	15.6%	15.6%
	Tell, with self as subject: e.g., I should give the doll eggs.	20.3%	1.6%	0.0%
Ask C: e.g., Ask (to) Sonia what should you/she give the doll?	Ask, with wrong subject: e.g., What should you give the doll?	53.1%	73.4%	34.4%
	Tell, with Sonia as subject: e.g., Give the doll eggs.	37.5%	17.2%	18.8%
	Repeat wh- clause, not as a question: e.g., What should you/she give the doll.	0.0%	0.0%	26.6%
Tell B: e.g., Tell (to) Sonia what should she give the doll.	Ask, as if wh- clause were direct report: e.g., What should you give the doll?	51.6%	45.3%	43.8%
Tell C: e.g., Tell (to) Sonia what should you/she give the doll.	Ask, as if wh- clause were direct report: e.g., What should you give the doll?	26.6%	26.6%	4.7%
	Ask, with self as subject: e.g., What should I give the doll?	1.6%	3.1%	4.7%
	Repeat wh- clause, not as a question: e.g., What should you/she give the doll?	17.2%	12.5%	23.4%

direct report mode, i.e., they were interpreting the construction as *Ask (to) Sonia, "What should you (Sonia) give the doll?"* The fact that the response had the question intonation, AND the fact that the second person pronoun was NOT changed support this argument.

It is interesting to note in this connection that Tanz (1976)[1] found almost 20% of her 3;6- to 5;1-year-old children sometimes responded to an instruction such as *Ask Tom where you should sit* with *Where you should sit?* She notes that this type of error could be accounted for by what we have called a direct report interpretation of the *E*'s instruction, i.e., interpreting it as "containing a direct quotation of a question rather than a subordinated question" (p. 91). She points out that to get this reading the child would have to fail to attend to two cues in the adult's instruction: (1) lack of question intonation, and (2) noninversion of subject and verb. She then rejected the hypothesis that this is what her children were doing on the grounds that it lacked generality, failing to explain their responses to two other types of sentences she used. However, in our study, since there is no (potential) cue from noninversion of subject and auxiliary verb in the complementizing wh- clause which the child would need to ignore in order to interpret the instruction as a direct report, such an interpretation becomes much more attractive.

Even stronger evidence in support of our contention that our children were interpreting the Ask B instructions as if they were direct report instructions comes from their responses to Tell B and Tell C constructions (see *Table 7.4*). Nearly one half of all responses to Tell B, *Tell (to) Sonia what should she give the doll*, were the same responses as given to Ask B, *What should you give the doll?* Since children changed the third person pronoun (*she*) in the instruction to the second person pronoun (*you*) in their responses, AND since they used the question intonation, they must have been interpreting the instruction as being one of direct report, i.e., as being *Tell (say) (to) Sonia the question ". . . .?"* This was the only type of error our children made on Tell B structures, and notice that they made two and one-half times as many of these direct report errors on Tell B as on Ask B even though the overall error rate is very similar on the two structures. As can be seen in *Table 7.4*, this type of error was also made on Tell C, although not as frequently as on Tell B. It is obvious from inspecting *Table 7.4* that this reasoning accounts for a large proportion of the errors on Ask and Tell constructions. The fact that children changed the pronoun in Tell B from *she* to *you*, coupled with the fact that they did NOT change the second person pronoun in Ask B, compels us to conclude that their errors are due to their interpreting these instructions as being direct report constructions. It is interesting to note that, although Carol Chomsky does not stress the fact, several of her children also *asked* to Tell instructions. Examples of this can be found on her Case 1, 2, and 3 structures (e.g., pp. 68, 73, and 94, respectively).

There are two factors which may play a role in our children's interpretation of these structures as being in the direct report mode. First, in the case of Tell constructions, the Arabic word for *tell* (?oul) also means *say*, the verb most commonly associated with the direct report mode, as in *John said, "Mary, put the book on the table*, as opposed to *John told Mary to put the book on the table*, or *John told Mary where to put the book*. Second, in both Ask and Tell B and C, as mentioned above, the complement wh- clauses, unlike English, are well-formed questions in terms of morpheme order, such that they could stand alone as questions.

Why, one might ask, were there less than half as many direct report errors on Tell C as on Tell B? Recall that the terminal morpheme on the complement verbs in the Ask/Tell C sentences was ambiguous as to person of the subject, thus meeting the "subject omitted" condition and allowing knowledge of the MDP to be tested. It would seem that the ambiguous subject marker on the verb was not as strong a cue for the direct report interpretation as was the explicit pronoun in Case B; thus the greater the diversity of responses in the ambiguous pronoun condition. Exactly how the explicit versus ambiguous pronoun morphemes play their differential roles in Arabic-speaking children's interpretation of these and other utterances deserves further investigation.

Let us now turn our attention to another category of errors, "Repeat" errors. Note that children made quite a few Repeat errors on Tell C, but none on Tell B. A Repeat error was classified as such, and not as a question, on the basis of the intonational contour and stress pattern of the response uttered by a child. This is best illustrated by looking at examples of differential stress which might be placed on instructions to the child.

(19)   ?oulɪ-la la Sonia shou lazaim taʕti l-laʕbai?
        Say (to) Sonia, "What should (you/she) give the doll?"

(20)   ?oulɪ-la la Sonia shou lazaim taʕti l-laʕbai.
        Tell (to) Sonia what should (you/she) give the doll.

The instruction was always given by *E*1 as in (20) without question intonation and stress. Children who repeated had to be interpreting Tell C as something like *Say after me (to Sonia) "What should give the doll,"* which, without the question intonation and stress, is nonsense. Chomsky observed similar errors. At least one of her children repeated on her Tell Case 3 (p. 70), and one repeated the wh-clause of her Ask Case 3 (p. 59). Three of our children, all 10-year-olds, consistently repeated on Ask C. Surprisingly, there was a slight tendency for our older children to repeat more on Tell C than the two youngest age groups. Even more difficult to explain is the fact that, to Ask C instructions, 26.6% of our 10-year-olds' responses were Repeats, while none of our 6- and 8-year-olds' responses were of this sort. It is as if some of our 10-year-olds were perceiving the entire test situation as a drill to repeat exactly what an adult says. It seems not entirely unlikely that older children might have had more classroom experience in being asked to do such things than younger children. There is probably more emphasis on memorizing, repeating back exactly what is given by the teacher in most Lebanese primary schools than in American primary schools (a vestige of the OLD French educational system). The fact that the verb *tell* means *say* may have also played a critical role.

Comparing our children to Chomsky's in terms of Ask comprehension "Stages" we find that three of our children, compared to eight of hers, were at Stage A, failing all constructions, and one of ours, compared to two of hers, was at Stage B, passing the simplest construction (A1), but failing all others.[2] Only one of our children, a 10-year-old, as compared to 14 of Chomsky's children, was at the most advanced (E) Stage, passing all constructions. Direct comparison with Chomsky's Stages C and D is impossible for two reasons. First, we have an extra construction type. Second, Chomsky's Stage D consisted of children who succeeded on the two easiest constructions, but asked with the wrong subject (*you*) on the most difficult construction. She called this "partial success," reasoning that since they at least asked instead of making the dominant error of telling, they were at a more advanced stage than children who told. Since our children's most common error to Ask constructions was to ask with the wrong subject (direct report interpretation) it can be argued that the underlying metric upon which our stages should be based is that of correctness of grammatical assignment. When stages were constructed in this way 18 children (7, 6, and 5 6-, 8-, and 10-year-olds, respectively) passed A1 and A2, but failed B and C. And 22 children (4, 9, and 9 6-, 8-, and 10-year-olds, respectively) passed A1, A2, and B, but failed C. Notice that the age distributions are as they should be, i.e., relatively more younger children in our third stage, and more older children in our fourth stage.

Notice two similarities between our Stage data and Chomsky's: First, we observe wide age ranges within stages. Second, children who succeed on a more complex structure also succeed on simpler structures. Of our 48 children, only one, a 6;0 boy, is a clear exception. He made no errors on Ask B, but *told* three times on Ask A2 and twice on Ask A1.

Attempting to discover stages in Tell which would integrate reasonably with our Ask stages is a complex task which thus far has not proved very fruitful. However, it seems reasonable to expect that a child who interpreted Ask B and C instructions as direct reports might also have been inclined to interpret Tell constructions as direct reports. Of the 23 children who did not interpret Ask B and/or C as direct reports, none interpreted Tell's as direct reports, while of the 22 children who did interpret Ask B and/or C as direct reports, six interpreted Tell's as direct reports.[3] Thus there is some consistency across Ask's and Tell's in this direct report interpretation tendency. Furthermore, there is considerable consistency in the way individual children responded within Tell constructions. For example, of the 16 children who made no errors on the Tell B constructions, only one failed Tell C. (Remember that we had predicted that Tell B would be easier because it contained an explicit surface pronoun, but empirically we found no significant differences.)

In summary, it is clear that complement clause complexity, defined as the number of surface elements deleted from the clause, is not an important determiner of Lebanese children's performance on Ask/Tell sentential complement constructions.

There is support for the notion that constructions where the MDP applies produce better performance than those which require its violation.

The foregoing conclusion is complicated by the fact that many children interpreted the two more difficult Ask/Tell constructions (those where predictions based on MDP violation obtain) as being direct reports, i.e., containing quoted speech. This very interesting fact makes unclear the role of MDP violation/application. Furthermore, since MDP violation is required precisely where the pronoun is deleted, it is obvious that children's performance depends upon the *nature* of the surface elements present or deleted in relation to other elements—on nonsyntactic, semantic, perhaps even pragmatic, factors. Direct report interpretations are the result of an interaction between pronoun present/deleted and Ask/Tell. Certainly, an explanation of performance based on the notion of surface completeness is a superficial one.

Five Ask stages emerged, with wide age variation within stages. While there was some tendency for children who interpreted Ask constructions as direct reports to do the same with Tell's, no combined, integrated Ask/Tell stages emerged from the data.

Notes

This research was supported by a Research Grant from the Ford Foundation awarded to the first two authors through the Center for Behavioral Research, American University of Beirut. We wish to thank E. T. Prothro, Director of the Center, for his support, and Sana Takla for her experimental assistance. Parts of this research formed the basis of the third author's M.A. Thesis at the American University of Beirut.

1. We are grateful to Thomas Roeper, who, after hearing our paper at the Symposium, brought Tanz's unpublished data and the similarity of our hypothesized explanation to hers to our attention.

2. "Passing" was defined as Chomsky defined it, i.e., being correct on at least 3 out of 4 exemplars of a construction.

3. A child was defined as exhibiting direct report interpretation on Ask if s/he interpreted as a direct report 3 or 4 out of 4 sentences of Ask B, Ask C, or both. A child was defined as exhibiting direct report interpretation on Tell if s/he interpreted as a direct report 3 or 4 out of 4 sentences of at least two of the four following construction types: Tell A1, Tell A2, Tell B, and Tell C.

Chapter 8

The Structure of Coordination in Children's First Language Acquisition of Japanese

Barbara Lust
Tatsuko Kaneda Wakayama

Previous research has identified constraints on the structure of coordination in young children's first language acquisition of English (Lust, 1977). This paper investigates constraints on coordination in young children's first language acquisition of Japanese; and compares these to those previously found in English. It attempts to define both common and distinct properties of the constraints in the two languages, and to assess their nature. In particular, it inquires whether certain putative universal properties of coordination structure in natural language determine some common part of the constraints on acquisition of the two languages.

The Structure of Coordination in Natural Language

One of the principal characteristics of coordination across languages is the possibility for reduction of redundancy in coordinate structures.

A *conjunction reduction schema* is assumed to describe this reduction in the grammars of some, if not all, languages.[1] This schema relates *sentential coordinations* (i.e., coordination between sentences) such as (1) to *phrasal coordinations* (i.e., coordination between nonsentential constituents, e.g., nouns, verbs, adjectives, etc.) such as (2) (cf. Stockwell, et al., 1973).

(1)   John sings and John dances

(2)   John sings and dances

While sentential coordinations such as (1) are generated directly, according to these grammars, other forms of coordination such as (2) are not; they are derived from sentential coordinations by the conjunction reduction schema.

Although it has been proposed that phrase structure rules alone may be sufficient to describe conjunction in natural language (e.g., Dougherty, 1970, 1971), arguments for the necessity of a conjunction reduction schema persist (e.g., Stockwell et al., 1973; Gleitman, 1969).[2] (See also Langendoen, 1975a, b and Sag, 1976 for current descriptions of this rule schema.)

The schema has been thought to be universal. Its relevance to Japanese coordination has been supported by Kuno (1967-1968, 1973), Nakau (1971), and Inoue (1969), for example. In Japanese, the schema would interrelate sentential and phrasal coordinations such as (3) and (4) respectively.

(3)   James-wa utau shi, James-wa odoru.
       (James sings and James dances)

(4)   James-wa utau-shi odoru.
       (Janes sings and dances)

Structure-dependence of coordination reduction. The redundancy reduction described by the conjunction reduction schema is structurally constrained. *Directionality of redundancy reduction* in general depends upon the constituent structure of coordinated elements. Thus in sentence (6), for example, the redundant element in the left conjunct is reduced (*backward reduction*), not the one in the right conjunct (*forward reduction*) as in sentence (2).

(5)   John *stayed* and Mary *stayed*

(6)   John and Mary *stayed*

In sentence (1) the redundant element "John" is left-branched in constituent structure, while in sentence (5) the redundant element "stayed" is right-branched in constituent structure. Backward reduction is ungrammatical for sentence (1) as sentence (7) shows:

(7)   *Sings and John dances.

Forward reduction is ungrammatical for sentence (5) as sentence (8) shows:

(8)   *John stayed and Mary

These data reflect a general "directionality principle" in natural language coordination correlating right-branched redundancy with *backward reduction* and left-branched redundancy with *forward reduction*. Firsrt noted by Ross (1970) for verb reduction, the principle was later extended to other grammatical categories by others, e.g., Sanders, 1975; Tai, 1969, 1971.

This structural constraint is putatively universal, thus explaining why verb reduction is *backwards* in Japanese, where the verb is final and thus necessarily right-branched, e.g., (9). This is opposed to English where the verb is *left-branched* and reduces *forward,* as in (10).

(9)   OV̸+OV

    A.   Hon-o kau-shi, pen-o kau

Book buy and pen buy

    B.   Hon-to pen-o kau.

Book and pen buy

(10)   VO+V̸O

    A.   Buy the book and buy the pen.

    B.   Buy the book and the pen.

An Independent Constraint on the
Direction of Coordination Reduction

Recently, however, a number of linguists working independently to describe the structure of coordination across diverse languages (Hankamer, 1971; Maling, 1972; Harries, 1973) have observed that forward and backward coordination reduction are not equivalent structurally.

These studies suggest that conjunction reduction deletion may be independently constrained universally, so that *deletion in coordinate structures always applies in a forward direction* regardless of branching structure. Only forward reduction may reflect a simple coordinate deletion operation. Ostensible backward reduction as in sentence (6) or (9) may result from a distinct (right-node-raising rule) (Hankamer, Maling), which applies to right-branched redundancy.[3]

It has been suggested that Japanese may offer no essential contradiction to this putative foward directionality constraint on coordinate deletion (Kuno, 1973:13; Harries, 1973).

In summary, according to this theory, a universal component of natural language, the conjunction reduction schema, interrelates coordination types (sentential and phrasal) by structurally constrained redundancy reduction. By a general constraint, constituent structure of redundant elements correlates with location of reduction site. A more abstract directionality constraint may characterize the deletion component of the conjunction reduction schema. Coordinate deletion operates in a forward direction.

Previous Research in English Language Acquisition

Previous research, on the structure of coordination in young children's acquisition of English, found constraints which appeared to reflect properties of the universal conjunction reduction schema reviewed above (Lust, 1977).

In this research in English, two- and three-year-old children (mean age 2; 6 in years and months) (N=23) were asked to imitate a set of simple coordinative sentences such as in (11) and (12) according to regularized elicited imitation techniques.[4]

(11)   SV+$V

    A.   *Babies* laugh and *babies* cry.
    B.   *The teddy-bear* walks and sleeps.

(12)   SV̸+SV

    A.   Mommies *jump* and babies *jump.*
    B.   The kitties and the dogs *hide.*

(Such sentence patterns were also administered in VO form by use of the imperative, e.g., VO+V̸O, "Eat cookies and eat crackers.")

Results of this study showed that *conjunction structure* had a significant effect on children's imitation. Sentential coordinations, e.g., (12A) above, were generally significantly easier for children to imitate than *phrasal coordinations,* e.g., 12B above, suggesting a general developmental precedence of sentential coordinations over phrasal coordinations in child language. This result was thought to support the relevance of a conjunction reduction schema to child language, since it demonstrates that children have sentential coordinations available as structural referents for phrasal coordinations in their developing language system.

In addition, results of this study showed that *reduction directionality* had a significant interactive effect on children's imitation of coordination in English. Phrasal coordinations with forward reduction patterns were significantly easier than those with backward reduction patterns. In addition, when children reduced redundancy in sentential coordinations, they did so when the reduction pattern was forward, e.g., (11A). (Fifty percent of errors on forward reduction patterns were reduction.) They rarely if ever reduced them when the reduction pattern was backward, e.g., (12A). These results were thought to further confirm the relevance of a conjunction reduction schema to coordination in child language, since they appeared to demonstrate a structure-dependent constraint on redundancy reduction in a forward direction, and this constraint has been claimed to be a characteristic of the conjunction reduction schema as seen above.

Constraints found on coordination in English child language, *viz.,* (1) a *conjunction structure constraint* determining early precedence of sentential coordinations and (2) a *reduction directionality constraint* determining forward direction of redundancy reduction, might reflect universal grammatical properties of the structure of coordination in natural language, viz., a conjunction reduction schema determining a relation between coordination types, and an independent forward directionality constraint on deletion in this schema.

At the same time, however, these putative reflections of grammatical constraints in child language may not be independent of a-linguistic cognitive principles (Sinclair, reported in Lust, 1977). Their precise nature remains at issue (e.g., the work of Bever, 1970, and Slobin, 1971a, as well as that of Piaget has been proposed to provide alternative explanations of aspects of these constraints).

Possible Universal Properties of the Constraints on Acquisition

Regardless of their nature (cognitive-linguistic or cognitive-a-linguistic) if these constraints found on coordination in child language in English are fundamental to the language acquisition process, they should apply universally to acquisition of distinct natural languages.

Previous research includes some suggestion that a forward reduction directionality constraint might hold in first language acquisition of languages other than English. Roeper (1973) found German children (4 and 5 years old) to have greater difficulty imitating backward reduction patterns such as (13), than forward reduction patterns such as (14).

(13)   *Backward reduction*

Nicht der Vater, aber der Junge macht die Tür zu.
Not the father, but the boy made the door shut.

(14)   *Forward reduction*

Die Mutter macht nicht die Tür, aber die Fenster auf.
The mother opened not the door, but the window up.

Study of coordination in first language acquisition of Japanese, however, can provide a strong test for possible universal properties of the constraints found in English acquisition, since Japanese differs structurally from English (as well as from German) in several crucial ways.

1.   Japanese is a highly case-marked language. It makes less use of word order than English. Because the conjunction reduction schema is defined on the basis of word order, it may be less natural in Japanese than in English.

2.   Japanese represents coordination by a series of inflections whereas English achieves it by an independent connective morpheme ("and").[5] Since the conjunction reduction schema is defined with regard to a connective morpheme, again, the conjunction reduction schema may be less natural in Japanese. For these reasons, children's language acquisition in Japanese may be less sensitive to the schema.

3.   Japanese is SOV in basic word order, whereas English is SVO. These linear order differences between Japanese and English result in reversed patterns of redundancy reduction in coordination. For example, as we saw in (9) and (10) above, for the case of verb-redundancy, Japanese reduces backward where English reduces forward. Thus, comparing acquisition of coordination reduction in

Japanese and English, makes it possible to assess differences in reduction directionality independently of differences in category or case of the redundant or deleted term. If we would find that a reduction directionality constraint also held in Japanese child language, we would have strong evidence that this factor is independent of lexical category or case.

4.   Moreover, Japanese is principally a left-branching language as opposed to English which is principally right-branching (cf. Kuno, 1973:7-8). That is, Japanese generates recursive terms to the left of a non-null site (e.g., A → Aα, where α is some non-null element) whereas English mainly generates them to the right (A → αA) (Chomsky, 1964a:123, fn 9).[6] In addition, Japanese has a rather rigid verb-final constraint. It is intuitively obvious that a language which is rigidly verb-final, and which may delay closure of a sentence (through a possible infinite number of left recursive embeddings on the initial nouns of the sentence for example) might be more tolerant of backward (or leftward) reductions than a language which is right-branching and which favors an initial sentence skeleton (subject-verb). Given the differences in constituent structure between Japanese and English then, it might be expected that acquisition of coordination in Japanese might not demonstrate the forward directionality constraint on coordination reduction found in English acquisition. However, if the forward directionality constraint found in English were in fact a reflex of the abstract constraint on the deletion component of the conjunction reduction schema and if this conjunction reduction schema characterizes Japanese, then the constraint should also hold in Japanese, unaffected by the constituent structure differences between the languages.

Simple Japanese Coordination: Study Number One

Method

To test whether *conjunction structure* and *reduction directionality* are significant in first language acquisition of Japanese as they are in acquisition of English, imitation of simple coordinative sentences was elicited from 38 Japanese children between the ages of 2; 5 and 5; 9 (mean age 3; 8) in the Tokyo-Yokohama areas of Japan. (There were 20 females and 18 males.)[7] In a design similar to the design of the English study reported above, the Japanese children were asked to imitate a set of Japanese sentences consisting of symmetric pairs of subjects and verbs, or objects and verbs (SV+SV; OV+OV).[8] Sentences were systematically varied in *conjunction structure* (sentential or phrasal) and in *direction of reduction pattern* (forward or backward). Each of the 4 reduction patterns shown in *Table 8.1* was given in both sentential and phrasal form; example sentences are shown on the table. All sentences were 11 or 12 syllables in length.[9] Each sentence type was replicated once. There were 16 sentences for each child and a total of 608 sentences for analysis.

Children were divided into 4 age groups, mean ages (2; 10) (3; 2) (3; 10) (5; 0).[10] They were interviewed in nursery schools or in their homes by a methodology as closely matched as possible to the English study methodology.[11]

Table 8.1

Reduction patterns of simple coordinative sentences and examples
in both sentential conjunction and phrasal conjunction*

Forward reduction		Backward reduction	
1.	SV+ṢV	3.	SV̸+SV
2.	OV+∅V	4.	OV̸+OV

Examples

Sentential conjunction		Phrasal conjunction	
1A.	To-wa hiraku-shi to-wa shimaru Door open and door close	1B.	Inu-wa hoeru-shi kamitsuku Dog bark and bite
2A.	Mari-o tsuku-shi mari-o keru Ball bounce and ball kick	2B.	Booru-o nageru-shi tsukamu Ball throw and catch
3A.	Tori-wa naku-shi mushi-wa naku Bird sing and cricket sing	3B.	Sumire-to tanpopo-ga saku Violet and dandelion bloom
4A.	Umi-o miru-shi yama-o miru Sea look at and mountain look at	4B.	Zubon-to seetaa-o kiru Pants and sweater put on

*The slash through an S (subject), V (verb), or O (object) symbol signifies point of redundancy in a sentential coordination or point of redundancy reduction (null site) in phrasal coordination.

Results

Table 8.2 shows the mean numbers of correct imitations in this first study (assessed by Analysis of Variance). The results show that the structural factors, *conjunction structure* and *reduction directionality, do* both significantly affect young Japanese children's imitation of coordinative sentences. However, the effects of these factors were reversed from those in English. Although the Japanese children were sensitive to *conjunction structure* ($F(1,34)=16.78$, $p<.001$), they found *phrasal coordinations* significantly easier than *sentential coordinations* (means correct were 1.33 and 1.07 respectively). (That is, children found coordinations such as in the (B) sentences in *Table 8.1* significantly easier than sentential coordinations such as in the (A) sentences here.)

The *reduction directionality* factor is also highly significant as a main effect ($F(1,34) =72.42$, $p < .001$) in Japanese. It does not interact with conjunction structure as it does in English, but affects both sentential and phrasal coordinations. Moreover, it is highly significant in the reverse direction. Japanese children find *backward* coordination reduction patterns significantly easier than *forward* reduction patterns. That is, children found coordinations such as 3 and 4 in *Table 8.1* significantly easier than coordinations 1 and 2. The mean number of backward coordinations correct was 1.49; of forward only .92.

These effects held in general over all age groups although children improved significantly in successful imitation of coordination in each age group after the first two (mean number of imitations correct in each group was .81, .93, 1.31, 1.78 respectively). The conjunction structure effect significantly interacted

Table 8.2
Mean number correct of simple Japanese coordinative
sentences at each age level by conjunction structure,
reduction directionality, and constituent structure

	Sentential		Phrasal	
	forward	backward	forward	backward
Mean Age 2; 10*				
SV+SV	.500	.700	.500	1.100
OV+OV	.300	1.000	.700	1.700
		.625	1.00	
Mean Age 3; 2				
SV+SV	.111	1.000	.889	1.444
OV+OV	.667	1.000	.889	1.444
		.695	1.165	
Mean Age 3; 10				
SV+SV	.700	1.400	1.000	1.900
OV+OV	1.000	1.600	1.100	1.800
	1.175		1.450	
Mean Age 5; 0				
SV+SV	1.778	1.889	1.444	1.889
OV+OV	1.667	2.000	1.556	2.000
	1.834		1.722	

*Age in years and months

with age $(F(3,34)=4.11, p=.014)$; with the oldest age group finding sentential and phrasal coordination similar in difficulty.

In Japanese imitation, there was little spontaneous *reduction* of redundancy in sentential coordinations, and little *elaboration* of phrasal coordinations. This was in contrast to the English study where both reduction and elaboration had occurred (although there had been significantly more reduction than elaboration). Only two percent of sentential coordinations (4% of errors) were reduced by Japanese children. Reduction occurred mainly in the second age group (mean age 3; 2) accounting for 9% of errors on sentential coordinations here, and occurring equivalently on backward and forward reduction patterns. Only 1% of phrasal conjunctions (3% of errors) were elaborated in Japanese.

Discussion

According to the results above, acquisition of coordination by young Japanese children does not demonstrate a precedence of sentential coordination over phrasal coordination (or even a synchrony of these two). Unlike acquisition of coordination by young children acquiring English, Japanese acquisition demonstrates a precedence of phrasal coordination over sentential coordination. Under the assumptions of this study, these results signify that, unlike coordination in child language in English, coordination in Japanese child language does not reflect the structure of a conjunction reduction schema (at least for the coordination types we studied here). The very small amount of reduction and elaboration errors in Japanese children's imitations as compared to English supports this interpretation. Japanese children do not demonstrate interrelation of the sentential and phrasal coordinations studied here.

There are a number of technical problems in comparing these results to those in the previous study of English acquisition (see fn 9 and 10 above). The developmental primacy of phrasal coordinations in Japanese may, for example, be explained by the fact that although phrasal coordinations in the Japanese study had the same number of syllables as sentential coordinations, they had consistently fewer words. In the absence of a grammatical constraint, they would be expected to be easier to imitate for this reason alone.[12]

However, coordination in Japanese child language is also unlike that in English in that Japanese children reverse the preference for forward reduction patterns shown by English children and exhibit a clear preference for backward reduction patterns of coordination. Given the assumptions of this study, coordination in the language of Japanese children once again does not demonstrate accord with the structure of the grammatical conjunction reduction schema since, as we saw above, an abstract *forward* directionality constraint characterizes deletion in this schema.

Why, however, would the conjunction reduction schema not characterize child language in Japanese while it did so in English, if it is universal in grammar for natural language as has been proposed? Notably, it is quite possible that contrary to what has been proposed, the conjunction reduction schema does *not* characterize the correct grammar for Japanese. Various coordination structures may be generated independently in Japanese grammar by phrase structure rules alone (cf. Dougherty, 1970, 1971). Although this is a matter for independent linguistic analysis, preliminary arguments for this conclusion are obvious in terms of the differences between Japanese and English cited above. Because Japanese is a highly case-marked language, for example, it may achieve coordination variation by case-marking alone. More importantly, it may be that the ostensible "coordinating" particles used in the Japanese sentences in this study are not in fact coordinative in the way that the English connective "and" is (E. Jorden, personal communication).[13]

Notably, if a conjunction reduction schema (as defined above) does *not* describe the Japanese coordination in the study above, then it could not be expected to constrain Japanese first language acquisition of coordination. If the constraints found in English acquisition do reflect the conjunction reduction schema, and this schema does not characterize Japanese, then it would follow that *neither* of these constraints, i.e., the preference for sentential coordination or the preference for forward reduction, would necessarily appear in acquisition of coordination in Japanese. This explanation of the absence in Japanese of the constraints found in English acquisition would be supported if we would find a coordination structure in Japanese which clearly did involve a form of conjunction reduction; and if for this structure a preference for forward directionality of reduction did show developmental primacy in Japanese child language as it had in English child language. The following study sought to test this possibility.

Japanese Coordination By "mo":   Study Number Two[14]

Japanese does allow a type of coordination by the morpheme "mo" which appears to involve coordinate deletion, e.g., (15). Unlike the phrasal coordination in *Study Number One* above, it cannot easily be described by phrase structure rules alone.

(15)   John-wa ringo-o katta, banana mo
        John apple ate, banana also

If it cannot be independently generated, sentence (15) must be related (both syntactically and semantically) to a sentential coordination such as (16).

(16)   *John-wa* ringo-o *katta, John-wa* banana-o *katta.*
        John apple ate, John banana ate

"Mo" sentences such as (15) can be described as resulting from deletion of redundant elements in a sentence such as (16) without regrouping of remaining elements (Harries, 1973). The deletion is forward in accord with the forward directionality constraint on coordinate deletion.

If this structure of conjunction reduction by simple forward deletion does characterize "mo" forms such as (15) in Japanese, and if the grammatical structure of conjunction reduction does constrain young children's acquisition of coordination, then Japanese child language should evidence constraints on "mo" coordination similar to the constraints on coordination found in English language acquisition and different from the constraints found on other forms of Japanese coordination in *Study Number One* above. Namely, child language should demonstrate a *conjunction structure* effect by which children acquire reduced "mo" coordinations such as (15) subsequent to (or simultaneously with) related sentential coordinations such as (16); and child language should demonstrate a *reduction directionality* effect by which the *forward* reduced "mo" forms are developmentally precedent to other reduced forms of coordination.

Method

To test whether Japanese child language would demonstrate these two constraints on coordinations with "mo," 43 children in the Tokyo-Yokohama area of Japan (age 2;5 to 5;9; mean age 3;8) were asked to imitate reduced "mo" coordinations such as 1 and 2 on *Table 8.3,* as well as the sentential "mo"

Table 8.3

Reduction patterns and examples of simple coordinative sentences using "mo" in Japanese

	Examples
Forward reduction	
1. SV+S mo	1. Kuruma-wa hashiru, densha-mo Car run, train also
2. OV+O mo	2. Suika-o taberu, budoo-mo Watermelon eat, grape also
Backward reduction	
3. [S+S] V	3. Otona-mo kodomo-mo oyogu Adult and child swim
4. [O+O] V	4. Kudamono-mo yasai-mo kau Fruit and vegetable buy
Sentential coordination	
5. SV̸+SV (mo)	5. Hato-mo tobu-shi suzume-mo tobu Pigeon fly and sparrow fly
6. OV̸+OV (mo)	6. Kami-mo kiru-shi kire-mo kiru Paper cut and cloth cut

coordinations to which they were assumedly related (e.g., 5 and 6 on *Table 8.3*).[15] In addition, the children were asked to imitate backward phrasal coordinations such as 3 and 4 (on *Table 8.3*), to which the split "mo" coordinations corresponded. Children's imitation of the forward reduced "mo" coordination pattern 1, SV+Smo, could thus be compared to their imitation of the backward phrasal coordination [S+S]V, which is similar to coordination in *Study Number One*. Their imitation of the forward reduced "mo" coordination in 2, OV+Omo, could be compared to their imitation of the backward phrasal [O+O]V coordination. All sentences were 11 or 12 syllables in length as in *Study Number One*.

There were 23 females and 20 males in four age groups (mean ages 2; 9, 3; 2, 3; 9, 5; 0). Each child was asked to imitate two examples of each of the 6 "mo" grammatical patterns on *Table 8.3*, providing 516 sentences for analysis for this study. Again, ANOVA were applied to the data.[16]

Results

Table 8.4 shows means for these analyses. Unlike reduced Japanese coordinations in *Study Number One, reduced "mo"* coordinations (e.g., 1 and 2 on *Table 8.3*) did not differ significantly from *sentential coordinations* (5 and 6) in difficulty; although the phrasal coordinations (3 and 4) were significantly easier than the sentential coordinations as they had been in *Study Number One* $(F(1,39)=6.48$, $p=.02)$.

With regard to the directionality effect, *the forward reduced "mo" coordinations* were in general, significantly more difficult for the children to imitate than the *backward phrasal coordinations* $(F(1,39)=6.26, p=.02)$ as forward phrasal coordinations had been in *Study Number One*. The mean number of

Table 8.4
Mean number correct of simple Japanese coordinative
sentences using "mo" at each age level

| | Reduced coordination | | |
	Forward reduction by "mo"	Backward reduction (Phrasal coordination)	Sentential coordination
Mean Age 2; 9			
SV+SV	.273	.455	.455
OV+OV	.455	.455	.364
	(.364)	(.455)	(.410)
Mean Age 3; 2			
SV+SV	.600	1.600	1.300
OV+OV	.900	1.300	1.100
	(.750)	(1.450)	(1.200)
Mean Age 3; 9			
SV+SV	1.636	1.636	1.727
OV+OV	1.636	1.545	.909
	(1.636)	(1.591)	(1.318)
Mean Age 5; 0			
SV+SV	1.818	1.909	1.909
OV+OV	1.909	1.909	1.455
	(1.864)	(1.909)	(1.682)

backward phrasal coordinations correct was 1.35; of reduced "mo" coordinations, 1.16. However, this directionality effect with the "mo" sentences significantly interacted with age $(F(1.39)=4.41, p=.01)$. In the youngest age group, and again at the oldest age groups, "mo" coordinations and background phrasal coordinations appeared similar in difficulty.

Moreover, the Japanese children frequently elaborated the "mo" coordinations although they had rarely done so with the phrasal coordinations of *Study Number One*. That is, children frequently (35% of errors) converted a sentence such as example 1 on *Table 8.3*, to a sentence such as (17):

(17)   Kuruma-wa *hashiru,* densha-mo *hashiru*

Only 2% of the phrasal coordinations (type 3 and 4) were elaborated (similar to *Study Number One*).

In addition, ten percent of errors on the reduced "mo" sentences consisted of a meaning-preserving relocation of the rightmost "mo" term to form a phrasal coordination. For example, given "Kuruma-wa hashiru, densha-mo" (*Table 8.3*, example 1), children provided a sentence such as (18), i.e., SV+S → [S+S] V:

(18)   Kuruma-mo densha-mo hashiru

When the elaboration (+relocation) imitation types are scored as successful, reduced "mo" coordinations are seen as significantly easier than the backward phrasal coordinations to which they were related (F(1,39)=5.50, p=.02). Mean number of reduced "mo" coordinations either correct or elaborated (or relocated) was 1.56.

Discussion

The results of this second study suggest that acquisition of Japanese coordination by "mo" is developmentally constrained in ways more similar to acquisition of coordination in English, than to acquisition of the Japanese coordination in *Study Number One* above. First, imitation data suggest that forward reduced "mo" coordinations (e.g., 1 and 2 on *Table 8.3*) are acquired synchronously with *sentential coordinations.* Notably, in English, although sentential coordinations preceded phrasal coordinations developmentally in general, forward direction phrasal coordinations, in particular, were synchronous with sentential coordinations. On the contrary, in Japanese *Study Number One*, both forward and backward phrasal coordinations were acquired significantly earlier than sentential coordinations, thus appearing to be independent of them developmentally.

Also unlike coordination in Japanese *Study Number One* and more like coordination in English acquisition, reduced "mo" coordinations are frequently elaborated, confirming their relation to sentential coordinations in child language. Errors on the reduced "mo" coordinations consisted of a larger amount of elaboration to sentential coordination, e.g., (17), than of conversion to phrasal coordination, e.g., (18). This may further signify the primacy of sentential coordinations for these "mo" coordinations.

Second, reduced "mo" coordinations, which are *forward reduction patterns*, appear to be acquired early in development of Japanese coordination (when their elaborations are considered correct), similarly to English coordination acquisition where forward reduced coordinations appear to be acquired earlier than backward reduced coordinations and synchronously with sentential coordinations.

As stated above, "mo" forms of Japanese coordination may differ from other forms of Japanese phrasal coordination (such as in *Study Number One*) by requiring some form of coordinate deletion in their description. It may be that the greater commonality in acquisition pattern between these "mo" forms and English coordination (i.e., they both demonstrate similar developmental constraints on *conjunction structure* and *reduction directionality*) can be explained by the greater commonality in their grammatical structure (i.e., they both may be described by some version of a conjunction reduction schema). The differences in developmental constraints in Japanese *Study Number One* from both Japanese *Study Number Two* and the English study may be due to difference in grammatical structure of these coordinations. Japanese coordination in *Study Number One* may not involve a conjunction reduction schema, but independently generated phrasal coordination alone.

General Discussion

Commonalities in Acquisition of Japanese and English Coordination

The elicited imitation studies above suggest that in both Japanese and English, children's acquisition of coordination is sensitive to the factor of *conjunction structure*, i.e., to whether coordination is sentential or phrasal. Correspondingly, acquisition is sensitive to whether redundancy is present or absent in coordination. In addition, in both Japanese and English, children's acquisition of coordination is sensitive to the *direction of redundancy reduction* in coordination, i.e., to whether reduction is forward or backward. Correspondingly, children's acquisition is sensitive to the syntactic location of redundancy in coordination. Both of these factors determine constraints on child language in Japanese and English in that they determine order of development of coordination structures, and limit redundancy reduction.

Differences in Japanese and English Acquisition of Coordination

The value of each of these factors for acquisition is reversed in Japanese and English for basic coordination types (*Study Number One*). This reversal appears to reflect distinctions in grammatical structure between the two languages.

The conjunction structure factor. As we suggested above, in Japanese *Study Number One*, a developmental precedence of phrasal coordination over sentential coordination, which reverses the developmental pattern of English acquisition, appears to reflect the absence of a conjunction reduction schema for these coordinations in Japanese grammatical structure.

The reduction directionality factor. In the absence of the grammatical structure of a conjunction reduction schema, the branching or constituent structure of a language might be expected to be a principal determining factor in children's acquisition of coordination. The strong preference for backward reduction patterns in coordination in Japanese child language may reflect young Japanese children's sensitivity to the basic leftward branching structure of the Japanese language.

In particular, the Japanese children's preference for backward reduction patterns (*Study Number One*) consists of a preference for coordinate structures with a unique verb. This verb is represented redundantly in sentential coordinations (*Table 8.1*, 3A and 4A for example) or singularly in phrasal coordinations (3B and 4B in the table for example). Since the verb is rigidly sentence-final in Japanese, the preference for backward reduction patterns consists of a preference for patterns with unique sentence-final constituent. Since leftward branching structures require identification of some constant right-most non-null term to the left of which recursive devices operate, children's preference for backward coordination patterns (such as 3 and 4 in *Table 8.1*) could be interpreted as evidence of their attempt to determine a constant right-most term in accord with the left-branching structure of the language. If this is true, Japanese children are sensitive to a highly abstract property of the constituent structure of their language, namely recursion directionality.

Since all of the backward coordinations in *Study Number One* had a unique final verb, however, it remains possible that children's preference for backward reduction patterns in *Study Number One* is explained by a primacy of the "verb" category in coordination in Japanese child language; it may be easier for children to remember a redundant or reduced verb than a redundant or reduced noun.[17.] The results of *Study Number Two*, where the factor of verb category reduction was not confounded with the factor of reduction directionality (both backward and forward reduction patterns were tested for verb reduction), showed that reduction directionality has a significant effect independent of the category of deleted term. This suggests that the results of *Study Number One* may reflect the directionality factor rather than the verb category factor. However, further experimental work is necessary to confirm this. If the Japanese children's strong preference for backward reduction patterns is due to children's sensitivity to the recursion directionality of their language, then children should also show this preference in coordination reduction of other phrase structures which are not verb-final, e.g., NP, AP, PP, etc.

Universal Properties of Language Acquisition

The results of these studies on Japanese acquisition bear on our interpretation of the previous English acquisition study, and on our definition of possible universal properties of constraints on acquisition of coordination in a first language.

Linguistic universals. The constraints found on acquisition of coordination in Japanese and English cannot be simply described as reflexes of a putatively universal conjunction reduction schema. The conjunction reduction schema may not apply to coordination in all languages or to all coordination in a language, contrary to what has been sometimes proposed. The developmental ordering of sentential and phrasal coordination may vary depending on whether or not a conjunction reduction schema grammatically describes the coordination involved. A precedence of sentential coordination over phrasal coordination (or synchrony between these) may occur only where the conjunction reduction schema characterizes the grammatical structure of the coordination.

The reduction directionality constraint also cannot be simply described as a reflex of a constraint on deletion in the putatively universal conjunction reduction schema. The Japanese results suggest that the recursive branching structure (right or left) of a language may constrain children's sensitivity to reduction directionality (forward or backward). It may do so in all cases, or only where a conjunction reduction schema does not apply. The precedence of forward over backward reduction in acquisition of coordination in English may reflect children's sensitivity to the principally right-branching nature of the English language, just as precedence of backward reduction in Japanese may reflect a sensitivity to the principally left-branching nature of Japanese. (English-speaking children may seek a constant non-null left-most term from which to generate recursive terms rightward.)

Since the conjunction reduction schema is thought to apply to English coordination, however, it remains possible that the properties of deletion in this schema may explain the directionality constraint on English acquisition. Moreover, the results of the second Japanese study, on "mo" coordinations, tentatively suggest that a developmental precedence of forward reduction may occur even in a left-branching language, for coordination structures which are described by conjunction reduction. Thus in this case the directionality effect may in fact reflect the conjunction reduction schema. Japanese children, however, here *elaborate* forward reduction patterns whereas English children *reduce* them. That is, Japanese children "correct" a forward reduction. These Japanese imitation data may suggest a possible interaction of a constraint on conjunction reduction (forward direction of reduction) with a constraint determined by the branching structure of the language (against forward reduction and for a non-null right-most term).

Cognitive a-linguistic universals. It remains possible that the constraints found on acquisition of coordination in Japanese and English may be at least partially explained by principles of cognition which are not specific to language. The developmental precedence of forward reduction of redundancy which appeared in English and again in Japanese "mo" coordinations accords with the general developmental constraint on cognition defined by Piaget as "nonreversibility" (Sinclair et al., 1976, and reported in Lust, 1977). This principle may cohere with certain grammatical principles of coordination.

Alternatively, it has been suggested that the preference for forward reduction patterns in acquisition of coordination may result from an a-grammatical "cognitive perceptual" principle of language acquisition by which *children prefer sentences with an uninterrupted initial sentence frame.* Thus, it is claimed, English-speaking children reduce redundancy in SV+SV coordination, e.g., *John came and John stayed → John came and stayed*; and they do not reduce redundancy in SV+SV coordination, *John came and Mary came → John and Mary came* because the latter reduction would interrupt an initial sentence frame. This "cognitive perceptual" principle has been proposed to be "universal" in language acquisition. It corresponds to a perceptual principle which has been defined for adult language, whereby an early stage of sentence perception is believed to consist of identification of a "canonical sentoid" (Fodor, Bever and Garrett, 1975:344). Here a "canonical sentoid" is thought to consist of a subject-NP and a verb.

It is clear that such a principle alone will not explain our acquisition data across languages. In Japanese, children significantly prefer *backward* reduced coordinations over forward (SV+SV $>$ SV+SV). Thus, in terms of the proposed cognitive-perceptual principle, they *prefer* interruption of an initial sentence frame, over noninterruption.

Notably, however, in Japanese a "sentence frame" is structurally distinct from a sentence frame in English. A Japanese sentence-frame is achieved sentence *terminally* by virtue of the grammatical structure of Japanese, viz., its branching structure and its rigid verb-final constraint. Japanese children's strong preference for backward reduction patterns and a unique sentence-final verb may in fact reflect some version of a cognitive-perceptual principle by which children seek to determine a "sentence frame." Comparisons of Japanese and English data, however, show that the nature of the "sentence frame" which children seek is clearly grammatically determined. Our cross language data show then that such a cognitive-perceptual principle, if universal, must interact with principles of grammatical structure in constraining first language acquisition.

Notes

We thank Virginia Valian for essential assistance to this research. We are also indebted to the following in Japan: Professors Hikohito Hiraide and Emiko Inoue, Miss Tusune Hirano and Mrs. Matsuyo Funada, Mrs. Noriko Terakawa, Mrs. Fumiko Kaneda, and Mr. and Mrs. Hidetatsu Kaneda. In particular we thank Miss Hiroko Kitamoto and Mrs. Fumiyo Yamazaki for their assistance in interviewing the young children of our study. We also appreciate the assistance of Mrs. Ai Okubo, the comments of an anonymous NIMH review committee, and, at a late stage of this paper, the insightful advice of Professor Eleanor Jorden. This research was supported by NIMH small grant MH 29443-01; and by NIH Fellowship No. 5 F22 HD01226-02.

1. Conjunction reduction has been described as a "schema" rather than a "transformation" because of its structure-building power and because it must apply to variables (cf. Stockwell et al., 1973).

2. The critical arguments for a conjunction reduction schema include cases of coordination involving derived constituents, and cases of "right-node-raising" where it appears that nonconstituents may be coordinated.

3. Right-node-raising (RNR) is the grammatical rule which reduces terminal right-branched redundancy by Chomsky-adjoining a copy of the redundant element, thus creating a new node, and deleting all lower occurrences of the element (cf. Maling, 1972).

4. The elicited imitation task was developed by Slobin and Welsh (1973). In the task a child is asked to say a sentence "just the way" the adult says it. The assumptions of the task are that the child reconstructs the adult sentence in imitation, processing it through both comprehension and production systems and thus revealing properties of these systems in the child. It is known that both length and grammatical structure may cause variation in the child's performance.

5. Certain connectives in Japanese, which we did not study, are morphemes, e.g., *soshite* (and then).

6. As has been previously observed, it is probable that no natural language is exclusively either right or left branching (Chomsky, 1964a).

7. There were no significant differences between imitation data of males and females in either of the Japanese studies we report here (tested by ANOVA). These data are thus pooled.

8. It should be noted that the Japanese OV coordinations differ from the English VO coordinations not only in their permutation of order, but also in that the English VO sentences are imperatives; the Japanese OV sentences are not. The Japanese "OV" sentences are subjectless. (These may result from subject ellipsis; or Japanese sentence structure may

simply not require a subject (E. Jorden, pc).) The imperative was not used in Japanese because it requires additional inflection.

9. As in the English study, several constraints were placed on sentential and phrasal coordinations so that, for example, these would be as equivalent as possible. For example, constraints were imposed so that nominal particle marking and verb inflection would not differ between corresponding sentential and phrasal coordination forms. Thus, for example, since SV+$V must reduce to [S *wa* V+V], the sentential coordinations included the *wa* particle on each subject. Moreover, coordinations were designed to be semantically symmetric and nontemporal.

Sentences were presented in random order. Vocabulary adjustments were made if necessary for a child.

Several methodological differences were necessary in the Japanese study, however. (1) English sentences were 7 syllables in length. It was not possible to construct the set of simple coordinative sentences in 7 syllables in Japanese. (2) In addition, sentential and phrasal coordinations in the English study had been equated not only for syllable length but for word length where possible. (This was achieved by using determiners in NP's in phrasal coordinations for example.) This appeared not to be feasible in Japanese (which doesn't use corresponding NP determiners). Thus Japanese phrasal coordinations have consistently fewer words than sentential coordinations although the same number of syllables. (3) Also, Japanese uses several coordinating connectives which disambiguate the general coordination achieved by the connective "and" in English, and which are more narrowly constrained both syntactically and semantically than the English "and." Thus for example, while "and" was used in all English coordinative sentences, Japanese required distinct connectives for NP coordination as opposed to VP or sentential coordination. The *to* connective for NP coordination was chosen because this connective seemed to allow the same range of ambiguity as the English "and," one meaning corresponding to an expansion to sentential coordination, and one meaning corresponding to phrasal coordination (Kuno, 1973:112). The *shi* connective was chosen to represent sentential coordination (and verb phrase coordination) because it has been described as the Japanese connective closest to "pure" coordination (Kuno, 1973:203, 206 208). Accordingly, the order of clauses connected by *shi* is commutative; and we assume that the conjunction reduction schema (in either English or Japanese) must act on a pure (i.e., symmetrical, nonsubordinating) coordination by "and." (4) Developmentally, the markers used in these Japanese sentences (*to* and *shi* as well as *wa*, *ga* and *o* markers for topic, subject and object) have been noted to appear within or about the second year (Okubo, 1968; McNeill, 1966a; Sanches, 1968). In observational data, *to* has been noted to occur early (1; 11 mos., Okubo; 2; 2, Sanches) as well as *o* (2; 1, Sanches). Regarding *wa* and *ga*, McNeill noted *ga* to occur about 2; 4 and *wa* about 6 months later; Okubo however noted *wa* to occur at 1; 6 and *ga* at 1; 9; Sanches noted them both at 2; 3-2; 4. The verb inflection marker *shi* has been noted to occur later (2; 5 Okubo) and is the last to develop of the markers considered here.

10. English data were grouped in terms of developmental language level (as measured by MLU). Although speech samples were collected on all the Japanese children in these studies, it appears that the MLU measure cannot be simply applied to Japanese child language.

11. Young children were interviewed in their homes, where a natural speech sample was collected. Mothers presented the sentences for imitation. Older children were interviewed in nursery schools by an experimenter, using similar methodology. Experimenters, who were native speakers of Japanese, were the second author, or one of two Japanese persons trained by her. Data were transcribed by the trained experimenters in Japan, scored in the United States by the second author and verified by the first. In addition, as a measure of reliability, a random selection of 10 interviews across all age groups was independently transcribed and scored by an independent trained native Japanese speaker in the United States. Concurrence between first and second transcription and scoring was 95%. Attenuation was 20% of Ss

interviewed, due to the elimination of children who did not adapt to the imitation task or whose language development level was too low to allow imitation.

12. The sentential coordinations might be expected to be more difficult in Japanese because they involved the connective, *shi,* which is known to develop later than other connectives (cf. fn 10 above). However, the precedence of phrasal coordinations held for both noun coordinations (e.g., 2 and 4B on *Table 8.1*) which used the *to* connective and for verb coordination (e.g., 1 and 2B). There was no significant interaction of this difference with the conjunction structure effect). Verb coordinations such as 1 and 2 also use the morpheme, *shi.* Thus, the conjunction structure effect can't be due to the *shi* particle alone.

13. E. Jorden notes for example that use of the connective *shi* has the connotation of "building up to a climax." (personal communication).

14. We thank Maska Oguar for encouraging us to test these sentences.

15. The "mo" marker has been noted to occur early developmentally (1; 8 Okubo; 2; 1 Sanches).

16. The methodology for this study matched that of *Study Number One.* The reliability estimate on transcription and scoring for this second study was 98% (based on a random set of 10 interviews); the attrition rate was 22%.

17. It might be thought that this result—preference for backward reduction patterns—could be explained on the grounds of the corresponding regroupings which result from reduction. Forward reductions involve regrouping of two verbs, backward reductions involve regrouping of two nouns, in phrasal coordination form (see examples on *Table 8.1*). However, since this preference for backward reduction patterns held for both sentential and phrasal coordinations, this regrouping difference cannot fully explain the results. No regrouping is involved in sentential coordination.

There may be a more general factor involved here, however. Even within a sentential coordination, there may be some advantage to varying nouns rather than verbs. This deserves to be studied further. Correspondingly it might be thought that the preference for backward reduction patterns can be explained in terms of the connectives involved. Both sentential and phrasal forward reduction patterns involve the marker *shi* which develops later than the other connectives as noted above. However, backward reduction patterns in sentential coordination form also involve the connective *shi.* Thus this explanation alone is not sufficient either.

Chapter 9

The Acquisition of
Action Representations
in American
Sign Language

Marcia Steyaert
Ruth Ellenberger

In the past decade, we have witnessed an explosion in linguistic investigation of both child language acquisition and sign languages, such as American Sign Language (ASL), the manual communication system used by the majority of the deaf in North America. Although each area has been investigated for its own sake, it was also hoped that knowledge gained through these studies might contribute to the understanding of language and assist in the formulation and assessment of linguistic universals; and indeed, such hopes have begun to be realized. Numerous studies in child acquisition of a variety of languages (many are summarized in Slobin, 1971a and Brown, 1973) have revealed that, despite some individual variation among children learning the same language and the great dissimilarities among many of the languages studied, there are still some striking similarities in the way that children acquire their native tongues.

Recent investigations of American Sign Language have produced considerable evidence that this manual-visual language can and should be regarded as a language in its own right, not just as a simple extension of pantomime and "natural" gesture or as a manual representation of English. ASL has been shown to serve all the communicative functions usually attributed to spoken languages. It also possesses many of the structural characteristics usually proposed to define true human language, e.g., recombinability of lexical and sublexical units, productivity, and systematicity (Bellugi and Klima, 1975). In addition, as will be seen, it can be learned as a native language by children exposed to it (Bellugi and Klima, 1972; Boyes-Braem, 1973; McIntyre, 1974; Wilbur and Jones, 1974; Ellenberger and Steyaert, in press).

As natural language expressed and received through visual-manual, rather than aural-oral means, sign language has afforded the linguist the opportunity to determine the effect of mode of communication on language structure, and once variation due to modality has been isolated, to formulate linguistic universals that can characterize *all* human language, regardless of mode of communication. For example, because ASL shares so many characteristics with spoken languages, and can thus be regarded as a natural language, Friedman (1976b) was able to argue that some other putatively universal features of human language, such as arbitrariness, discreteness, and use of a vocal/auditory channel (Hockett, 1966), are *not* necessary properties of language but only of language in the oral/auditory modality.

Just as the study of adult sign language has provided valuable information about the nature of human language, the study of child acquisition of sign language as a native language can certainly provide useful input to the study of language acquisition in general, again by permitting linguists to study acquisition independent of any particular mode of communication. The few studies on sign language acquisition which have been conducted indicate that, although differences due to mode of communication do exist, speaking and signing children do exhibit many similarities in acquisition of semantic relations (Bellugi and Klima, 1972; Wilbur and Jones, 1974), negation (Lacy, 1972a), and questions (Lacy, 1972b).

The current study focuses on representation of action, in which ASL differs strikingly from spoken languages in that action descriptions in ASL are in certain respects less arbitrary than their counterparts in spoken languages. This difference raises an interesting question for the psycholinguist: What effect does a nonarbitrary relationship between symbol and referent have on language acquisition? In addition, because the visual modality presents the signer with a large variety of means of representing actions (ranging from simple pantomimic re-enactment to the highly systematized forms of a sign language), another question arises: In what order, if any, are these different means of action representation learned by a child exposed to them?

The current study traces the development of these means of representing action in the communication of a deaf child who was learning American Sign Language as a first language. As will be seen, the child's development of action representations shows a progression from use of very simple to highly sophisticated means, including adult-like use of spatial structuring.

Data were obtained from a series of monthly[1] videotapes of a deaf child of deaf parents who learned ASL as a first language and relied on it as his primary means of communication. Both the subject and his parents have profound hearing losses and use sign as the primary means of communication in the home. It should be noted that only children who have deaf parents learn ASL as a native language.

The language development of this child was followed between the ages of 43 and 71 months, as part of a longitudinal study of deaf children of deaf parents. The films recorded spontaneous conversation between the child and his mother (or occasionally, an investigator) in the child's home. All interpretations of signed sequences cited in this paper were verified by adult deaf signers who were quite familiar with children's signing styles.[2]

In this paper, English glosses will be used to represent signs. Although somewhat standardized, it is important to note that these English glosses often only approximate the meaning of a given sign. Many of the handshapes used in signs are the same as signs for numbers or symbols of the manual alphabet, so for the sake of convenience, handshapes in signs will be described in terms of the letter or number symbols they resemble, although this resemblance is often coincidental, i.e., unrelated to the meaning of the sign itself, or even to the spelling of its most common English gloss (see Appendix 1).

Background Information

Before discussing the child's acquisition of action representations, it will be helpful to describe some aspects of adult action representations. In ASL, signs representing physical actions are often stylized reproductions of the actions themselves, or of important aspects of them. For example, in one commonly used sign for *walk*, two "B" hands reproduce the alternating motion of the feet in walking. Such stylized reproductions of actions are unlike pantomime, however, in that they are standardized, respect the formational constraints of ASL,[3] and require less context to make their meaning "transparent." Both signs and pantomime are used by adult signers, and although there are some cases in which it is difficult to distinguish sign from pantomime, Bellugi and Klima (1975) note that "from the point of view of signers . . . there appears to be a perceived difference between the extremes of what is clearly signing and what is clearly pantomiming" (p. 179), with obvious pantomimes not being considered part of sign language itself.

In signed representation of an action, it is sometimes possible to incorporate into the sign itself reference to participants and places involved in the action. For example, if a signer wants to indicate that Harry gave George something and they are both present, he can direct the sign *give* from Harry toward George. If they are not physically present, he can point to a location,[4] signing or spelling George's name to indicate that this refers to him, and similarly specify another location as referring to Harry. (These reference locations are commonly placed in space at various angles to the signer's body.) The fact that Harry gave George something can then be represented by moving the sign *give* from Harry's location to George's location, thus incorporating the reference locations into the action sign itself.

Semantically, signs such as *give, tell,* and *send* involve reference to both source and goal; the sign normally moves from the reference location of the source to that of the goal. Certain other signs, such as *break, wash,* and *sew,* are normally performed at a single location representing the person, object, or body part acted upon. For example, the sign *break* done on the leg indicates a broken leg. In this paper, spatially modifiable signs like *give* will be referred to as source-goal signs; spatially modifiable signs like *break* will be called locational signs. When possible, both types of signs tend to be spatially modified; in fact, source-goal signs rarely occur in citation form,[5] i.e., the form used when a sign is made out of context. Thus, in locational and source-goal signs, one can modify the sign's placement in space so as to designate the participants of the action.

In some action signs, each hand visually symbolizes a participant in the action. In such signs, the handshapes used may indicate something about the nature of the participants in the action. For example, in the sign *crash*, in which two "A" hands meet abruptly, each "A" hand represents one of the colliding objects. The "A" handshape is used in the citation forms of many such signs and gives little information about the participants other than that they are solid objects. If the signer wants to impart more specific information about the participants, he can replace the "A" by another handshape, such as the "three," which represents a vehicle, usually an automobile. Use of "three" handshapes in the sign *crash*, then, would indicate that it was two cars that crashed. These symbolic handshapes, which are meaningless unless incorporated into action representations, have been called classifiers (Kegl and Wilbur, 1976). In addition to their use in well-established signs, as discussed above, classifiers may be used in representing motions for which there are no standardized action signs, e.g., a car moving along a winding road or going over a steep hill.

The signer can also alter the motion of a sign, such as *crash*, to incorporate more specific information about the motions of the participants. For instance, if there had been a collision between a moving and a stationary object, the signer could represent this collision by crashing a moving "A" hand into a motionless "A" hand. As demonstrated by the above examples, it is possible to modify a sign's handshapes and their relation to each other to further specify the participants in an action.

In ASL, then, there are two major classes of action sign modifications used to specify the action's participants: changes in the sign's internal structure, and changes in its placement in space. The modifications which any given sign will permit are limited by its formational and semantic properties; thus, ASL action representations are not simply pictures drawn in the air, but are highly systematic.[6]

Nevertheless, it is clear that depictions of actions in ASL are in some sense more concrete and pictorial and less arbitrary than their counterparts in spoken language, though usually not so iconic as to be comprehensible to someone unfamiliar with the conventions used. (See Hoemann, 1975 for discussion).[7] One might expect that such a representational system, because of its somewhat pictorial nature, could be quite easily grasped by a child, and would thus be acquired at an early age by a child learning ASL as a first language. Certainly, the visual mode itself might be expected to facilitate language acquisition, because in contrast to spoken language, the articulators are fully visible and can thus be more readily imitated. In addition, the nonarbitrary relationship between some signs and their referents could be expected to further assist the language learner.

Indeed, although further documentation is needed, it seems that the visual modality does facilitate the child's production of language. In the few sign language acquisition studies available, it was found that a signing child's first sign may emerge two to three months earlier than a speaking child's first word (Boyes-Braem, 1973; McIntire, 1974; Wilbur and Jones, 1974). McIntire (1974) also reported that at 10 months, an age at which a speaking child is likely to produce his first word, a signing child may have a vocabulary of 20 signs and be producing two-sign utterances. At age 18 months, when the speaking child typically produces his first two-word utterances, signing children are producing utterances containing three or more signs.

Despite the facilitating effects of the visual modality, however, the present study of a deaf child will illustrate that, as in the acquisition of complex syntactic structures in English (Chomsky, 1969) some aspects of the action representation system are apparently not acquired until rather late. In this case, they were acquired only near the end of the period studied.

Discussion

The subject's representation of action in the earliest tapes, beginning at age 43 months, was characterized by use of pantomime and citation-form signs. The pantomime used at this time frequently involved role-playing, in which the child acted like another person or animal. For example, when he pretended to be a dog, he pawed the air with his hands and walked around on his hands and knees. It was not always clear whether such pantomime was intended as communication or was simply play. Pantomimes representing single actions, such as chewing, were also used. This latter type of pantomime resembles that sometimes used by adults, either to represent single actions which have no formal signs, or for humorous purposes in story-telling. However, the child used such pantomimes in contexts in which an adult would probably use a formal sign.

Almost all of the action signs used in this early period, which include *play*, *eat*, and *brush teeth*, are among those which are not usually subject to the spatial modification described above. Source-goal signs such as *tell*, *give*, and *show*, which seldom occur in citation form, were not found at all in these tapes. Locational signs, such as *bite*, *break*, and *sew*, occurred only rarely in the early tapes. It may be that source-goal and locational signs were not used at this time because spatial modification can result in great variation in the appearance of a sign. Because of this variation, the child may not yet have succeeded in abstracting out the recurring features of such signs or mastered their complex reference system well enough to feel confident in using them.[8]

The next group of tapes, beginning at age 54 months and separated from the earlier ones by a period of several months, was characterized by less use of pantomime, especially that in which the child assumed the identity of an animal, for instance, and imitated its general behavior. The pantomime which did occur more closely resembled that of the adult, in that it could be segmented into a series of discrete actions.

Source-goal signs such as *give*, which did not occur in the earlier tapes, and locationally modifiable signs such as *break*, which then occurred only rarely, occurred frequently in this second group of tapes. While these signs did not yet incorporate arbitrarily established reference locations used to represent people or things not physically present, they were moved between or performed on people and objects in the signer's immediate surroundings. For example, the subject indicated that he wanted to give something to someone across the room by moving the sign *give* from himself toward that person.

Another tendency evident at this time was for the child to provide some sort of concrete backup or context for his action signs. One way in which this was done was the use, within a single utterance, of both a pantomime or gesture and a sign representing the same action. For example, the child performed the sign *bite* on his mother's knee, and then leaned over and pretended to bite it.

Another type of concrete backup noted was the frequent performance of action signs on appropriate places in pictures or on concrete objects. For example, in a story in which a dog was jumping through a series of hoops, a series of *jumps* was done between the hoops on the page. When talking about an automobile collision, the child made the sign *crash* with one hand hitting a toy car, instead of his other hand.

In several instances, the sign itself was concretized in some way. The sign *eat*, in which a flat "O" hand is brought up to the mouth, was actually inserted into a wide-open mouth, rather than just brought up near the lips. The sign *bite*, in which a closing hand represents the action of the mouth, was performed in front of the mouth instead of in its usual location on the arm in neutral space.

In the earlier group of tapes, the subject, although probably aware of the iconicity of the action signs he used, gave no evidence of such awareness. The appearance of these various types of concretization in these later tapes suggests that the subject was becoming aware of the relationship between an action and the formalized way it is represented in a sign and was playing with that relationship.

Moving the sign *give* from the general vicinity of one person to that of another, as described previously, utilizes aspects of the signer's environment in a way which is wholly acceptable and conventional in adult signing: moving a source-goal sign from source location to goal location. However, an adult signer would not insert the sign *eat* into his mouth, except perhaps for humorous purposes. The child was apparently learning to use the iconic relation between real world actions and signs, but the manner in which he did this was not always consistent with adult usage.

The most interesting phenomenon seen in this group of tapes was the development of the ability to provide additional information about the participants in an action by modification of the handshapes and/or motion of a sign, as described earlier. In the following examples, it is clear that the child was using each hand to represent one participant.

In one example, the subject represented one skier following another down a hill by placing his hands side by side in "B" shapes, so that the palms faced each other, and then moving them on wavy parallel paths down and away from himself, with one hand placed slightly behind the other. He periodically interrupted this skiing action to indicate the identity of the lead skier. This was done by placing a fingerspelled "K," the first initial of the skier's name, on top of the leading "B" hand. After each such interruption, the "K" hand again assumed the "B" shape, and the skiing action was resumed. At the beginning of this description, the child pointed to himself to indicate that he was one of the participants in the action; by designating the leading hand as the other skier, he made it clear that he followed his companion down the hill. Two "B" handshapes held facing each other are used in the adult sign *road*, probably representing the margins of the road. However, adults do not commonly use such "B" handshapes to represent two individuals following separate paths, as the child did in the above example.

Another example involved modification of the sign *ski*, normally made with the hands held parallel in the "X" configuration and moving forward. The episode involved the subject snowplowing to keep from colliding with a tree. His efforts failed and he broke his skis against the tree. At one point in this story, the two "X's" of the sign converged on each other from the sides, indicating the snowplowing position of his skis. The two "X's" then collided, and the sign *break* was made to indicate that the skis broke. The child had analyzed the sign *ski* into its two components, one representing each foot, and had used this knowledge in producing an acceptable modification of the sign.

The other examples of this phenomenon also involved either skiing or skating collisions. In one case, the subject waved a "K," indicating the name of the same skiing companion, and then signed *tree* with the other hand while converting the "K" into the usual "A" handshape of the sign *crash*. This "A" hand was then crashed into the tree. By substituting the sign *tree* for one "A" handshape of *crash*, he indicated that the object his friend hit was a tree. He thus identified both participants in the action and the roles they played in its execution.

In a final example, he identified the participants in an action by using two different, significant hand configurations throughout the execution of the sign. One hand was held in the "X" configuration of the sign *ski* to indicate a skier, while the other formed the sign for tree. The "X" collided with the tree and hooked on the thumb, indicating that the skier had become entangled in the tree's branches. By this type of modification, the child again was able to characterize the participants in the action and the roles they played.

In the earlier tapes, the subject generally either used pantomime to depict action sequences or used single or unmodified signs. In these later tapes, he was able to use the signs more flexibly and sometimes simultaneously to depict complex action sequences. He seems to have realized that in many action signs the hands symbolize two separate objects and was able to use this knowledge to produce meaningful modifications of his signs. These modifications reveal that the child had developed the ability to analyze signs into their meaningful components and to combine them in ways that more clearly represent the nature of an action and its participants, even though his modifications were not always those normally used by adults.

The ability to structure the space in which action signs move, as described at the beginning of this paper, was the most important new development evident in the subject's narratives in the next and final group of tapes, which begin at age 61 months. In some instances, the subject used what we will call "shape descriptors" to set up a spatial framework for his action signs. Shape descriptors are commonly used following nouns to indicate the shape and/or size of an object; for example, two "F's" starting together and moved outward to the sides represent a long, slender, solid object. The general forms of these shape descriptors are standardized, although some modifications are possible to indicate details of size and shape. Shape descriptors can also be placed in space to designate reference locations for the objects they describe.

In one case, the child was describing a barrier over which his horse jumped. He first signed *rock* (an "X" hand under the chin) followed by a shape descriptor in the form of two "C" hands placed off to one side, thereby establishing a location for the rock. He repeated the sign *rock* and placed a similar descriptor off to the other side to indicate a second rock. Then he signed *wood*, followed by a shape descriptor in the form of two "C" hands starting together and moving off to the sides where the rocks were located. This represented a thick log placed across the rocks. He then signed *horse*, placed one arm in roughly the position established for the log, and moved the sign *jump* over the log. The child thus clearly indicated through his structuring of space that the horse jumped over a barrier formed by a log laid over two rocks.[9] This spatial structuring is common in adult language when used as a framework for action signs or when describing the spatial relationships of several objects, such as the furniture in a living room (Huttenlocher, 1975).

Another characteristic of this final set of tapes was the frequent and creative use of classifiers. As mentioned earlier, classifiers are standardized handshapes which may be used in some action signs to represent various entities such as cars, planes, and people. In contrast to the substitutions used in the previous stage (e.g., *tree, ski*), they are usually meaningless unless they occur in action representations. The child first learned to modify existing action signs; he then learned to create his own action signs in a conventionalized manner through the use of classifiers.

For example, the subject often used the standard "three" handshape to represent a car in such actions as one car running over another, a car getting stuck, and cars being piled in a junkyard. In one instance, he described a car getting stuck and the driver continuing his journey on foot by moving his hand along a single path while changing the handshape from that of the car classifier to that of the person classifier (a "V" handshape). By such use of these two classifiers, one beginning at the point where the other left off, the child was able to indicate the continuity of the action. Such classifiers provide one way for the child to represent simultaneously the nature of both the moving entity and the action itself.

With the acquisition of spatial structuring and use of classifiers in this final group of tapes, the child had learned the more complex aspects of action representation in ASL, and although his action representations may not yet have been as complex and organized as those of the adult, he had now acquired the basic syntactic means necessary for action representations in his language.

Conclusion

Several clear trends were observed in the child's developing system of action representations. The earliest action signs used seemed to be the citation forms of signs which are not normally spatially modifiable. In the second group of tapes, there was frequent use of spatially modifiable (source-goal or locational) signs. These signs were modified to indicate people or objects which were physically present but did not yet incorporate arbitrarily established reference locations. Also at the time, action signs were often accompanied by some type of concretization. These concretizations suggest that the child had realized that there can be a relationship between a real action and the formalized way it is represented in a sign, and was playing with this relationship. He had evidently also recognized that in some action signs, each hand symbolizes one participant in the action, and was able to modify his signs accordingly, altering the shape or motion of a hand to provide additional information about the participant it represents. However, he did not yet respect all the adult-language conventions for doing this. It was only later that the child acquired the ability to significantly modify action signs by the structuring of space and to create new signs through the use of classifiers.

While one might expect spatial modifications to appear earlier because of their pictorial nature, they are apparently relatively late acquisitions, perhaps because such representations may require a fairly advanced mastery of cognitive skills involving spatial relationships. Also, setting up a spatial framework as a background for the subsequent representation of an action requires a type of advance planning which may be beyond the capabilities of a younger child.

Thus, the child's acquisition of action representations seemed to manifest a clear developmental progression from early use of citation forms of signs not usually subject to spatial modification to acquisition of adult-like spatial structuring.

The existence of a systematic developmental progression should not be surprising to anyone familiar with studies of spoken language acquisition. Children learning spoken languages do not acquire them all at once, nor does the child learning ASL immediately master the entire system. However, the progression observed in this study seems to involve factors, such as iconicity, which are not directly relevant to spoken language acquisition.

For instance, the ability to break a whole into its parts and the learning of the conventions for producing new combinations are fundamental to the acquisition of both spoken and sign languages. However, in spoken languages the parts relate to their real-world referents and to each other in quite arbitrary ways. In ASL action representations, however, these relationships are often not completely arbitrary. For example, the child's ability to produce the meaningful modifications of the sign *ski* which were cited above depends on recognition of the iconic relationship between the sign and its referent. This has no clear counterpart in spoken-language acquisition.

In spoken and in sign languages, a child's ability to describe spatial relationships is limited by his cognitive development. However, ASL differs from spoken language in that a signed description of characteristics of a scene actually involves a formalized reproduction of aspects of that scene. Again, this has no direct analog in spoken language acquisition.

The differences between an arbitrary and an iconic action-description system make certain other comparisons with spoken language acquisition somewhat problematic. As one example, the modifications of action signs cited here might be regarded as a type of inflectional system, with a locational sign, for instance, being regarded as inflected for one of its arguments. Children acquiring inflected languages have been observed to overuse a single inflected form, e.g., using a third-person inflected verb for first, second, and third person (Rūke-Dravina, 1973:263). The overuse of one form is conceivable in a spoken language, in which the inflections are arbitrary. However, in most cases it is difficult to imagine a signing child overusing a particular inflected form—for instance, signing *wash* on his face to indicate washing his feet—given the iconic nature of this inflection.[10]

This is not to say that the acquisition of signed and spoken languages cannot be compared at all. First, although this study is concerned with a relatively nonarbitrary part of the language, other aspects of ASL are as arbitrary as spoken languages. Second, researchers of language acquisition in either modality must concern themselves with such basic and unresolved issues as the ability to analyze the linguistic signal into its components, and the relation between cognition and language. It is probably at this very fundamental level that the acquisition of action representation in signed and spoken language can most profitably be compared.

One promising area for future research growing out of this study would be inquiry into the relationships among motor development, cognitive development, and linguistic expressions representing actions in spoken languages and American Sign Language. Another possible area for future research would be the influence on child sign language of modifications made by parents in their signing to children; for example, the previously-noted tendency to use concrete backups for action signs may simply result from imitations of similar parent-to-child signing. At present, no research on the topic of linguistic input in sign language acquisition has been reported. Because language development can differ considerably between children, it would also be interesting to compare this child's development with that of other children learning American Sign Language as a first language, to determine whether trends similar to those found for this child characterize their language acquisition as well.

Finally, it seems that results of these studies could profitably be compared with results from studies of hearing children, and that such comparisons would be valuable in the formulation of *true* universals of child language acquisition.

Notes

The research reported herein was performed pursuant to a grant from the Bureau of Education for the Handicapped, U.S. Office of Education, Department of Health, Education, and Welfare to the Center of Research, Development and Demonstration in Education of Handicapped Children, Department of Psychoeducational Studies, University of Minnesota. (Grant No. OE-09-332189-4533(032) and 300-76-0036)

1. Intervals between filming sessions were sometimes longer than a month, due to vacations and illnesses.

2. We wish to thank Vicki Anderson, Shirley Egbert, and Carol Finke for their assistance as translators and informants in this study.

3. For discussion of some of these phonological constraints, see Battison, Markowicz, and Woodward (1975). Some discussion of distinctions between sign and pantomime is given in Newkirk (1975).

4. Pointing is not the only means for establishing reference locations. Other commonly-used conventions for this purpose include direction of gaze and body shifts. See Friedman (1975, 1976a) and Baker (1976).

5. The citation form of a sign is its "dictionary" form, the form used when it is made out of context.

6. Although the principles governing this system are not yet fully understood, research in this area is currently in progress (Friedman, 1976a), and adult signers are quite consistent in their grammaticality judgments on this matter.

7. It should be noted that not all aspects of ASL are as iconic as action representations; many other aspects of ASL are nonpictorial and arbitrary.

8. It is possible that the use of small toys as stimuli in these films may have encouraged physical manipulation at the expense of linguistic output. The unfamiliarity of the filming situation may also have adversely influenced the language on these early films.

9. At this stage, English-like word order (without use of spatial structuring) was also used as a means of signed descriptions of actions. English word order is not typical of the ASL to which this child was exposed at home. The use of such order probably resulted from the child's school program, in which signs in English word order were used as the primary means of communication.

10. Other investigators (Fischer, 1973; Bellugi and Klima, 1972) have observed morphological overregularizations in children's signing comparable to those often noted in spoken language acquisition. The data for this study contained a number of possible examples, but all were sufficiently ambiguous to preclude any useful comparisons.

APPENDIX 1

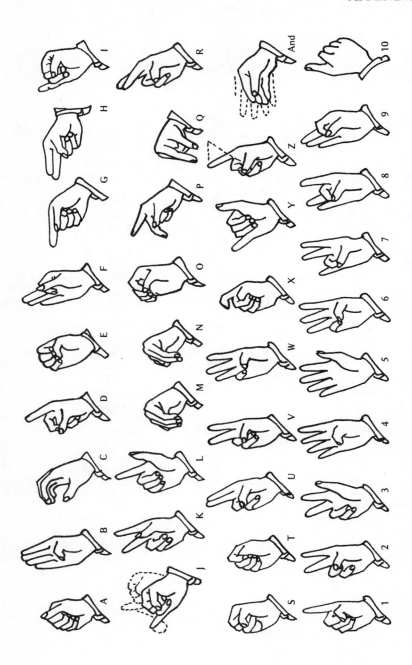

Part
2

Second
Language
Acquisition

Chapter 10

The Comparative
Study of
First and Second
Language Acquisition

Bernard Spolsky

Many linguists, like other scholars, prefer their field not to be corrupted by any suggestion of relevance to practical matters; for them, linguistics should remain a pure science, its study motivated only by the desire to increase human knowledge. There are others, however, who claim that it can offer a panacea for many of the problems they hear of, and who therefore rush to offer their services to handle any difficulties in language planning or teaching. Each of these positions is, I believe, equally wrong, for while it is true that linguistics can often develop knowledge of use to the solution of practical problems, especially in the area of education, the relation between the theoretical knowledge and its practical implication is seldom direct.

Some part of the difficulty might well have derived from the term applied linguistics with its implication that linguistics is to be applied to something. In too many cases, theoretical linguists tended to assume that their linguistic theory should be used to solve directly the problems of some practical area like foreign language teaching or the teaching of reading. Generally, they have turned out to see the problem so narrowly that their solution has done as much harm as good. In the field of language teaching, for instance, the structural linguists worked effectively to replace a system based on one limited view of language (the translation method) by an equally rigid and psycholinguistically invalid approach (the audiolingual method). When this system too turned out to be inadequate, there were many who thought that all that was needed was to come up with a new one based on the latest theory of language. Much more productive than such an approach is to start with a specific problem and then look to linguistics and other relevant disciplines for their contribution to its solution. Language teaching, for example, takes place in a school and is as much influenced by sociological, economic, political, and psychological factors as it is by linguistic ones.

Within this context, I choose to approach the problem today from the point of view of a field that I prefer to call educational linguistics. The scope of educational linguistics is the intersection of linguistics and related language sciences with formal and informal education. It is a field that needs to draw on the various branches of linguistics and to derive from them implications for educational practice. (Spolsky, in press.)

In this context, it is reasonable to start by asking what is the relevant educational problem that knowledge about language acquisition might be expected to help solve. The central aim of any language education is to increase the student's ability to communicate verbally, both productively and receptively. There are three major aspects to such modification: the enrichment of the child's original variety, the addition of another variety, or the suppression of a variety. Other classifications are made: for example, between mother-tongue teaching, second language teaching, and foreign language teaching. Each of these may be further defined and refined according to the variety, the function for which it is intended, and the level of competence aimed at. Various areas of linguistics have their contribution to make to the description of the task and its possible accomplishment. Linguistic theory will necessarily dominate the whole process making clear exactly what is meant by language in the whole process. Sociology of language will be of critical importance in recognizing the functional differentiation of the varieties concerned and the social pressures that account for the patterns of language use in the child's immediate environment and in the society for which he or she is being educated. And psycholinguistics will be expected to cast light on the process of the development of linguistic and communicative competence itself.

From the field of psycholinguistics in general and from the studies of language acquisition in particular, the educational linguist asks three related questions: (1) What is the normal course of the development of language in an individual? (2) Given the normal range of individual variability in the development of communicative competence, what factors account for this variation? (3) Which of these factors are susceptible to control by an educational system? The answers to these questions are clearly basic to language education, for they both set its limits and suggest the kind of intervention that might permit helping each individual child reach these limits.

The Normal Course of Language Development

The general lines of a child's development of language are reasonably well established. During the first few months of his life, the human infant produces a wide range of sounds. Some of these sounds are identified by mothers and by some investigators as being differentiated and able to express such notions as hunger or discomfort. Also during this stage, the infant becomes able to react differently to different voices. In the period from six to ten months, the child's vocalizations become phonetically more complex using a wide range of vowels and consonants that provides opportunity for some imitative practice. Between eight to ten months, evidence is seen that the child can understand various linguistic signals: gestures, words, phrases, and other instructions. From about that age, they gradually develop ability to differentiate sounds. By about ten to twelve months, the child starts to understand commands.

The first "word" usually occurs about the twelfth month. For about the next six months, there is a low addition of vocabulary, each one word or unit functioning like a full sentence and having, in different situations or with different accompanying gestures, different meanings. In the second half of the second year, there is a rapid increase of vocabulary and the emergence of patterned speech. The nature of the first pattern has been analyzed by a number of observers as consisting of two word-classes and the possibility of combining them into two-word sentences. The two-word sentence stage raises the basic questions about the nature of child language acquisition, with the nativists arguing that it presents evidence of the innate nature of linguistic rules and the learning theorists attempting to suggest mechanisms by which it could be learned; the weight of argument appears to favor the former. By the end of the third year, evidence suggesting a much more complex grammar has emerged, allowing for three-word sentences with considerable structural complexity. In the next two years, there is rapid progress in the development of syntax; by the age of five, the child's syntax is reasonably close to adult, and he or she can usually communicate with a stranger. Even at this stage, there still remain considerable differences between the child's grammar and adult grammar. Studies of comprehension have shown that there is a gradual learning of more complex structures for the next five years at least. The acquisition of vocabulary continues for a long time after that. Evidence also suggests that semantic development is extremely slow; some lexical generalizations only start developing about the age of eight.

Only recently has there been much research into the development of more complex communicative competences. There is good evidence on the development of more than one language in an individual. The classic study of child language is still Leopold's study of his own bilingual daughter. He summarizes the process as follows:

> In the initial stage the bilingual presentation merely meant a larger vocabulary to choose from. The child chose either the German or the English item at her own discretion, leaning at first more on German, later more and more decidedly on English, and welded one language instrument out of the two presentations. . . . The split into two contrasting languages, distinguished by the person addressed, first showed rudimentarily and vascillatingly towards the end of the second year. Consciousness of dealing with two languages began early in the third year. The active separation of the two languages did not start in earnest until the very end of the third year. Increasingly, from then on, the learning of English and German proceeded separately.   (Leopold, 1953)

Other studies of childhood bilingualism make clear that a child can acquire more than one language at a time; there is a period of confusion or delay, but in normal cases, each language ultimately develops separately, its strength determined by various sociolinguistic factors influencing the environment in which the languages are acquired and the attitudes developed to them. Even when children learn only one language, it is clear that they also learn the stylistic requirements of different situations. While the bulk of the acquisition of stylistic variation probably occurs after the age of five, children by then will probably have developed a number of controlled variations depending on the person they are speaking to. For instance, they will often have learned to use a form of baby talk when speaking to dolls and small animals, and have developed different styles for speaking to strangers.

With the age of starting formal education, a whole new set of demands is added. Teachers and peers each require new and conflicting varieties; the introduction of the written language adds a new channel and usually also new linguistic rules; there is a rapid increase in the demand for verbalization of concepts; and there is a new set of sociolinguistic rules, like one telling you to keep quiet except when the teacher asks you to speak.

In general outline, this is the course of normal development; within this range, the child builds its own communicative competence, making use of the combined working of its innate language acquisition ability and its exposure to meaningful language.

The Question of Variation

There is no question but that there is considerable variation in the communicative skills developed by individuals. Some people have a much wider range of skills: they can control several languages and several varieties of language. And there is a great variability in the level of skill reached by individuals: few indeed have the powers of expression of a Shakespeare; and as literature teaches while it tests, not everyone is capable of reading and appreciating literature. The nature of this variability, the factors that account for it, and the way it might be altered, are the principal concerns of educational linguistics. Before we look at this in more detail, we might ask about the potential implications of various answers.

If, as the most extreme nativist position holds, all aspects of language acquisition depend on innate abilities and properties, there would appear to be no point in language education. To the extent that language acquisition is unaffected by the external environment, or that it is purely genetically based, there is little point in talking about other factors, or in looking for ways of controlling or approving any individual student's skills. A modified nativist position is possible: it might be argued that linguistic competence (in the Chomskyan sense) is what is purely innate, while linguistic performance and communicative competence are dependent both on linguistic competence and on other factors, including environmental ones. If this is so, then the study of linguistic competence is important to educational linguistics in the way that it delimits the area in which intervention is irrelevant. At the same time, the educational linguist is interested in the kind of factors that govern the development of varied linguistic performance and communicative competence.

Another simple view would be a strictly environmental one. If all aspects of language are learned, whether the learning is as simple as in Skinner's model or as complex as proposed by Staats (1971), then there are presumably no limits to be set on the potential of language educators; once the mechanisms of learning can be understood, any kind of modification is possible.

Much more complexity is implied by an approach that admits any degree of mixture of innate development (say, development that is tied to maturity and timing) and learning, for it would be necessary to isolate the effect of each of these. One such approach is held by those who seem to believe that first languages are "acquired" in some simple way, but that second languages need to be learned in quite different ways. In what follows, I shall assume a multifactor explanation though, given the present vagueness in definition of communicative competence and the crudeness in available measure of an individual proficiency, there would seem to be slight hope of any precise allocation of degree of relevance to each of the identified factors.

As has been mentioned earlier, contemporary psycholinguists have tended to stress the nativist position, finding in the acquisition of language clear evidence of an innate predisposition. One implication of their position is a biological and genetic explanation of variability in the level of competence achieved by an individual. Behavioral psychologists on the other hand stress the role of environment, building their models of language learning around notions of reinforcement, conditioning, and generalization that they derive from general learning theory. Such an approach implies the ease of changing language behavior by training. A third position, related in its emphasis on environment to the second, is that of the sociolinguists, whose basic interest in socially correlated language variation leads them to accept easily the existence of a causal relationship between social factors and the existence of a causal relationship between social factors and linguistic development.

While the contrast in the underlying philosophy of each of these approaches is clear, it is possible, as Osser (1970) suggests, to conceive of reconciliation. Such a reconciliation might involve holding that every child has equal inherited propensity for the development of linguistic competence, but that differing environmental conditions lead to eventual differentiation in language performance. There is good reason to favor Osser's suggestion that biological factors play a greater role in the development of prelinguistic vocalization and in the acquisition of basic language structure, while social and environmental factors are more important in the acquisition of more elaborated styles and in the learning of socially appropriate varieties. Another way to characterize the general division between the two might be to suggest that innate factors will be more concerned with the form in which linguistic knowledge is stored (the kinds of rules and features that form an individual's grammar) while social factors and environment will control the amount and kind of linguistic knowledge and the ability to use it.

Let us start in any case with the factors that are internal to the learner and with those that might be called biological. Even if we accept that the propensity for language is inherited, and if we define propensity for language so as to include language universals, we can still allow room for biological genetic variation in individual cases. First, there are the clear cases of genetic variation: cases of congenital defects that affect the development of language and speech. For example, when the brain does not develop fully, the resulting mental retardation is accompanied by impairment of various aspects of language function.

A strong proponent for the importance of genetic factors in language learning (and in other learning) is Arthur Jensen (1969), who has argued that there are two levels of learning. The first is "associative" learning, while the second level, a higher level, is required for "cognitive or conceptual" learning. These two levels of learning, he says, depend on different neural structures that are genetically provided. One of the many difficulties with this position, with its clear racial overtones, is that what Jensen considers "cognitive or perceptual learning" appears to be basic to any language acquisition, whether of a standard or nonstandard variety. For it to be true, there would need to be evidence of difference in structure between the various social varieties; and no such evidence has been produced.

Moving from genetic to general physiological factors, there are clearly a number of anatomical and physiological features that are necessary to the full development of normal human language. Pathological conditions, whether genetic or traumatic, will necessarily interfere with its acquisition. Luria's work (1973) in neurolinguistics has made clear the main lines of correlation between the physiology of the brain and language abilities. Another striking piece of evidence for physiological correlation is Lenneberg's presentation (1967) of the close parallels between the development of language and the development of other motor skills. Connected to the notion of the relation between physiological maturation and language acquisition is Piaget's theory of successive cognitive stages. If we assume a built-in biological clock, then we cannot expect external influences to have a major effect. Thus, an extreme nativist position might rule out the influence of environment and the value of intervention. In gross terms, there is some truth in this: whatever you do, you can't teach a baby to talk before it's ready; and while you can produce certain behaviors before the competence for them has appeared, this behavior is no more counterevidence than is a parrot's "speech" evidence that birds can learn human language. But, in finer detail, it also seems clear that the biological state is a matter of potential rather than actual ability: it means that the organism is ready to acquire the next stage of competence, provided only that it is exposed to appropriate environmental stimulus.

This analysis fits in with the notion that a process of hypothesis testing underlies much of language acquisition. The child is ready with a set of hypotheses about the nature of language, and is ready to test the accuracy of these hypotheses and to modify them. But this can be done only when he or she is exposed to relevant examples. The critical question is how much and what kind of exposure is necessary. For if a great deal of exposure is needed, then one could easily explain individual differences as resulting from the amount of exposure: thus, children in homes where there is little talking would be expected to acquire language more slowly or less completely. Convincing evidence on this position has not yet been presented.

Without going further into basic causes, I should like now to look at a number of other learner (and so internal) factors that are likely to influence language acquisition. These are ability, motivation, learning strategy, and personality. None of them are prime factors. Ability is at least in part genetic, motivation depends on attitude, and learning strategies are themselves learned. But using each as a separate heading permits us to find out more about the business of acquiring language. By ability, I refer here both to general intelligence and to specific language aptitude. A first distinction might usefully be made between the normal, informal acquisition of a language (whether a first or a second or a subsequent one) and the formal learning of a standard variety or second or foreign language in school. Take the formal learning first. Intelligence, as Jakobovits (1970) points out, is usually considered the ability to learn: this being so, it is no wonder that I.Q. correlates clearly with school foreign language learning, explaining about fifteen to twenty percent of the variance. Even more significant in a school situation is the general factor that Jakobovits labels foreign language aptitude and that he believes accounts for about one-third of the total variance. According to John Carroll's (1965) analysis, foreign language aptitude includes at least four distinct abilities: (1) the ability to discriminate sounds and to store auditory data over something longer than a few seconds; (2) the ability to recognize (but not necessarily label) the grammatical functions of words and sentences; (3) the ability to memorize material, whether meaningful or meaning-less; (4) the ability to infer linguistic patterns from new linguistic contexts.

A little reflection suggests that these abilities, so basic to formal foreign language teaching, also have their part in normal first language acquisition. A child must not just discriminate between the various auditory data, but store them; he must be able to recognize the functions of words in sentences; he must be able to memorize; and he must be able to infer linguistic rules without supervision. In what way, then, does aptitude for foreign language learning differ from aptitude for acquiring a first language? Or, put another way, why should a test measuring the factors that Carroll proposed be a better predictor of foreign language learning than a simple measure of first language proficiency? For it is reasonable to assume that these factors might be just as well measured by their effect on the development of first language proficiency as by themselves. The answer, I believe, is that the test, itself a formal school activity, measures not just the abilities, but also the willingness or ability to use them in a foreign language classroom, another formal school activity. The factors are underlying ones, but measuring them involves measuring this additional factor too.

Motivation is another general term that includes in it a number of deeper factors. In foreign language learning, it can be translated as perseverance, and is then quantifiable as the amount of time a student is prepared to spend learning.

Jakobovits presents five factors contributing to perseverance: (1) need achievement, (2) attitude toward the teacher, (3) interest in second language study, (4) attitude toward foreign culture, (5) ethnocentrism and anomie. For this last factor, the basic statement is that of Lambert and others (1962):

> *This theory, in brief, states that an individual successfully acquiring a second language gradually adopts various features of behavior which characterize another linguistic and, as is often the case, another cultural group. The learner's ethnocentric disposition and his attitude towards the other group are believed to determine his success in learning a new language.*

In a number of basic studies, Wallace Lambert and his colleagues have drawn attention to the major importance of what they call integrative motivation to the learning of foreign languages. They suggested that there are two classes of motivation for language learning, instrumental and integrative, and that the presence of the latter is necessary to successful mastery of the higher levels of proficiency.

While the cluster of attitudinal and motivational factors is more relevant to formal school language learning than to the informal acquisition of a first or second language, there are hints for this latter situation, especially in the attitudinal factor. Need achievement is related to performance in a school subject, as are the next three factors: attitude toward teacher, interest in second language study, and attitude toward foreign cultures. With slight modifications, these same factors might be expected to relate to success in any school subject. But the fifth is specific to language study: one learns the language better if one wants to use it for group membership than if one needs it for any other purpose.

There is a connection between integrative motivation and the need to communicate. The more one wants to be part of a group, the greater the need to learn its language. John Macnamara (1971) refers to this when he discusses the failure of classroom language teaching as compared to street language learning. In the street, he says, "the reward for success and the punishment for failure is enormous. No civilized teacher can compete. But more to the point, the teacher seldom has anything to say to his pupils so important that they will eagerly guess his meaning" (p. 475). As the immigrant child on the street or in the classroom is forced by his need to communicate to acquire the new language, even more the infant is presumably eager to make sense out of the world around him and gain, through language, better control over what is done to him and more productive membership in the social group in which he is growing up. Motivation, then, is a complex set of factors, internal to the learner but showing close ties with his environment, that has considerable influence on the acquisition of communicative competence; as it varies in strength and kind, so individual learners are likely to vary in the proficiency that they attain.

Other Factors

It is somewhat artificial to distinguish between the learner factors discussed so far and the inherent or environmental causes which lie behind them. What we are dealing with here are not distinct categories, but a continuum that might be ordered according to the possibility of ease of external manipulation. We have talked so far about factors that are either innate or so basic as to make intervention difficult. We go on next to look at those aspects of the environment that are external to the learner but not usually under the control of the school and finally at the instructional variables that the school is assumed to be able to control.

There are a set of factors which, although outside the normal sphere of formal education, are in fact susceptible to control. Among the child's experiences, the earliest likely to have influence on language acquisition, as in other aspects of physical and cognitive development, is prenatal and early nutrition. Studies suggest that fetal malnutrition affects not just birth weight itself but that a significantly large proportion of low birth weight children turn out to be mentally subnormal. There is indeed evidence to suggest that malnutrition impairs the development of complex intellectual skills and adaptive capacities.

The next significant period of interaction is in the home during early childhood. To what extent does variation in the home experience affect language development? The first kind of result is obvious: children acquire the language or languages and variety or varieties to which they are exposed. Relevant research has been summarized by John and Moskovitz (1970). During the prelinguistic stage, the rate of a child's vocalization can be increased experimentally. Studies that show that more talk is directed to children in normal homes than in institutions perhaps help account for the poor language development of children in institutions. It has also been shown that from the age of eighteen months on, children in U.S. middle-class homes produce more sounds than lower income children. Social class and ethnic differences in performance on vocabulary tests show up from about the age of three. But these results might reflect the kinds of tests used than motivational variables in the test situation. Studies of syntactic development have yielded contradictory results, often hampered by failure to recognize the different varieties of language being acquired. A number of studies do, however, ascribe an important role to parent-child dialogue in language development. Macnamara's theory of language learning argues for the importance of the parental role. He suggests that a child works out the structure of a language by first determining meaning, then finding the relation between meaning and expression. This depends, he says, on the provision of many clues: a mother talks to the child usually about things that are present to his senses, she uses exaggerated intonational patterns, and she accompanies her speech with gestures and facial expressions. If these processes are so important, it is clear why there is such a potential for variation. Various cultural and ethnic groups have different attitudes to verbal expression. The traditional Jewish emphasis on verbalization would thus help explain why the economic poverty of the east European ghetto was accompanied by linguistic richness, rather than the impoverished speech that so many scholars assume goes with poverty. Beyond these group differences, great degrees of individual variation could also be expected to result from the kind of language use that takes place in the home and from the attitude to verbalization.

It will be clear that these matters bring us to the general question of the relation of social class to language development. In recent years, there have developed two conflicting views which characterize the position taken by most U.S. scholars. The first, which may be called the language deficit theory, is held by a number who have worked on studies of poverty; it assumes the existence of shortcomings in the language capabilities of poverty children. A contrary argument, often called the language difference position, has been taken by linguists; they say one is dealing not with deficit but with a different variety of language. The seeming deficit is a result of testing the children for their use of a variety of language that they do not in fact use.

The way these two positions have arisen is clear. As long as one assumes (and such assumptions are common among American educators) that there is only one variety of English, the standard language, and as long as one measures the performance of lower class or minority children in this variety, one finds deficits. It is easy to conclude then that the children have limited vocabularies or control a limited number of grammatical structures. There is, of course, a deficit if the child is compared to a speaker of standard English. To this extent, the deficit theory is an accurate description of the minority child's language situation. But the supporters of the theory go further: they assume either that the minority child controls no variety of language in which he is not deficient, or that the variety he controls is itself inferior in some intrinsic way. These two extensions are denied by linguists. Their work has generally made it possible to observe and study the complexity and richness of the nonstandard varieties that these children often control, and have further found no real support for the notion that one language or variety is intrinsically inferior to another.

With the idea of inferior languages is often confused the notion of distinct codes or styles presented by the British sociologist Basil Bernstein. Bernstein points out the error in equating his notion of a restricted code with the notion of linguistic deprivation. His interest is not in differences of competence but in differences in use:

> It is not that working-class children do not have in their lexical repertoire the vocabulary used by middle class children. Nor is it the case that the children differ in their tacit understanding of the linguistic rule system. Rather what we have here are differences in the use of language arising out of a specific context. One child makes explicit the meaning which he is realizing through language for the person to whom he is telling the story, whereas the second child does not do this to the same extent.   Bernstein, 1970:26

Bernstein believes that these different forms of communicative style have a social origin, depending on the strength of social collective bonds. These codes, which are matters of performance and not competence, establish a cultural control over the speaker's options. The code, he believes, has an effect on educability, for children who are "limited to a restricted code primarily because of the subculture and role system of the family, community, and work" are likely to rely on extra-verbal means of expression, to perform poorly on verbal I.Q. tests, to have difficulties with abstraction, and in general to gain little benefit from school. Formal education requires of these children that they change their code and the way they relate to their community. It handicaps them further, for as Bernstein says, "at the same time we offer these children grossly inadequate schools with less able teachers."

Factors Under School Control

Whatever degree of variation in individual communicative competence might be inherited, a great deal of the variation is likely to be accounted for by environmental factors which are, as we have just seen, outside the normal control of the school. To this extent, it can reasonably be suggested that language education is not just a matter for the educational system, but is very deeply and clearly influenced by a variety of social, political, cultural, and economic factors.

What then can a school do to modify the communicative competence of its pupils? What kinds of changes can it produce? It can try to enrich a variety, to teach a new medium or channel, or to teach a new style. In carrying out these various changes, it can basically manipulate two factors: the pupil's motivation and his exposure to a variety. Take motivation first. If we use Lambert's distinction between instrumental and integrative motivation for foreign language acquisition, it becomes clear that the school can provide various kinds of motivation leading its pupils to change their linguistic repertoires. The strongest of these is the need to communicate: by forcing the pupil to modify his variety of language, or to acquire a new one, before he will be understood or will understand what is going on around him, the school seems to be providing the strongest possible motivation for the change. But it is actually more complex than this. Consider the kind of policy adopted by many schools which punish children for speaking languages other than the school language. There are equally strong but less negative means of motivating: the key point is to provide a situation (a time or a context) in which the target variety is useful for communication. One of the most effective of such ways is to use it for instruction; that is, rather than trying to teach the variety, to use it to teach in. Central here is the naturalness of the requirement: the child can accept as reasonable that there are people, places, and times which demand a certain variety, and he will learn that variety as long as he wishes to communicate with those people, in those places and at those times. The relevant strength of the different kinds of motivation is likely to change with changes in the prestige of a language. In Quebec, Parisian or continental French remains the status language, while French-Canadian was associated with social disadvantage, but the recent improvement in the political position of the French-Canadian has led to increased learning of French by English speakers. Because it lacks control of this more basic kind of motivation, the school usually tries to work on the learner's instrumental motivation. One such approach is to explain to the pupil the value of the variety he is being encouraged to learn, pointing out that he will need it for some later stage of his education, of his career, or for greater enjoyment of leisure. More generally the school is forced to take advantage of the pupil's general desire to succeed in what he does, apportioning grades, praise, blame, and prizes to encourage harder work and more earnest application.

The school itself can usually do little to change motivation, but it might do much more than it does to recognize individual differences in kind and degree of motivation. What it does control much more is the learner's exposure. It is often the case that school is the first place where the child is exposed to the new or modified variety. Many children meet the standard language or the standard variety for the first time when they come to school and probably the majority are expected to use the more formal autonomous styles only as part of their formal education. In extreme cases, school is the only place within the society where the school variety, with its high demands of purity and correctness and its often artificial set of special conventions, is to be found.

While there is no variation in the fact of exposure, there is of course considerable variation possible in the amount and manner. A first manipulable variable in language education is the time devoted to it: how much and how often is the learner exposed to the language or variety he is expected to acquire? It is a reasonable assumption that, other things being equal, the more he is in contact with the variety, the more he will be likely to acquire it. One might also ask what arrangement of time would be most beneficial. It is often argued, for example, that the teaching of a second language should start as early as possible. The strongest form of theoretical argument in favor of this policy depends on the notion that natural language acquisition takes place only while the child is young: that biological maturity involves a hardening of the ability to acquire language. H. H. Stern (1967) has summarized the evidence for early starts and concludes much more cautiously than one might have expected: "nor is psychological evidence for an early start in the teaching of languages before puberty nearly as obvious as popularly believed." The starting age, he believes, is a matter much more of the intended aim rather than of some natural advantage of an early start. There seems to be no reason against starting to expose a child to a second language or standard dialect early on but an early start is not as vital as is sometimes conceived. Ervin-Tripp (1974) has reported on the superior language learning strategies of older children than younger, and Krashen's distinctions between formal and informal instruction help account for the advantages that adult learners have in many situations.

What seems likely to be important is the manner and speed of presentation of the new variety. Depending on goals and situation, there is likely to be an optimal gradient at which the child is presented with and called on to use a new variety. At one extreme, there is the traumatic experience of the lone immigrant thrust into an environment where he knows not a word of the new language with which he is surrounded; at the other, the occasional five-minute lesson devoted to a classical language as in the attempts to help English children appreciate Latin roots in English. Between there is a whole continuum of possibilities, varying not just in the dimensions of time sharing (how much of the time available is given to each variety) but also the kinds of communicative demands (oral or written, active or passive), and topics, situations, or participants to which the varieties are allocated.

As well as variations in time, variations in exposure are possible. I use exposure as a neutral term, referring to the way in which the new variety, or any aspect of it, is presented to the learner. But there are a number of different kinds of exposure possible, again forming a continuum. Start at the level of a single event: a critical aspect of a language learning or teaching event is presumably the internalization of the new rule or item, or the testing of the hypothesis, the step toward the development of full communicative competence. Learning a variety involves a vast number of such internal events, and follows the experience of an even larger number of exposures to external data relevant to the internal decision.

Perhaps this could become clearer if we look at an example. Any piece of linguistic knowledge is part of the complex whole, and it is quite artificial to isolate any simple unit. Consider however a stylistic or social rule, the sort that speakers of a nonstandard variety are expected to develop with the standard variety. We'll take the fact that standard English has a number of different forms in place of the substandard *ain't*. What are the various ways in which a speaker who uses *ain't* might be taught to use the standard forms? A number of basic strategies might be employed: (1) modeling—the speaker might be exposed only to speakers who do not use the stigmatized form, but use the standard forms; (2) explanation—the speaker is informed of the nature of the behavior required of him; (3) practice—the speaker is called on in some way such as modeling or explanation to produce the desired forms; (4) reinforcement—the speaker is negatively reinforced when he produces the stigmatized form or positively when he produces the desired forms.

Any language teaching is a combination of these: any language learning event takes place as the result of one of them. From the point of view of the learner, language learning is basically a matter of exploring: trying out hypotheses about means of communication. The confirmation or disconfirmation of the new hypotheses takes place either when the learner encounters an utterance or understands one or in the reaction of the person with whom the learner is communicating. Once a child has worked out that there is some power of speech to control action or understand the needs of others, he is constantly exploring the nature of this power, finding out when it works and how.

The basis of language pedagogy is to recognize this exploration and the way in which it takes place, and to find ways to make it more efficient or to control its direction. Recognizing this, many scholars have stopped talking about experiments in language teaching and have called for deeper understanding of the way in which language learning takes place.

Some studies have raised questions about the importance of variations in methodology. Larger studies such as those by Schere and Wertheimer, Smith, and Levin have shown less variability accounted for by method than many language teachers would expect or supporters of one methodology or another would hope. A well-known study by John Upshur (1968) showed very little if any influence of formal instruction on foreign students' improvement in English, and a recent paper by Suter (1976) reports "negligible relationships" between pronunciation accuracy of 61 English learners and the amount of formal classroom instruction they were given in pronunciation. Among the factors he found of importance were native language, amount of concern the learner expressed about pronunciation, and amount of interaction with native speakers.

It is the questions raised by studies such as these that have led scholars to recognize the importance of the study of second language acquisition to the field of educational linguistics.

It will perhaps be noted that I have not attempted in the discussion so far to present any clear distinction between first and second language acquisition. While one of the classic studies in the field, that by Werner Leopold, was in fact a study of the language development of bilingual children and thus could clearly be considered a comparative study of first and second language acquisition, the two fields have developed in some ways quite independently. The study of first language acquisition has seemed to be much closer to theoretical linguistics and to psycholinguistics; the study of second language acquisition, on the other hand, has been much more closely related to the practical concerns of language teachers and so has seemed much more like an applied field. In recent years, however, a number of scholars in the field of second language acquisition have attempted again to analyze the similarities and differences. Two papers in 1974 looked at the same issue very carefully. Barry P. Taylor (1974) argued that in fact first and second language acquisition depend on a cognitively similar process. Taylor does not believe that the physiological evidence of a critical period is conclusive. He considers that the psychological learning strategies involved seem similar, believes that the native language is something the second language learner can fall back on rather than a source of interference, accepts that cognitive maturity possibly makes some difference, and concludes that the main reasons for any differences are probably effective psychological variables. Susan M. Ervin-Tripp (1974) suggests that arguments for the existence of fundamental differences between first and second language acquisition have arisen largely because of the different kinds of study that have been conducted. Second language acquisition research, she points out, tends to be applied while first language acquisition research is much more theoretical. The evidence used in the study of first language acquisition has often come from case studies, with detailed analysis of an individual therefore possible. Those studying second language acquisition have tended to look at groups, their evidence therefore being statistical. Studies of first language acquisition have focused on the strategies of the learner, while a great number of studies of second language acquisition focus on the variable input to the learning situation. Finally, first language acquisition studies tend to take place in natural environments while second language acquisition studies tend to be concerned with what happens in a classroom. She argues for one great value in the study of second language acquisition: it can ethically be manipulated:

> We can readily control age of second language acquisition, but are dependent on social or physical accidents, with attendant confounding circumstances, to study hearing recovery cases or isolated children learning a mother tongue late.

In the paper, she reports on the result of a detailed study of some children learning a second language. She finds many basic similarities:

> "Second language learners, like children, remember best the items they can interpret"; "the basic preference of the child at first is for a principle of one meaning-one form, and he rejects two forms for it appears to be an identical meaning or reference situation"; and "the first features of sentences to be used in comprehension rules are those that survive in short term memory best."

Overall then, she noted a great number of similarities between the kinds of sentences produced and understood by children learning their first language and children learning a second language. Contradicting a widely held assumption, she found that in the age range of 4-9 the older children appeared to learn much faster than the younger.

A number of studies attempt to deal with differences or similarities in the order of acquisition of specific features. Dulay and Burt (1974a) report on a number of studies of the errors made by children learning English as a second language and consider that they are similar to those made by children learning English natively. The greatest number (87%) they considered to be "developmental," that is, like those that a native language learner makes, rather than a result of interference. They believe therefore that "the account of language acquisition offered by first language research has proved to be a most productive predictor of children's errors in second language acquisition" (p. 134). Similar results are reported in other studies such as Milan (1974) and Gillis and Weber (1976). When, however, one looks more carefully at the actual order of acquisition, certain doubts seem to arise. A second paper by Dulay and Burt (1974b) finds a number of differences that lead them to conclude that "we can no longer hypothesize similarity between second language and first language acquisition" (p. 255). Similarly, Bailey, Madden, and Krashen (1974) report results similar to Dulay and Burt's, showing some similarity in order of acquisition between adults and children learning English as a second language that is still different from the order in first language acquisition.

These seeming contradictions are perhaps to be explained by the somewhat limited scope of the research that has been done to date. Dealing with the wider question of the applicability of second language acquisition research, Tarone, Swain, and Fathman (1976) point out that a great deal of the work in second language acquisition has in fact looked at product rather than process. Working with a comparatively limited number of morphemes, there is found evidence of what is widely called the "interlanguage" of second language learners at a given stage rather than evidence of the underlying process. The strategies and processes have not yet been fully studied; the individual variables (age, sex, etc.) have not been taken into account; the environmental variables have not been fully investigated, and the basic methodology of data collection remains under-developed and the validity of instruments unclear. The methodology of the studies and the statistics they use have been seriously questioned in a recent paper by Rosansky (1976).

The concentration of students of second language acquisition on product rather than process is perhaps best exemplified by the great attention they choose to pay to something that a number of them label "interlanguage." The first clear exposition of the notion was in a paper by Corder (1967). In that paper, Corder proposed that a study of what he called the second language learner's "transitional competence" would reveal systematic errors arising not from interference from the native language so much as giving evidence of the nature of the learner's "approximative system." Within a few years, clearly under the impact of studies of first language acquisition as much as following Corder's lead, error analysis replaced contrastive analysis as a principal activity of those concerned with research in the area of language learning. A clear change of approach and goal was also evident: those who had worked in the field of contrastive analysis clearly considered themselves applied linguists, their assumption being that contrastive analysis would make it possible to prepare more efficient materials. Those working in error analysis, on the other hand, consider themselves much more students of psycholinguistics whose studies might lead to some understanding of the nature of second language acquisition and not necessarily to some immediate way to improve second language teaching.

It is perhaps because of this distinction in approach that the notion of interlanguage has become comparatively popular. Interlanguage, first used by Selinker (1972), is generally defined as a "system" that is "distinct from both the native language and the target language," Selinker, Swain, and Dumas (1975). A good deal of work in second language acquisition has been to attempt to establish the existence and nature of these interlanguages. There is an interesting change of perspective. Whereas to traditional language teachers (and probably to most students) a learner's control of a language at a given stage is assumed to be transitional, with both teacher and learner concerned to move it closer to the target, the student of interlanguage appears to be much more satisfied to accept it in its own right as an object for synchronic study. Serious problems of course arise from the fact that these learner's transitional systems do not turn out to be either stable or widespread. The degree of variation that is found causes concern. For example, Cancino, Rosansky, and Schumann (1975) found evidence of considerable variability in the order of acquisition. Looking at Arab students learning English, Scott and Tucker (1974) looked very hard to find some degree of regularity in their errors. Their conclusions suggest some confusion. They

> found errors that were sufficiently frequent and regular, as well as instances of correct usage apparently following standard English rules, for us to assume that we were dealing with a rule-generated language system. . . .

On the basis of their studies at two periods of time, they thought it reasonable to claim that they were dealing with "two approximate systems" although, recognizing all the differences that did occur, they recognized that they were dealing with "twenty-two idiosyncratic dialects."

In the study of speakers of four languages (Arabic, Spanish, Persian, and Japanese), Diane E. Larsen-Freeman (1975) found a high level of agreement in the kinds of errors made, but still a great deal of evidence of apparent individual and language group variation. To deal with some of these contradictory results, Lonna J. Dickerson (1975) proposes that interlanguages, like real languages, should be seen as having variable rules:

> Like native speakers, second-language learners use a language system consisting of variable rules. Their achievement of the target language comes about through gradual change by using, over time, greater proportions of more target-like variants in an ordered set of phonetic environments.   (p. 407)

These arguments have been extended by Wayne B. Dickerson (1976), who demonstrates that the observations of five Japanese speakers learning English /l/ over a year provide data showing the kind of patterned variation and wave change postulated by Labov to explain language change. On the basis of this analysis, he argues that we are dealing with variable rules working in a native grammar (Japanese-English), which might be referred to as interlanguage provided interlanguage is defined to include variable rules. He proposes variability analysis rather than error analysis, and suggests that the failure of contrastive analysis has resulted from its refusal to accept variable rules.

As may be apparent from some of the earlier references, a good deal of the difficulty of this area arises out of first assuming an interlanguage, a presumably complete grammar that has been internalized by the learner, but attempting to establish its existence by using fairly limited tests of errors made with certain morphological elements. As a result of this sketchy sampling of a learner's knowledge, the picture that emerges remains as confused as some of the statements made about second language acquisition.

Perhaps one of the greatest weaknesses of studies of second language acquisition is that they still are concerned with too simple a view of the process. As Tarone, Swain, and Fathman point out, they seldom go beyond syntactic questions and are often limited to analysis of the order of acquisition of specific morphemes. In this, they are like many of the earlier studies of first language acquisition, with attempts to write simple grammars for learners. One can certainly sympathize with Adjemian (1976), who calls for "painstakingly designed studies repeated at various intervals, yielding both longitudinal and setting-specific data" (p. 319). Those studying first language acquisition have found it necessary to move to much more complex approaches: to attempt semantic, cognitive, and pragmatic explanations of the process, and to argue that each type of explanation may be important at the various stages of development. Studying second language learners in action could, as Ervin-Tripp pointed out, be a very valuable way of learning more about the whole process of language acquisition; and recognizing the more complex models needed in first language studies will be a vital step in clarifying some of the confusions of present second language acquisition research.

Chapter 11

Linguistic Input in First and Second Language Learning

Stephen J. Gaies

From research in applied linguistics and related disciplines has emerged in the last generation a radically altered view of the nature of first language acquisition. According to the nativist view, the language learner, whose innate predisposition to acquire language is activated, at a given stage of maturation, by exposure to primary linguistic data in the language to be acquired, scans that data in order to discover how certain linguistic universals are manifested in that language, categorizes the data, and induces from it a set of hypotheses or sentence-generating rules to account for that data and to produce novel utterances consistent with it. These hypotheses which the child forms undergo constant revision; the language acquisition process thus involves a succession of "grammars" or rule-systems developed by the learner to contend with increasing exposure to the language to be acquired and which he/she modifies at least partially in response to feedback received from linguistic interaction with adult speakers of the language.

There are certainly factors which suggest that the adult attempting to learn a second language is in an irrevocably different position from that of a child acquiring his/her native language. Furthermore, it is undeniably true, though for reasons which are far from fully understood, that adult second language learning is nowhere nearly so universally successful as first language acquisition. Many applied linguists, however, agree with Corder (1967) that "it still remains to be shown that the process of learning a second language is of a fundamentally different nature from the process of primary acquisition" (p. 164). Indeed, investigation of the utterances of adults learning a second language both in "natural" situations and through formal instruction suggests that like children acquiring their native language, adults actively process and organize the target language data to which they are exposed. Data are scanned for underlying regularities, and through the application of a number of processing strategies, adults attempt to induce rules for the data to which they are exposed and to generate utterances of their own in the language. Many "errors" made by adults learning a second language are systematic, and they reflect an underlying hypothesis about the language. The kind of error which was explained by behavioral theory as an imperfect imitation, an incorrectly learned habit, can in fact be more adequately explained as the product of an adult's hypothesis about the structure of the target language which happens not to correspond to the actual rule in the full target language system.

Within the framework of the nativist approach to first (and, by implication, second) language learning, the focus, then, is on the learner. This relocation of the primary mechanism of the acquisition process in the learner has been accompanied by a parallel de-emphasis of the role played by external or environmental sources, which the behaviorists had insisted were the sole determinants of behavior change (i.e., learning). In the view of the behaviorists, the child learning language was considered to be enormously dependent on the particular set of overt verbal stimuli to which he/she was exposed; the individual's attempts to imitate the specific utterances heard and the nature of the reinforcement which greeted those efforts were thought to shape the development of a verbal repertoire and would thus constitute the heart of the acquisition process. The early nativist view (McNeill, 1966b), on the other hand, drastically minimized the importance of the particular linguistic data to which the learner is exposed as a critical factor in the acquisition process. Rather, it is through the innate ability of the learner to induce regularities and to form generalizations from a mass of unorganized, random linguistic input that language is acquired.

More recent research, however, suggests that it is not solely by the learner that primary linguistic data is organized and that to imply, as McNeill has done, that the language learner is exposed to linguistically random data is inaccurate beyond the degree of mere hyperbole. As Landes (1975) concludes from a review of the research, "it is clear that adults are not only sensitive to and affected by the need to communicate with their children, but that interaction patterns between parents and offspring change with the increasing language skills of the child" (p. 376). It is the opinion of Landes, among others, that it is therefore a mistake to treat the nature of the actual linguistic input to which a learner is exposed as basically irrelevant to the acquisition process.

Let me briefly review some of the research in question. First, as regards evidence for the assertion that adult-child verbal interactions are linguistically different from adult-adult discourse, the most striking evidence is the existence of "baby talk," which Ferguson (1964) defines as "a special form of language which is regarded by a speech community as being primarily appropriate for talking to young children and which is generally regarded as not the normal adult use of language" (p. 103). Modifications of the full adult system in the form of reductions, deletions, and replacements are seen to account for the characteristic simplicity of "baby talk."

According to Ferguson, many informants feel that their use of "baby talk" makes it easier for children to learn to talk. It may well be that "baby talk" serves as a transitional model for young children as they progress from initial vocalizations toward the beginning of genuine language acquisition. The claim is a complicated one to defend, however, since, as Ferguson points out, "baby talk" is also used with pets and infants, and it can hardly be argued that an infant or pet is being taught to speak.

On the other hand, substantial adjustment of normal adult language also occurs when adults address young children who *are* learning their first language. Early evidence of linguistic adjustment can be found in Brown and Bellugi (1964), whose study involved the verbal interactions of a single mother-child pair. The mother's sentences were generally short and grammatically simple. Drach (1969) found that the average adult-adult utterance contains twice as many transformations and ten times as many subordinate clauses as the average utterance addressed by an adult to a 26-month-old child. Further, adult-child verbal interactions involve a much higher percentage of imperatives and interrogatives; Ervin-Tripp (1971) stated that interrogative sentences account for between 25-50% of a total corpus of adult-child utterances. Drach also found that utterances in adult-adult interactions are considerably more variable than utterances addressed by adults to children in terms of morpheme count; in addition, the average utterance length of adult-adult speech, as measured by morpheme count, is two and one-half times that of the average adult-child utterance.

Similar evidence comes from Snow (1972), who reported that mothers use fewer subordinate clauses and compound verbs when speaking to two-year-old children. Compared to that addressed to two-year-olds, the speech addressed to ten-year-olds involves longer sentences, less repetition, and more pronoun substitution. Furthermore, "mean preverb length scores (of mother-child interactions) were lower, indicating less left branching and self-embedding" (Snow, 1972:556). Research by Phillips (1973) involving thirty mother-child pairs confirms the hypothesis that speech addressed to young children is syntactically less complex. This is also the conclusion of Granowsky and Krossner (1970), whose work examined the language used by teachers in kindergarten classes.

Brown, Salerno, and Sachs (1972), as well as Snow (1972), have shown that the trend toward syntactic simplification which can be observed in parent-child speech is also characteristic of the speech addressed to young children by nonparent adults. Finally, Gleason (1973) and Shatz and Gelman (1973) found evidence that as early as age four, and certainly by age eight, children themselves modify their language when addressing younger children.

As measured by sentence length, transformational complexity, and a number of other variables, then, the syntax of the language which adults use with young children clearly suggests a deliberate effort toward simplification.

As for the claim that adult linguistic input varies according to a child's age, the evidence is much more sketchy. Snow (1972) found that the language addressed to two-year-old children is grammatically simpler than that used with ten-year-olds (in fact, Snow asserted that mothers' speech to ten-year-olds is comparable in syntactic complexity to adult-adult verbal interactions). Phillips (1973) claimed that from age eighteen months, children begin to be addressed in increasingly complex language. Fraser and Roberts (1975) asserted that this trend toward increased syntactic complexity, as measured by mean utterance length, continues until the child reaches two and one-half years of age; no change was observed thereafter, however.

Though the documentation is incomplete and in places somewhat contradictory, it remains nonetheless reasonable to suppose that between ages two and ten, children are exposed to increasingly complex linguistic data. The actual schedule according to which this takes place, however, remains largely unknown. So, for that matter, are two other issues: first, the relative importance of adult linguistic input versus input from child-child interactions and adult linguistic performance not specifically addressed to children, and second, the question of whether linguistic simplification is geared to the chronological age or perceived linguistic competence of the child learning language. It is, however, a reasonable working assumption to view the relative simplicity and organization of adult linguistic input as having a facilitating effect on the acquisition process, in that the child may more easily discover the basic sentence patterns and major constituent categories of the target language when the load placed on his/her cognitive abilities and memory are not excessive.

In the case of second language learning which takes place in formal instructional settings, there is by definition the assumption that the learner's exposure to and experience with the second (or foreign) language is in some way guided and organized. Given what is known thus far about the organization and structuring of the input data in first language acquisition, one is confronted by the paradoxical situation of knowing that the input data in first language acquisition, which was thought to be essentially random, is in fact structured, but of not knowing whether the input data in presumably structured presentations of a second language is indeed similarly adjusted and organized. It was the purpose of the study to be reported on in this paper to find evidence to address this paradox. The specific question investigated was the following: in terms of syntax, is there any indication that the linguistic data to which formal learners of English are exposed through the oral classroom language of their teachers is adjusted and graded in complexity analogously to the language addressed to first language learners?

In the present study, the syntax of the oral classroom language of eight ESL (English as a Second Language) teacher-trainees was examined. The subjects were teacher-trainees enrolled in a Practicum course offered by the Program in Applied Linguistics at Indiana University. Three of the subjects were highly proficient nonnative speakers of English who had had some experience teaching English in their home countries. The others were native speakers of English whose prior teaching experience was quite limited.

The subjects taught adult ESL classes as part of the Practicum course requirements. These classes, which are offered each semester, meet hourly four evenings a week for a period of ten weeks. In the Fall of 1975, when the data for the present study was collected, instruction was offered at four different levels. Each of these four levels was taught by two teachers, who shared the teaching responsibility equally.

Each of the subjects agreed to let the researcher tape three of his/her classes: one each at the beginning, middle, and end of the ten-week period. In addition, the weekly meetings of the Practicum class, in which the subjects and their instructors discussed general and specific problems and approaches in teaching English to speakers of other languages, were taped so that samples of the language which the subjects used with each other—i.e., among linguistic peers—could be obtained.

From each of the twenty-four classroom tapes, a 500-word sample was selected for analysis. In each case, the sample consisted of the first 500 words contained in sentence-length utterances spoken by the teacher during the actual class period. For the baseline language data collected in the Practicum class meetings, the first 500 words spoken in sentence-length utterances by a subject to the class as a whole and with the class's attention constituted the sample for that subject.

The samples were transcribed and analyzed by the researcher. Analysis proceeded by segmenting the samples into T-units. A T-unit is defined as "one main clause plus any subordinate clause or nonclausal structure that is attached to or embedded in it" (Hunt, 1970:4). This unit of syntactic analysis is objective and easy to compute, and in the last ten years it has gained increasing recognition as a far more valid index of syntactic complexity than other measures, including sentence length. A particularly attractive feature of the T-unit as an index of syntactic maturity (complexity) was revealed by O'Donnell, Norris, and Griffin (1967), who noted a close relationship between T-unit length and the number of sentence-combining transformations required to generate a T-unit.

Altogether, measures on six dependent variables were computed for each sample. *Table 11.1* presents a comparison of the means of the subjects' classroom language and their speech among linguistic peers. The data indicates an overall process of syntactic simplification in the classroom language. The subjects spoke in shorter clauses and used fewer subordinate clauses per T-unit when addressing their students than they did when speaking to highly proficient interlocutors. Multivariate analysis of variance performed on the data revealed that the overall difference in syntactic complexity was highly statistically significant ($p=$ < 0.0001).

Table 11.2 compares mean performance of the subjects according to the level at which they were teaching. What emerges from the data is an unmistakable relationship between the syntactic complexity of the subjects' classroom language and the level of proficiency of their students. At any level, the syntax of the teachers' oral classroom language is more complex than at the level immediately below it and less complex than at the level immediately above it; and *this is true for every one of the six criterion variables.*

Table 11.1

Comparison of the syntactic complexity of subjects' baseline
(Practicum class meetings) language and their oral classroom language

			Variable			
	w/T	c/T	w/c	AJ/100	AV/100	N/100
Source						
Baseline	10.97	1.60	6.84	11.59	20.27	28.54
ESL classroom	6.19	1.20	5.10	2.54	5.33	11.16

w/T	words per T-unit
c/T	ratio of clauses to T-units
w/c	words per clause
AJ/100	adjective clauses per 100 T-units
AV/100	adverb clauses per 100 T-units
N/100	noun clauses per 100 T-units

Table 11.2

Comparison of the syntactic complexity
of subjects' oral classroom language by level

			Variable			
Level	w/T	c/T	w/c	AJ/100	AV/100	N/100
L1 (Beginner)	4.30	1.02	4.20	0.00	0.76	1.60
L2 (Upper Beginner)	5.75	1.14	5.04	1.46	3.64	6.92
L3 (Intermediate)	6.45	1.24	5.18	2.26	8.40	13.54
L4 (Advanced)	8.26	1.38	5.98	6.47	8.51	20.91

At L1, the two subjects used T-units whose mean length was only 52% as great as the average T-unit used by the two teachers at L4. The mean length of clauses used by the subjects teaching at L1 was only 70% of the mean clause length in the data of the two subjects teaching at L4. Finally, the difference in ratio of clauses to T-units at the two levels also indicates the difference in the language used by the teachers at these levels. It should be noted that since every T-unit contains one main clause, the minimum possible ratio of clauses per T-unit is 1.00. The subjects teaching at L4, then, used subordinate clauses roughly nineteen times as often as did their counterparts teaching students with no proficiency in English at the time classes began.

Multivariate analysis of the data revealed the following: (1) the level of proficiency which a class of students was assumed to have is a statistically significant ($p = <0.0227$) factor determining the syntactic complexity of the classroom language used by the teacher, and (2) the syntactic complexity of the oral language used by a teacher at one level is significantly less than mean performance of the teachers teaching at more advanced levels (the only exception was between the Intermediate and Advanced levels, where the same trend was apparent, but not to a statistically significant degree).

To summarize, the study just described investigated whether the classroom language of teachers in a formal language learning setting reflected some degree of syntactic adjustment and whether these adjustments, if indeed they were found to exist, moved progressively, like those discovered in the primary linguistic input in first language acquisition, toward greater approximation of the full adult target language norm. From the data obtained, the answer to both questions is affirmative.

It is widely believed, however, that linguistic adjustment of the kind observed in the classroom language of the subjects in the present study is characteristic of virtually all verbal interactions between speakers of a language and less than fully proficient interlocutors. This is the view of Ferguson (1971), who postulated the principle that speech communities tend to have conventional varieties of "simplified" speech which speakers regard as appropriate for use when their interlocutors do not have full understanding of the language in use. One variety, to which the name "Foreigner Talk" has been given, is, like "baby talk," thought to be the product of conscious choices on the part of speakers of a language and is generally felt to be a transitional form of communication between linguistic unequals.

In other words, the syntactic adjustments made by foreign language teachers represent a single instance of the kind of linguistic adjustment typically made on behalf of *all* adults learning—formally or not—a second language. The primary linguistic input to which formal second language learners are exposed via their teachers' classroom language is indeed syntactically adjusted as is the case with the primary linguistic data with which first language learners operate, but this simplification is no less typical of the speech addressed to adult learners in language usage settings where the intent is not specifically instructional.

Is the implication, then, that the contribution of the foreign language teacher's classroom language is merely neutral in the sense that it does not controvert the nature of the linguistic data to which all language learners, both first and second, are exposed? I think not, but the motivation for saying this is not based on syntactic adjustment alone, but rather on another dimension of teachers' classroom language which is specifically the result of the instructional setting in which it occurs.

A number of studies have shown that many of the verbal interactions between parents (most generally mothers) and children acquiring language involve communicative strategies or devices on the part of the adult which are tantamount to what Landes (1975) calls "training sessions." Among the different strategies which have been observed, four are worth mentioning here:

Repetition: This technique is thought to have potential accelerating effects on language acquisition. As Snow (1972) explained:

> *Short term memory limits the time available for processing input. Repetition of a sentence would give added processing time, thus increasing the child's chances of successfully processing the sentence.*   (p. 563)

Kobashigawa (1969), who studied the same corpus examined by Drach (1969), found that 15% of the statements, 35% of the questions, and 60% of the imperatives addressed by a mother to her 26-month-old son were repeated with no long intervening pauses or activity.

Prodding: This strategy characterizes instances when a parent makes it verbally clear that he/she wants the child to say or repeat something. Such verbal directions typically take the form of "Can you say . . . ?" or "Say . . . ." A related device is *prompting*, in which, for example, a mother will show a child a picture of something which the child knows the word for and will say, "This is a *what*?" or "What's this?"

Modeling: This refers to those occasions in which it is evident from the situation that the mother intends to demonstrate or teach her child something. In contrast to prodding or prompting, modeling takes place when, for example, a child does not know the name of something in a picture and the adult supplies the appropriate lexical item.

Correction or instruction by expansion: While most studies of language acquisition devalue the role of corrective feedback, there is considerable sentiment to regard parental expansions of children's utterances—what have been termed "imitations in reverse," and which are presumably performed by an adult to check his/her understanding of the child's utterance—as very possibly contributive to language development. An expansion recognizes the truth value of a child's statement, while at the same time it demonstrates to the child how that statement is encoded by his/her speech community at the very moment when the child is likely to be most attentive to such information. In contrast to children's imitations of parental utterances, which are not grammatically progressive, it has been asserted by at least one researcher (McNeill, 1966b) that in some cases, children's imitations of parental expansions are grammatically progressive roughly 30% of the time. Additional empirical evidence for this was provided by Nelson et al. (1973), who found that the syntactic development of an experimental group of forty-month-old children was significantly enhanced by their exposure to expansions which recast the subjects' sentences by providing a new syntactic structure.

Now, it is precisely these kinds of "training sessions" which are characteristic of foreign language classroom verbal activity. Preliminary observation of the data from the present study indicates that these four strategies are used by all subjects in the classroom, but particularly so by the two subjects teaching at the Beginner level. These kinds of verbal interactions between a speaker of a language and a learner of a language are communicative and/or pedagogical in nature, and they are essentially consistent with any individual teaching methodology. They are, in fact, so intimately a part of the teacher's normal classroom activity that the role they may play in the learning process is probably taken too much for granted.

Their use by foreign language teachers, however, like the tendency to simplify the syntax of the language which they address to their students, suggests that the foreign language teacher may serve the same or a similar function in second language learning that the parent does in first language acquisition. To whatever degree the primary linguistic input supplied by parents in first language acquisition is a critical feature of the acquisition process—i.e., serving some instructional function, whether by conscious design or not—the linguistic and communicative/pedagogical strategies which characterize teachers' classroom language might similarly shape and guide the formal second language learning process. In addition, the "training sessions" which result from the use of these strategies in a teacher's verbal interactions with his/her learners would thus be a major criterion distinguishing formal from unstructured or "natural" second language learning, since in the latter these strategies would presumably be considerably less frequently employed by speakers of a language whose contact with a learner of the language has no explicit pedagogical goals. It is my feeling, however, that it is reasonable to suggest that the nature of second language teachers' classroom speech is such that in terms of the linguistic input to which second language learners are exposed through formal instruction, further support is lent to the hypothesis that first and second language learning are in many ways qualitatively similar and should not be assumed to proceed in a fundamentally different manner.

Chapter 12

Acquisition of English Prepositions by Monolingual and Bilingual (French/English) Ontarian Students

Raymond Mougeon
Michael Canale
Susanne Carroll

This paper compares results of analyses of English preposition usage by two groups of Ontarian elementary students both at the grade 2 and grade 5 levels. The first group consists of bilingual Franco-Ontarian students from Welland and Sudbury. The second group is composed of monolingual English students from Toronto.

The data on preposition usage by the bilinguals are interesting in several respects. First, having controlled for language dominance (English or French) among the bilinguals, we are in a position to examine the possible influence of patterns of language dominance on English preposition acquisition from age 7 onward. Second, it has been reported in several studies that second language learners' proficiency in English preposition usage correlates highly with their overall proficiency in English (cf. Oller and Inal, 1971; Stubbs and Tucker, 1974). On its own merit then, preposition usage is an important area of research in the field of second language acquisition. Third, given our base line data on preposition usage by English monolinguals, the data on the bilinguals' usage permit comparison of first and second language learning strategies (interlanguage transfer, overgeneralization, omission, etc.), and of the sequencing of English preposition acquisition. The data on the monolinguals' preposition usage are also of interest in view of the lack of studies devoted to first language development from age 5 onward (cf. Palermo and Molfese, 1972) and the lack of a unified data base on the development of English preposition usage for this age group.

Methodology

Sample

The bilingual group is composed of 15 grade 2 and 14 grade 5 students enrolled in French language schools in Welland and Sudbury, Ontario. A total of 14 females and 15 males were selected. Socioeconomic stratification based on parental occupations yielded a weighted sample of four working class, five middle class, and six upper-middle class students in grade 2, and a sample of four working class, six middle class, and four upper-middle class students in grade 5. Self-reports on language usage in the home (in parent to child, child to parent, and child to child communication) indicated that among the grade 2 students, seven subjects had French as their dominant language and eight English. Among the grade 5 students, two of the subjects were English-dominant bilinguals and the remaining 12 were French-dominant. In both Welland and Sudbury francophones are outnumbered by anglophones: according to the National Census of Canada (1971) francophones make up 17% of the population in Welland and 27% in Sudbury (cf. Mougeon, Canale, and Bélanger, to appear, for discussion of the sociolinguistic profile of these communities).

The monolingual group is composed of four students in grade 2 and four in grade 5 at an English language school in Toronto. An equal number of males and females were selected at each grade level. All the students come from upper-middle or professional class environments. Due to lack of research funds we have been unable to weight the monolingual group with students representing other economic groups.

Data Collection

The data were obtained through recorded interviews conducted at the schools with each subject. The interviews ranged in length from 30 to 45 minutes and were semi-directed to cover such topics as leisure activities, school and home life, personal experiences and aspirations, story-telling, etc. All interviews were transcribed and checked for accuracy of transcription.

Tallying Procedures

Tallying of the standard and nonstandard uses of English prepositions found in the transcribed interviews took place in three steps.

First, the authors established every occurrence of a context in which use of an English preposition was required—see Brown's (1973:255) discussion of an "obligatory context" as a test item. Not counted as obligatory contexts were: (1) occurrences of particles, prepositions not followed by an NP or, in the case of the sandhi-form *to*, by an infinitive; (2) ambiguous uses (example: *I like traveling in the plane = by plane* or *in a specific plane?*); (3) occurrences that are part of a larger nonstandard or ambiguous structure (example: *She went in Papa bear's bed = She got into Papa bear's bed?*); (4) instances in which the student immediately self-corrects; (5) repetitions within the same prepositional phrase; and (6) occasions of the preposition *of* in the expressions *kind of, sort of,* and in the prepositional constructions *in front of, on top of,* etc.

Second, the authors judged preposition usage in each obligatory context as either standard or nonstandard. These judgments were arrived at jointly, based on two of the authors' native intuitions. Nonstandard usages were grouped as substitutions (examples: *I went at the slide* for *to the slide*), omissions (example: *He went   hide*), redundant uses (example: *It could lay three million eggs by a day*), and misuses (example: *He dressed into an Eskimo* for *as an Eskimo*). In the tables which summarize our findings on preposition usage (cf. Results section), we have included as errors only those nonstandard usages grouped as substitutions or omissions.[1]

Third, the prepositions to be examined were classified according to the senses they expressed. For example, *at* in its locative (+LOC) sense, as in *at home,* was distinguished from *at* in its temporal (+TEMP) sense, as in *at night; to* used to introduce an indirect object (+IO) (example: *give it to someone*) was distinguished from *to* (+LOC) (example: *go to school*) as well as *to* followed by an infinitive (+VP) (examples: *I want to go, you gotta stay*); *by* (+LOC) (example: *he lives by us*) was kept distinct from *by* used in its instrumental (+INSTR) sense (example: *go by plane*), etc. Note that we analyzed only those types for which we found five or more obligatory contexts. Thus, not listed in the tables to follow are some of the above prepositions used in other senses (example: *at* in expressions such as *at all, at last, look at someone*), as well as infrequent prepositions such as *after, before, between,* etc.

Results

Tables 12.1 and *12.2* summarize our findings on preposition use by the grade 2 and 5 bilinguals.

Two aspects of these findings merit attention. First, assuming that a percentage of error of 10% or less indicates acquisition of a given item (a cross-sectional adaptation of Brown's (1973:271) longitudinal acquisition criteria), we note that the grade 2 bilinguals have not fully acquired nine of the 19 prepositions listed in *Table 12.1,* whereas the grade 5 bilinguals have acquired all but four of the 14 prepositions listed in *Table 12.2.* Second, assuming that the range of percentages of error may be taken as some indication of the order in which the prepositions are being acquired, we find that the order of acquisition indicated in *Table 12.2* is quite similar to that represented in *Table 12.1.* Thus, we note that those prepositions having a percentage of error of less than 10% in *Table 12.1* likewise have a percentage of error of less than 10% in *Table 12.2.* Furthermore, the four prepositions that have a percentage of error greater than 10% in *Table 12.2*—i.e., *into, to* (+LOC), *by* (+INSTR), *at* (+TEMP)—likewise are among the prepositions having percentages of error higher than 10% in *Table 12.1.* The behavior of *by* (+INSTR) seems erratic since it is the only one of the four prepositions just mentioned for which a higher percentage of error was found for the grade 2 bilinguals than for the grade 5 ones. (This erratic behavior may be a

Table 12.1

Acquisition of English prepositions by grade 2 bilingual students

Preposition	Total items	Total errors	% errors
Into	66	65	98
To (+LOC)	93	45	48
Through	6	2	33
By (+LOC)	7	2	28
About	11	3	27
Out of (+INSTR)	13	3	23
At (+TEMP)	15	3	20
To (+IO)	53	10	19
By (+INSTR)	7	1	14
On (+TEMP)	10	1	10
In (+TEMP)	22	2	9
From	14	1	7
Of	73	5	7
On (+LOC)	139	9	6
To (+VP)	268	16	6
With	75	2	4
In (+LOC)	181	7	4
At (+LOC)	42	1	2
For (+IO)	66	1	2

Table 12.2

Acquisition of English prepositions by grade 5 bilingual students

Preposition	Total items	Total errors	% errors
Into	48	41	85
To (+LOC)	113	27	24
By (+INSTR)	9	2	22
At (+TEMP)	9	1	11
From	21	2	9
For (+IO)	54	3	6
In (+TEMP)	16	1	6
In (+LOC)	139	7	5
Over	18	1	5
At (+LOC)	61	3	5
On (+LOC)	126	5	4
With	85	3	3
To (+VP)	301	3	1
Of	132	1	1

function of the low number of occurrences of this preposition in the grade 2 bilinguals' speech). Focusing only on the prepositions *into, to* (+LOC), and *at* (+TEMP), we observe that they are ordered the same with respect to one another in both *Tables 12.1* and *12.2*.

It is perhaps worth discussing the suggested order of acquisition for the locative prepositions listed in *Tables 12.1* and *12.2* in light of H. Clark's (1973) "complexity hypothesis."[2] Within Clark's framework, the semantic complexity of locative prepositions increases with the number of dimensions (point, surface, volume) and the notion of directionality (no directionality, direction toward a location, direction away from a location) involved (1973:41). In this light, it is interesting that the locatives *at, on, in*, which do not involve directionality, are among the first prepositions acquired completely by the bilinguals. Also consistent with Clark's hypothesis are the bilinguals' late acquisition of *into* (involving three dimensions and direction toward) and relatively late acquisition of *from* (involving one dimension and direction away from). However, the fact that the locative *to* (involving one dimension and direction toward) is found to be acquired late by both the grade 2 and grade 5 bilinguals is inconsistent with the predictions made by Clark's hypothesis. We shall discuss the locatives *to* and *into* in further detail in a later section.

Let us now turn to the findings for the monolingual English students in grade 2 (*Table 12.3*) and grade 5 (*Table 12.4*). We observe that at the grade 2 level, of a total of 14 prepositions, only *into* has not been acquired completely, whereas by grade 5 all 12 of the prepositions in *Table 12.4* have been acquired. Once more, it appears that the locatives *into* and *to* are among the last prepositions acquired. In addition, although the data for *at* (+TEMP) are minimal in the case of the grade 5 monolinguals, this preposition seems to pose difficulties for the grade 2 monolinguals as it did for the grade 2 and grade 5 bilinguals (cf. *Tables 12.1* and *12.2*). As to the order of acquisition of locative prepositions suggested in *Tables 12.3* and *12.4*, we note again that *at, in, on* seem to be acquired by grade 2 and that *into* and *from* tend to be acquired relatively late. Both of these findings are consistent with Clark's "complexity hypothesis" (cf. above). However, the tendency for the locative *to* to be acquired relatively late by the monolinguals is, as noted in the case of the bilinguals, inconsistent with Clark's hypothesis.

To conclude this section, one is struck by the similar order of acquisition of prepositions found for the monolingual and bilingual students. Such findings have been reported in studies of second language learners' acquisition of various grammatical items and have been cited as support for the hypothesis that second language acquisition = first language acquisition (cf. Dulay and Burt, 1974c and Ervin-Tripp, 1974, for references and discussion). However, to our knowledge the order of preposition acquisition has not been compared for first and second language learners of English.[3]

One other aspect of our findings deserves some comment. For almost all the prepositions listed for the grade 2 and grade 5 monolinguals and bilinguals, the relative frequency of error is lower for the monolinguals than for the bilinguals. This lag becomes more obvious when we compare the percentages of errors for the bilinguals who have English as their dominant language with those for whom French is dominant. As there were only two students in the grade 5 bilingual

Table 12.3

Acquisition of English prepositions by grade 2 monolingual students

Preposition	Total items	Total errors	% errors
Into	6	2	33
At (+TEMP)	10	1	10
To (+LOC)	43	4	9
On (+LOC)	27	1	4
With	30	1	8
Of	58	1	2
In (+LOC)	179	—	0
To (+VP)	75	—	0
For (+IO)	13	—	0
To (+IO)	12	—	0
About	11	—	0
In (+TEMP)	8	—	0
At (+LOC)	6	—	0
From	5	—	0

Table 12.4

Acquisition of English prepositions by grade 5 monolingual students

Preposition	Total items	Total errors	% errors
From	12	1	8
Into	12	1	8
To (+LOC)	60	3	5
Of	98	4	4
At (+LOC)	24	1	4
In (+LOC)	100	3	3
To (+VP)	101	2	2
On (+LOC)	48	—	0
With	32	—	0
For (+IO)	17	—	0
In (+TEMP)	7	—	0
At (+TEMP)	5	—	0

group who indicated English as their dominant language (cf. the Methodology section), we present only the results concerning the grade 2 bilinguals (*Figure 12.1*).

With the exception of *into*, the acquisition rate for the English-dominant bilinguals is almost identical to that for the monolingual English students. However, the French-dominant bilinguals seem to lag behind both of the other groups in their acquisition of *to* (+LOC), *to* (+IO), *at* (+TEMP), *to* (+VP), *of.* The lag in the acquisition of locative *to* is the most striking one and will be discussed below.

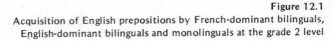

Figure 12.1

Acquisition of English prepositions by French-dominant bilinguals,
English-dominant bilinguals and monolinguals at the grade 2 level

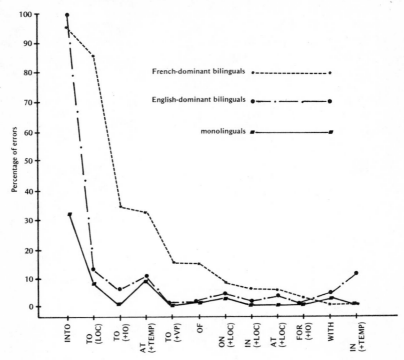

Two possible explanations for the lag in preposition acquisition found for
the French-dominant bilinguals come immediately to mind. First, the French-
dominant students are exposed to less English than the English-dominant and
monolingual students inasmuch as French is the language of communication in the
home. The fact that the English-dominant bilinguals compare well with the
monolinguals suggests that instruction in a language other than the one used at
home does not, at least to grade 2, adversely affect the rate of acquisition of
prepositions. Conversely, the findings in *Figure 12.1* suggest that the language of
communication used in the home constitutes a crucial factor in the acquisition of
English prepositions. This finding is consistent with Hébrard and Mougeon's
(1975) finding that for this same French-dominant group, there is an overall lag in
the acquisition of English syntax and vocabulary in comparison to the
achievement of the English-dominant students. It must be emphasized that in
neither Hébrard and Mougeon's study nor in this present research was the
language used in peer group communication investigated.

A second, perhaps complementary, explanation for the French-dominant
bilinguals' lag in preposition acquisition is interlanguage transfer (interference).

There are four aspects of our findings that suggest this possibility. First, it is clear from the results that the locatives *to* and *into* pose greater difficulty for the bilingual students (especially the French-dominant ones—cf. *Figure 12.1*) than for the monolingual students in both grade 2 and grade 5 (cf. *Tables 12.1-12.4*). However, other prepositions—such as *with*, the locatives *at*, *in*, *on*, and *in* (+TEMP)—appear to be acquired with equal ease by both the bilinguals (French- and English-dominant) and monolinguals.

Second, the bilingual students do not make the same types of errors as the monolinguals in the use of the locative *to*. At the grade 2 level, the bilinguals made a total of 45 errors in the use of the locative *to*, of which 39 involved substitution of *at* (1), four involved substitution of *in* (2), and two were omissions (3).

(1)   A.   I don't go very often *at* the park.
      B.   We went *at* Florida.
      C.   I said to bring me *at* the hospital.

(2)   A.   We're going *in* the farm.
      B.   We go *in* the bench.
      C.   We go *in* Toronto every week.
      D.   They go *in* the front of his house.

(3)   A.   We gonna go _____a parade.
      B.   We went _____Walt Disney World.

As for the grade 2 monolinguals, there was a total of four errors: one student substituted the prepositions *at, in, on, through* once each (4).

(4)   A.   Sometimes we go *through* our neighbors for supper.
      B.   We went *on* the pioneer village.
      C.   I play with my friends that go *in* the school.
      D.   Some people go *at* the net.

At the grade 5 level, the bilingual students committed a total of 29 errors involving locative *to*: 17 substitutions of *at* (5), nine substitutions of *in* (6), and three omissions (7).

(5)   A.   We went *at* my Grandma's.
      B.   My father was gone *at* a party.
      C.   I go *at* Towers and school.

(6)   A.   They gonna go *in* jail.
      B.   They go *in* the corner of the classroom.
      C.   She made plans to go *in* a motel.
      D.   I was going *in* Quebec.

(7)   A.   We made a big trip _____ Quebec.
       B.   I went _____ the principal's office.
       C.   We went _____ all the places.

The grade 5 monolinguals had a total of only three errors: all were omissions (8).[4]

(8)   A.   In July we're going _____ the cottage.
       B.   We're gonna go _____ the Rockies.
       C.   I started going _____ camp.

With respect to error types then, one observes a tendency among the bilingual students at both grade levels to substitute the prepositions *at* (strong tendency) and *in* (weak tendency) for the locative *to*.[5] On the other hand, it may be the case that the monolinguals in grade 2 resort to substitution of a variety of locative prepositions for *to* whereas the grade 5 monolinguals no longer do so.

Most of the nonstandard uses of the locative *at* pointed out above resemble the usage of the preposition *à* in French. Thus *à* can be used in a directional or nondirectional sense with expressions of location such as the names of cities, *l'école*, "school"; *la maison*, "home," *le magasin*, "store," etc. This semantic resemblance, in addition to the phonetic resemblance of *à* [æ] (in Ontarian French) and *at* [æːt] may account for the fact that the bilinguals generally substitute *at* for the locative *to* whereas the monolinguals in our study do not.

However, two points must be borne in mind when considering the possible interference of *à*. First, we do not know—neither from our data nor from the literature on acquisition of English as a first language—whether there may be some stage at which learners of English as a native language substitute *at* for locative *to* (as for example, Clark's "complexity hypothesis" would predict). This remains an interesting area of research. Second, there is no one-to-one correspondence between the nonstandard use of *at* found in the bilinguals' speech and the use of *à* in French. For example, the grade 2 and grade 5 bilinguals substitute *at* for *to* in sentences such as *We went at my aunt's* although there is no corresponding form with *à* in French (**Nous sommes allés à ma tante*); rather the preposition *chez* must be used (*Nous sommes allés chez ma tante*). Thus, each of these points suggests that the possibility of overgeneralization cannot be ruled out in favor of interference.

A third aspect of our findings suggesting interference from French involves the French-dominant bilinguals' substitution of *at* for *to* (+IO). Seven out of eight of these students' errors involve such a substitution—see (9) for examples:

(9)   A.   We write something *at* my mother.
       B.   She brought some food *at* her grandma.
       C.   They say it *at* someone.
       D.   *At* Mom, from Jill.

It is difficult to explain this substitution in terms of intrasystemic overgeneralization since *at* is not used to introduce an indirect object in English. Furthermore, we found no errors of this type in the speech of the English monolinguals. The possibility of interference is suggested by the fact that French uses the preposition *à* to introduce all noncliticized indirect objects, example: *Elle a apporté de la nourriture à sa grand-mère* (cf. 9B). Hence, once more the polysemous and very frequent French preposition *à* seems to have played a major role in the students' errors involving *to*.

Finally, certain aspects of the bilinguals' use of *into* also suggest the possibility of interference from French. As is clear from the results presented in *Figure 12.1* above, the English-dominant and French-dominant bilinguals make more errors in the use of *into* than do the monolinguals. Almost all such errors—whether committed by the monolinguals or bilinguals—involve substitution of *in* for *into* (example: *I went in the room*). The fact that in French there is no distinction similar to the one made in English between *in* and *into* may partially account for the lag in acquisition of *into* shown for the bilingual group. However, it must be noted that other factors may be involved: (1) overgeneralization of *in*, as suggested by the relatively late acquisition of *into* by the monolinguals; (2) the tendency (for adults) to overlook the *in/into* distinction in casual speech; and (3) the bilinguals' lack of exposure to formal English in the school.

Conclusion

Given the small number of monolingual comparison subjects and the lack of socioeconomic diversity within that group, our conclusions can only be tentative. However, in the absence of studies focusing on acquisition of a large number of English prepositions by first and second language learners, we offer the following concluding remarks.

Briefly, the order of acquisition of English prepositions would seem to be essentially the same for young language learners (through grade 5, say) be they monolingual or bilingual. This finding is interesting in two respects: it suggests a ranking of the prepositions examined according to the degree of difficulty they present for the young learner; and it suggests that interlanguage transfer plays no role in the sequencing of preposition acquisition for bilinguals.

However, this last point cannot be taken to mean that interlanguage transfer can have no effect on bilinguals' preposition acquisition, since we have found that the rate at which certain prepositions (for example, the locatives *to* and *into*) are acquired by French-dominant bilinguals is considerably slower than the rate of acquisition for these same prepositions by monolinguals and English-dominant bilinguals. Although the French-dominant bilinguals' relatively late acquisition of these prepositions may be explained in part by the students' limited exposure to English, this explanation does not fully account for the finding that certain prepositions (*with, at* (+LOC), etc.) seem to be acquired with equal ease by the monolinguals and both groups of bilinguals. We hypothesize that the more difficult prepositions such as the locatives *to* and *into* pose more problems for the bilinguals (especially the French-dominant ones) than for the monolinguals due to the lack of distinction in French between *to* and *at* (both expressed by *à*) and *in* and *into* (both expressed by *dans*). One of the predictions of this hypothesis would be that *to* and *into* are acquired by French-English bilinguals at a slower rate than they are by English monolinguals.

This being said, it should be pointed out that even in those cases in which interlanguage transfer offers a satisfactory explanation for a large number of bilinguals' errors, one cannot easily dismiss the possibility of overgeneralization working to the exclusion of, or in combination with, interlanguage transfer. For example, it is possible that in our own findings, the influence of French *à* is responsible for the bilinguals' nonstandard use of *at* with names of cities (example: *We go at Quebec, We go at Montreal*) whereas the process of overgeneralization has given rise to their use of constructions such as *We go at my cousin's, We go at my friend's*, etc., for which there are no equivalent structures with *à* in French. On the other hand, overgeneralization of *at* for *to* may have first given rise to constructions such as *We go at my cousin's, We go at the store*, etc., and the only influence of French has been to extend the use of *at* to constructions of the type *at Montreal, at Toronto*, etc. Similarly, overgeneralization of *at* to environments requiring *to* may be accelerated or reinforced by the lack of a distinction between *to* and *at* in French.

It seems to us then that in cases where either interlanguage transfer or overgeneralization offers a plausible explanation of the data, it does not follow that the possible influence of the other process should be written off. As has been pointed out frequently in the literature on second language acquisition (cf. Selinker, Swain and Dumas, 1975; Swain, 1975; Tarone, Cohen and Dumas, 1976) and in our own analyses of Ontarian French (cf. Canale, Mougeon, Bélanger and Ituen, 1977; Mougeon, Bélanger, Canale and Ituen, 1977), it is often difficult, if not impossible, to sort out the influence of either or both factors in second language learning.

Notes

The research reported on in this paper was supported by grants from the Secretary of State of Canada and the Ontario Institute for Studies in Education. We wish to thank Ellen Bialystok and Bernard Spolsky for helpful discussion of some of the ideas presented here. Of course we are solely responsible for all forms of error.

1. Redundant uses and misuses are not represented in the tables since there were too few cases of either type and they do not fit into the framework of the "obligatory context" test item.

2. Clark qualifies his hypothesis by suggesting that it may be restricted to a comprehension model of acquisition. Obviously, our data are based directly on speech production. Nonetheless, it seems that the question of whether or not the "complexity hypothesis" can be extended to a production model of acquisition is still an open one, and in this light our data may be relevant.

3. It is interesting to note that various researchers (e.g., Bailey, Madden and Krashen, 1974; Dulay and Burt, 1974d; Larsen-Freeman, 1976) claim to have found an acquisition

order of English morphemes common to second language learners (children and adults) regardless of native language background. However, if there is such a "universal order" of acquisition of these morphemes, one wonders why it is not the same order found by Brown (1973) for English monolinguals. See Rosansky (1976) for discussion of the methodology and statistical analyses employed in the second language acquisition studies.

4. It is possible that these three cases of omission involve nothing more than phonetic reduction of *to* which we were unable to distinguish from grammatical omission of *to*.

5. Although substitution of the locative *at* for *to* is still high among the grade 5 bilinguals (15/29 cases), there is a noticeable decrease in the frequency of this type of error by comparison to the grade 2 bilinguals (39/45 substitutions of *at* for *to*). The decline of this particular error continues throughout the academic years: Mougeon and Hébrard (1975a, b) found that there were few errors of this type in the speech of grade 9 bilinguals and none in the speech of grade 12 bilinguals from the same localities. However, based on recent interviews we have conducted in localities where francophones outnumber anglophones, substitution of *at* for *to* seems to persist through grade 12. It may be that the bilinguals' lower level of exposure to standard English in such localities is largely responsible for the fossilization of this nonstandard usage. See Mougeon, Canale and Belanger (to appear) for discussion of the role of demographic strength in language acquisition among Franco-Ontarians.

Chapter 13

The Developmental Aspects of Second Language Acquisition Revisited

Alberto Rey

The present investigation will attempt to determine if it is still possible to isolate some of the differentiating variables in the linguistic behavior of those who are at differing stages of second language acquisition if one does some minor but very critical methodological modifications of the Lambert (1956) study; and in turn test the usefulness of the WAT as a measure of bilingual proficiency. The modifications were as follows: (1) the target language was Spanish—Lambert's was French; (2) for the choice stimuli the Ss could respond in either or both languages—Lambert's Ss used either language, not both; and (3) the native speaker group was more strictly controlled and more similar to the nonnative groups in age and educational background—Lambert's native group consisted simply of "mature" native French speakers living in this country who know and daily use English.

The specific developmental aspects of bilingual proficiency studied were: (1) associational fluency, (2) free associations, (3) word-order influence, (4) stimulus provocativeness, (5) associational stereotypy, (6) vocabulary commonness, and (7) speed of primary response (latency).

Methodology

Subjects

Three groups of 10 Ss each were chosen to differ with respect to experience in Spanish. The groups were from the Cuban population of Miami, Florida and the native American population of metropolitan Washington, D.C. All of the Ss were between 18 and 23 years of age and college educated. The Ss were divided as to their experience in Spanish—American undergraduate junior or senior college level students majoring in Spanish (U), American graduate Spanish students (G), and native Spanish speakers (C). The nonnative Spanish speakers all had an average of B or better in their Spanish course work. All of the C subjects had been in the United States for 6 to 10 years and had two to four years of college education in the United States.

Procedure

The procedure and format followed for the WAT was the continuous free association method, the same method used by Lambert. For the first four words, the Ss were asked to respond with single word associations in either or both languages. After the Ss finished responding to the last "choice" stimulus word they were instructed to give as many associations as they could in the same language as the stimulus word for a period of 45 seconds. The stimuli were given in the series of five English followed by ten Spanish and finally by five English words. The a-b-b-a order was used to control for the effects of practice and fatigue as a function of time in the experimental session. The Spanish words were translation equivalents of the English words, which were selected from among the most frequently used and matched for frequency of occurrence, from Eaton (1940).

The WAT, as previously stated, consisted of "choice" stimuli and translation equivalents or "restricted stimuli. The choice stimuli were: *night, pequeño, musica,* and *poor.* The restricted stimuli chosen, in order of presentation were: *bad, home, brother, service, table, paz, silla, prosperidad, hijo, negocio, malo, casa, hermano, servicio, mesa, peace, chair, prosperity, son,* and *business.* The Ss' responses to the stimuli were recorded for later analysis.

Results

The data recorded were subjected to the series of different analyses mentioned earlier. Each analysis is presented in the form of a hypothesis.

Hypothesis A

As bilinguals progress in experience with a particular language, their number of associational responses to stimulus words in that language will be greater.

The average number of responses for each group in both languages was noted for the restricted stimuli to determine the groups' associational fluency. A higher number of responses to a stimulus word would be a result of that stimulus word's greater meaningfulness to the S. In other words, as one progresses in experience with a language, individual words become more meaningful to that individual. The average number of responses for each group may be seen in *Table 13.1.* Because of large within-group variability, the nonparametric Mann-Whitney U test (Mendenhall and Ramey, 1973), to test for reliability of group differences, was used. No significant differences were found for any of the S group pairings for either language, the highest level of confidence found was that for the C and G

Table 13.1

Mean number of responses for restricted stimuli

C group		G group		U group	
English	Spanish	English	Spanish	English	Spanish
90.8	85.7	87.9	80.3	93.8	85.7

group in Spanish, U (10,10) = 39, at greater than the 20 percent level. The similarity between the three groups in both languages can be interpreted positively as meaning that both the U and G groups achieved a native-like associational fluency in Spanish; however, since the U group's total number of associations in Spanish was not reliably smaller than either the G or C group, Hypothesis A was not confirmed.

Hypothesis B

As bilinguals progress in experience with a particular language, their numbers of associational responses in that language will be greater when given a choice of languages to use.

Table 13.2

Mean number and percentage of responses for choice stimuli

C group		G group		U group	
English	Spanish	English	Spanish	English	Spanish
173 (53%)	153 (47%)	138 (39%)	219 (61%)	162 (47%)	186 (53%)

All of the Ss were given two Spanish and two English words and asked to respond to the stimuli in either or both languages. This procedure was used to determine if the U group would give a smaller number or percentage of Spanish associations than the G group and if the G group would give fewer than the C group. *Table 13.2* represents the mean number and percentage scores for the "choice" stimuli. When these "choice" responses were analyzed to determine if one group gave a significantly larger mean number or percentage of Spanish responses than any other group, it was found that none of the groups had a reliably different score; the highest level of confidence was for the comparison between the C and G groups, U (10,10) = 37.5, at greater than the 17 percent level. It should be pointed out that the only reliably significant difference that was found was for the difference between the means of the English and Spanish responses of the G group, $U = 25 - p < .05$. Again, since the U group did not give a reliably smaller mean number of Spanish responses to the choice stimuli than either the G or C group, Hypothesis B was not confirmed.

Hypothesis C

As bilinguals progress in experience with a particular language, their speed of primary response will be faster.

The speed of primary response to each restricted stimulus word was noted, to the nearest tenth of a second, to determine the Ss' latency of response in English and Spanish. *Table 13.3* shows the speed of primary responses (the first or initial responses) for each group for the restricted stimuli of each language.

The average speed of primary response to the English stimuli were not found to be significantly different for any of the group pairings, all at U (10,10) >

Table 13.3
Average speed of primary response
for restricted stimuli (in seconds)

C group		G group		U group	
English	Spanish	English	Spanish	English	Spanish
3.7	4.4	4.3	3.9	·3.9	5.4

45, greater than the 36 percent level of confidence. The average speed of primary response to the Spanish stimuli were found to be significantly different between the C and U groups ($U = 27$, $p < .05$) and the U and G groups ($U = 32$, $p < .10$), with both the G and C groups being faster than the U group. It should also be pointed out that the U group also was significantly slower in their Spanish responses than in their English responses ($U = 32$, $p < .10$). Hypothesis C was confirmed.

Hypothesis D

As bilinguals progress in experience with a particular language, their associational responses in that language will be more affected by the habitual word order of that language.

Since there appears to be a habitual word order in each language, this order should be evident in the associational responses. The general adjective-noun order in English is that the adjective precedes nouns while in Spanish adjectives generally follow nouns. It was therefore predicted that the G group would more closely approximate the C group's word order than would the U group.

Each S was assigned a rating that indicated the percentage of adjective responses to the Spanish noun stimulus words—*paz, silla, prosperidad, hijo, negocio, casa, hermano, servicio,* and *mesa.* The average percentage scores for each group is listed in *Table 13.4.*

Table 13.4
Average percentage of adjective
responses to Spanish noun stimuli

C group	G group	U group
16.8	12.6	9.0

The C and U and the G and U group pairings were found to be significantly different—$U = 32.5$, $p < .10$ and $U = 30.5$, $p < .08$ respectively. The C-G groups were found to be not reliably different $U = 46$, $p > .40$. Hypothesis D was confirmed.

Hypothesis E

As bilinguals progress in experience with a particular language, their associational responses will approach the pattern of provocativeness of stimulus words shown by native speakers of that language.

If one stimulus word elicits more associational responses then that word may be considered more provocative. *Table 13.5* shows the total number of responses to each stimulus word of each group along with the corresponding high to low provocativeness ranking for each S group. It was predicted that the G group would more closely approach the Spanish ranking pattern of the C group than would the U group.

It was found that for the English responses the correlation coefficients between the C and U, the C and G, and the U and G groups were, respectively, .67, .84, and .73. The highest degree of correlation was for the C and G groups, but it should be noted that this was for the English responses, not the Spanish responses. For the Spanish responses the correlation coefficients were .78 (C and U), .73 (C and G), and .66 (U and G). The correlations were not in the general

Table 13.5
Provocativeness—total number and intra-group ranking for restricted stimuli

Stimuli	C group		G group		U group	
	Total	Ranking	Total	Ranking	Total	Ranking
Bad	73	9	78	8	85	7
Home	110	2	111	1	118	1
Brother	86	8	82	6	74	9-10
Service	68	10	69	10	81	8
Table	112	1	105	2	103	4
Peace	89	5	85	5	74	9-10
Chair	87	6-7	100	3	106	2
Prosperity	87	6-7	71	9	91	6
Son	105	3	97	4	102	5
Business	91	4	81	7	104	3
Malo	65	10	74	7	50	10
Casa	104	2	101	1	99	1
Hermano	80	6	83	5	89	4
Servicio	73	8	55	10	72	9
Mesa	122	1	90	3	98	2
Paz	83	5	69	9	75	7
Silla	89	4	86	4	76	6
Prosperidad	66	9	71	8	74	8
Hijo	98	3	97	2	90	3
Negocio	77	7	77	6	87	5

direction predicted since the C and U groups had the highest value. Hypothesis E was not confirmed.

It should be pointed out, however, that if one disregards the rankings and considers only the total responses for each of the Spanish stimuli, then the G group is more similar to the C group than the U group. For seven of the Spanish stimuli—*silla, prosperidad, hijo, negocio, malo, casa,* and *hermano*—the G group was closest to the totals of the C group for only three of the Spanish stimuli—*paz, servicio,* and *mesa.* Also, if one follows this type of analysis for the English responses, the same type or closeness of relationship may be observed—the G group is closer to the C group in the totals of eight of the stimulus words, while the U group is closer to the C group for only two of the words.

Hypothesis F

As bilinguals progress in experience with a particular language, their responses will exhibit a decrease in associational stereotypy in that language.

It was predicted that since individuals with less experience in Spanish would have a more limited vocabulary, those individuals would therefore exhibit more stereotypy in their associational responses. That is to say, the U group would exhibit the most stereotypy, the G group would exhibit less, and the C group would exhibit the least stereotypy.

To determine the degree or amount of stereotypy present in the responses, each S's first two responses were noted. If *grande* were given as a first or second response to *mesa* by all 10 Ss in each group, then *mesa* would receive a stretotypy score of 10. A maximum score of 20 would be achieved if all of the Ss in a group gave the same first two responses, while a 0 would mean that none of the responses were repeated by any of the Ss. *Table 13.6* shows the mean stereotypy scores for both the English and Spanish stimulus words.

Table 13.6
Mean stereotypy scores for restricted stimuli

C group		G group		U group	
English	Spanish	English	Spanish	English	Spanish
10.6	10.1	9.8	10.8	8.6	9.3

None of the group pairings proved to be significantly different for either language, with the C and U groups' English stereotypy scores having the greatest level of confidence, $U = 35, p > .13$. Hypothesis F was not confirmed.

Hypothesis G

As bilinguals progress in experience with a particular language, the commonness of the associational responses in that language will decrease.

The first two and last two responses of each S for both the English and Spanish stimulus words were used as a sample of that S's responses. Each of these

None of the group pairings were found to be significantly different in the commonness of the Spanish responses, with the G and U mean comparison having the highest level of confidence, $U = 36, p > .15$. The differences between the means that proved to have a high level of confidence were for the English responses was then assigned a value based on the English and Spanish word-frequency tabulations listed in Eaton (1940). A value of 1 was assigned to a response if it appeared among the first 500 words, a value of 1.5 for responses among the second 500 words, and so on up to the least frequently used words.

Table 13.7
Mean commonness ratings

C group		G group		U group	
English	Spanish	English	Spanish	English	Spanish
2.33	2.59	2.77	2.35	2.98	2.38

responses, where the C group gave significantly more common responses than either the G or U groups, $U = 31, p < .09$ and $U = 12, p < .002$. Also, both the U and G groups' Spanish responses were significantly more common than each group's own English responses, with $U = 18, p > .01$ and $U = 32, p > .1$. Hypothesis G was not confirmed.

Summary and Conclusions

In this investigation three groups of Ss at different stages of skill in the Spanish language were asked to give continuous free associations to a set of Spanish and English stimulus words. The three groups of Ss consisted of a native American group of undergraduate Spanish majors at a junior or senior level of Spanish, U; a native American group of graduate students majoring in Spanish, G; and a native Spanish (Cuban) group of undergraduates at the junior and senior college level in the United States, C. The three groups were found to be reliably different in only two of the seven areas analyzed: speed of primary response and word-order influence.

A comparison of the results of this study to those in the Lambert (1956) study shows some very interesting contrasts. Of the seven hypotheses tested in the present investigation, only two were confirmed—word-order influence and speed of primary response. Of these two confirmed hypotheses, only one was actually tested in the Lambert study, word-order influence, which was not confirmed, since the general conclusion was that the two nonnative French groups were equally affected by the habitual French word-order. Of the remaining five hypotheses not confirmed here, four were confirmed in the Lambert study—associational fluency, free associations, stimulus provocativeness, and vocabulary commonness.

The nonnative Spanish groups (G and U) were found not to differ significantly from the native Spanish group (C) in the first five areas previously mentioned, while there weren't any significant differences found between the G and C groups in any of the areas tested. These group similarities could be due to: (1) a high level of foreign language proficiency that can be achieved through variables other than education in the foreign language (in the case of the G and U not being significantly different and approaching the native fluency of the C group in five areas), (2) the possibility that the Spanish language proficiency of the C group has suffered somewhat because of the length of English language contact (as much as ten years of living and studying in the United States) or (3) the possibility that the word association test (WAT) is not sensitive enough or valid as a measure of foreign language proficiency.

Detractors of the WAT could point to the present investigation and find problems encountered in the use of word associations as a guide or index to bilingual achievement since only two hypotheses were confirmed and, in turn, suggest other types of tests that might have shown better indexes of achievement. This investigator would argue with these individuals that the WAT is a completely valid, extremely objective, and a readily quantifiable test of bilingual proficiency. It is quite possible that because of the very fact that it is so objective that the results of this investigation contrasted with those of the Lambert study. The differences in the results were probably not due to the deficiencies in the WAT but due, at least in part, to the stricter controls of the native foreign language (Spanish) Ss mentioned in the beginning of this study, which resulted in much more similar S populations. The finding that two differentiating variables were found in the linguistic behavior of individuals who were at different stages or levels of bilingual proficiency enforces the value of the WAT as a measure of bilingual proficiency.

If one then accepts the value of the WAT as a measure of bilingual proficiency, since it did measure or isolate two differentiating variables in the linguistic behavior of individuals who were at different stages of second language acquisition, and if one accepts the explanations offered for the similarities between the groups, the importance of the S group differences still remains to be discussed. The Spanish word-order influence and the speed of primary response to Spanish stimuli were both found to be significantly different between the C and G groups. This finding means that both of these variables were equally important in determining bilingual proficiency. Although Lambert (1956:99) does mention the importance of speed of primary response or automaticity—"A central characteristic of the process of thinking in a language is its automaticity as seen in behavior, a characteristic which the apprentice lacks in his second language," he only found that word-order influence equally affected both the undergraduate and graduate students and both were less affected than the native group. The importance of the finding of the present investigation that word-order influence was a differentiating variable used to distinguish between the U group and the C and G groups is that it stresses the relatively late influence a foreign language's habitual word-order has on students of that foreign language. In regard to the importance of the other differentiating variable found in this investigation, speed of primary response, this finding further substantiates the views on the importance of speed of primary response as a test of bilinguality. "The relative speed of response ... may be fruitfully used either as a single test of bilinguality or in conjunction with a complete battery of tests" (Lambert, 1956:103). This researcher would agree with the importance of this test for bilinguality but would strongly stress the importance of using a complete battery of tests on the word associations of individuals to determine the true picture of the complexity of bilingualism.

Chapter 14

The Acquisition
of German as a
Second Language

William D. Keel

In this paper we will examine certain significant errors which students from different language backgrounds (English, Thai, Arabic, Kazakh and Spanish) exhibit in their acquisition of the phonological system of Modern Standard German. Our purpose will be to determine in what way these errors bear on the principles of phonological theory, in particular the construct "complement of," a central notion in the recently advanced theory of atomic phonology (cf. Dinnsen 1976a, b; Dinnsen and Eckman, 1976). We will argue that the evidence from the phonological errors surveyed in this study support an extension of the application of the construct "complement of." Previous research has established the validity of the construct "complement of" for the proper characterization of rule generalization. In this paper we will argue that complement relations obtain not only between rules, but between individual segments. We will then show that the range of phonological substitutes for difficult to learn phonological segments is limited by the nature of the complement relations which obtain between phonological segments.

During the last few years we have witnessed significant changes in the views of psychologists and linguists on second language acquisition. Our attention is no longer focused solely on the description of a linguistic system to be acquired, but on how the learner perceives and interprets that system in the process of language acquisition. The errors which the language learner makes reveal his hypotheses concerning the structure of the new language with which he is confronted.

> *Underlying second language learning are cognitive processes that seem similar to those that determine the acquisition of the first language by the child and that characterize various types of "simplified" or "reduced"*

> *speech forms such as pidgin languages. Errors are not to be viewed as pathological manifestations to be eradicated, but constitute instead the most direct evidence of the learner's hypotheses and strategies.*   Valdman, 1975:219

While no final determination has been made concerning the similarity of first language acquisition and second language acquisition, there appears to be general agreement that the second language learner participates actively in the learning process. In such a cognitive model of second language acquisition Valdman posits a Language Learning and Acquisition Device (LLAD) (Valdman, 1975:221-222) which functions to mediate between the second language data and the learner's rules which characterize that data.

Data   →   LLAD   →   Rules

Cognitive model of second language learning.

Such an assumption has far-reaching implications for second language instruction (cf. Valdman, 1975). However, we are interested in the implications that such a model of second language learning may have for linguistic theory. If we assume that the language learner is formulating generalizations or hypotheses based on the second language data, then his attempts to produce utterances in the second language will expose those categories of grammar where the second language learner's hypotheses differ from those of the native speaker. We will argue that such differences in the phonological systems of native and nonnative speakers revealed by the errors of second language learners derive from a principle which is basic to the theory of atomic phonology.

In what follows, we will consider the difficulties which nonnative speakers evidence in acquiring the system of obstruent consonants in Modern Standard German and then proceed to a discussion of the implications of these difficulties for the assumptions of atomic phonology.

Labial		Coronal				Velar		
p	b	t	d			k	g	Stop
f	v	s	z	š	ç	x		Fricative
pᶠ		tˢ						Affricate

Obstruent Consonants of Modern Standard German

[This table differs from that found in Moulton, 1962:27. ž has been omitted since it only occurs in infrequent foreign words. I have added the labial and coronal affricates since it is generally argued that they exhibit the distributional character- istics of single consonants in German.]

Kazakh—German (Rabinowitsch, 1971). Speakers of Kazkh (a member of the northwestern group of Turkic languages) have particular difficulty in acquiring the labial obstruent consonants in learning German. Specifically, the Kazakh labial obstruent system only distinguishes a voiceless stop [p] and a voiced stop [b]. In attempting to produce the German labial fricatives the Kazakh student substitutes his [p] for German [f] and his [b] for German [v]. We thus find such common pronunciation errors as:

['ape] instead of ['afe]   *Affe* "ape"
['berden] instead of ['veːrdən]   *werden* "to become"   (p. 238)

The phonological problem remains even though the articulation of [f] and [v] presents no major difficulty. This is evidenced by the frequent occurrence of hypercorrect forms such as:

[fer'fekit] instead of ['perfekt]   *Perfekt* "perfect, n."
['ariveit] instead of ['arbaet]   *Arbeit* "work"   (p. 239)

Similarly, the Kazakh speaker substitutes [p] for the German labial affricate [f], e.g.:

['apel] instead of ['apᶠel]   *Apfel* "apple"
['porte] instead of ['pᶠortə]   *Pforte* "gate"   (p. 239)

Within the class of coronal obstruents the Kazakh speaker is able to distinguish all the German obstruents except for the affricate [tˢ]. However, in this case the Kazakh speaker substitutes the voiceless fricative [s] for the affricate, rather than the voiceless stop [t], e.g.:

['zese] instead of ['zetˢə]   *setze* "I set"   (p. 240)

The dorso-palatal fricative [ç] and the velar fricative [x] in German are replaced by Kazakh students with the voiceless stops [k] and [q], respectively:

[daq] instead of [dax]   *Dach* "roof"
['dekir] instead of [deçər]   *Dächer* "rooves"   (p. 240)

Iraqi Arabic—German (Lerchner, 1971; Kühnel, 1971). The speaker of Iraqi Arabic encounters similar problems in acquiring the German phonological system. As in Kazakh the phonological distinctions in the labial obstruents are limited to two. However, in place of the Kazakh opposition *voiced/voiceless* we find the opposition *continuant/noncontinuant*. Thus, for German [p] the Iraqi Arabic student substitutes his [b] and for German [v] he substitutes his [f], e.g.:

[ba'biːr] instead of [pa'piːr]   *Papier* "paper"
[faen] instead of [vaen]   *Wein* "wine"   (Kühnel:54-55)

For the labial and coronal affricates [pᶠ] and [tˢ] in German, speakers of Iraqi Arabic substitute the voiceless fricatives [f] and [s], respectively. (Kühnel: 55, with no examples given.) For the dorso-palatal fricative [ç], Arabic [š] is substituted.

Thai—German (Lange, 1971). For Thai speakers learning German the phonological difficulties follow a similar pattern. With the absence of voiced labial and coronal fricatives in Thai, the students substitute the voiceless fricatives: [f] instead of German [v] and [s] instead of German [z]. (Pp. 180-181, no examples given; Thai speakers who know English as a second language encounter further problems due to graphemic correspondence of German [v] and English [w].)

For the labial and coronal affricates the Thai students substitute the voiceless fricatives. Thus, German [pᶠ] and [tˢ] are replaced by [f] and [s], respectively (p. 181).

The nonanterior obstruents in German are particularly difficult for Thai speakers. The noncoronal obstruents [g], [x] and [ç] are all replaced by [k]. (In this class Thai only distinguishes an aspirated and an unaspirated voiceless stop, p. 180-181.) Interestingly, Thai students substitute the native coronal affricate [tš] for the German fricative [š] (p. 180).

Peruvian Spanish—German (Zierer, 1961). The principal difficulty for Spanish speakers learning German is the acquisition of phonological distinctions in the vowel system of German. As far as the obstruent system is concerned the problems are minimal. However, we again encounter substitutions for the German affricates: [f] instead of [pᶠ] and [s] instead of [tˢ] (p. 27).

[funt] instead of [pᶠunt]	*Pfund* "pound"	
[soːk] instead of [tˢoːk]	*zog* "pulled"	(pp. 27-28)

In addition, Spanish speakers have some difficulty with the velar and dorso-palatal fricatives

In addition, Spanish speakers have some difficulty with the velar and dorso-palatal fricatives [x] and [ç] for which they substitute the voiceless velar stop [k]:

[buːk] instead of [buːx]	*Buch* "book"	
[zik] instead of [ziç]	*sich* "3rd person reflexive pronoun"	(p. 27)

English—German (Moulton, 1962). English (American) students similarly have relatively few problems with the German obstruents (if we ignore phonetic details). The major difficulty is presented by the fricative pair [x] and [ç]. Most students will substitute [k] for [x]:

[tuːk] instead of [tuːx]	*Tuch* "towel, cloth"	
[hoːk] instead of [hoːx]	*hoch* "high"	
[dak] instead of [dax]	*Dach* "roof"	(cf. p. 28)

Beginning students (English speaking) also substitute [k] for [ç] at first:

[ik] instead of [iç]   *ich* "I"   (cf. p. 31)

When students learn to differentiate German [x] and [ç] according to their distribution after back and front vowels, respectively, they begin to substitute their [š] for the German [ç]:

[iš] instead of [iç]   *ich* "I"   (cf. p. 31)

As with students of other language backgrounds English speakers experience difficulty acquiring the labial and coronal affricates [pᶠ] and [tˢ]. (Moulton (1962) regards these segments as clusters.) Paralleling the substitutions of the older groups surveyed, the English speakers replace these affricates with the voiceless fricatives [f] and [s], respectively:

[flaome] instead of [pᶠlaome]   *Pflaume* "plum"
[feːrt] instead of [pᶠeːrt]   *Pferd* "horse"
[suːk] instead of [tˢuːk]   *Zug* "train"
[saːl] instead of [tˢaːl]   *Zahl* "number"

(Many Germans living in the Middle and Low German dialect areas do not pronounce standard initial [pᶠ-]; they substitute [f] for the affricate reflecting the lack of the affricate in those dialects.)

Summary of Phonological Errors

	Phonological Substitutions				
German Obstruents	*Kazakh*	*Arabic*	*Thai*	*Spanish*	*English*
p	—	b	—	—	—
b	—	—	—	—	—
f	p	—	—	—	—
v	b	f	f	—	—
pᶠ	p	f	f	f	f
t	—	—	—	—	—
d	—	—	—	—	—
s	—	—	—	—	—
z	—	—	s	—	—
tˢ	s	s	s	s	s
k	—	—	—	—	—
g	—	—	k	—	—
x	q	—	k	k	k
ç	k	š	k	k	k
š	—	—	tš	—	—

Table of Phonological Substitutions

From the above table we can see that in every case the labial and coronal affricates ([pᶠ] and [tˢ]) were reanalyzed by the language students as the voiceless fricatives [f] and [s], except by speakers of Kazakh who had no voiceless labial fricative in their native inventory. The second group of obstruents which posed major difficulties was the pair of fricatives [x] and [ç]. In this case the most frequent substitution was the voiceless stop [k]. Thai, Spanish, and English speakers failed to distinguish the two fricatives on the basis of their distribution following back or front vowels. Kazakh and Arabic speakers maintained the distributional distinction, but substituted uvular and velar stops [q] and [k] in the case of Kazakh, and the fricatives [x] and [š] in the case of Arabic. A further point of difficulty, for the speakers of the non-Indo-European languages surveyed, was the labial voiced fricative [v]. In this case the voiceless labial fricative [f] was the typical replacement, with Kazakh speakers substituting the voiced labial stop [b] in the absence of any labial fricatives. Substitutions restricted to one language group were: Kazakh speakers— [p] for [f]; Iraqi Arabic speakers— [b] for [p]; Thai speakers— [s] for [z], [k] for [g], and [tš] for [š]. The obstruent [b], [t], [d], [s], [k] posed no difficulty for any of the non-German-speaking groups.

Two obvious points which can be made with regard to the survey are: learners of German have difficulty with phonological distinctions which are absent in their native language, and failing to analyze the distinction correctly—forming the wrong hypothesis—they substitute a phonological segment from their native language in place of the target language segment to be acquired. Such statements are typical of those found in studies within a contrastive analysis framework (cf. Moulton, 1962).

The question we would like to pose in this paper is *why* do nonnative speakers learning German substitute the particular segments discussed above to the exclusion of others, which at first glance seem quite plausible? That is, does the choice of the substitute segment derive from any general principle in linguistic theory? This is particularly interesting given the parallelity of substitutions made by speakers from several language families.

Typically, contrastive analysis studies characterize such learner substitutions as the "corresponding" or "closest" segment with respect to the difficult to acquire segment. While such statements are certainly true, assuming one agrees on the definition of the terms "corresponding" and "closest," they lack explicitness and provide no basis for choosing between two or more segments, which are plausible substitutes for the new segment.

For instance, all of the student groups surveyed had difficulty with the labial affricate [pᶠ]. Those students whose language contained both [p] and [f] *invariably* substituted the fricative for the affricate. Only in the case of the Kazakh students, where [f] was not part of the native inventory, do we find [p] as a substitute for the German affricate. It seems that while both [p] and [f] are *plausible* substitutes for [pᶠ], [p] is chosen only in the absence of [f].

Apparently, the segments involved are subject to a hierarchy which is based on some universal principle. This is no doubt related to Jakobson's (1968) implicational universals of first language acquisition. That is, the acquisition of *fricatives* implies the presence of *stops* in the child's language (Jakobson, p. 67). Initially, the child substitutes the "corresponding" stop for the fricative [p] – [f], [t] – [s], etc. (p. 68). Similarly, the acquisition of affricates implies the presence of the corresponding stop and fricative in the child's language. Until an affricate is acquired the child substitutes either the *stop* or *fricative* of the same series (labial, velar, etc.). That is, either [p] or [f] are substituted for [p^f] (pp. 74-75).

While Jakobson's implicational universals of first language acquisition account for *most* of the phonological substitutions encountered in this survey ([p] for [f], [k] for [x]-[ç], etc.) they, too, are not explicit enough to provide us with a proper characterization of the acquisition of the German affricates. Jakobson's statement regarding first language acquisition of affricates allows either the corresponding stop or fricative to replace the affricate. The evidence presented here indicates that we must constrain the possible substitutes for the affricates in second language acquisition, so that only those substitutions which can be empirically confirmed are predicted.

The most uniform substitution involves the coronal affricate [t^s]. All learners commonly made the substitution of [s]. The question immediately arises: Why not [t]? Certainly the possibility of one of these groups substituting [t] for [t^s] seems plausible. In the parallel case of the labial affricate [p^f] we find [f] the general choice as a substitute, with [p] chosen only in Kazakh where [f] was not in the native inventory. If our introductory assumptions concerning the role of the second language learner are correct, then an adequate linguistic theory will have to account for this apparent lack of choice in the substitution of difficult to learn phonological segments.

If we compare the feature specifications—including redundancies—of the segments concerned, a pattern in these choices begins to emerge:

t	s	t^s
+consonantal	.	.
−sonorant	.	.
+coronal	.	.
+anterior	.	.
−voice	.	.
−continuant	+continuant	−continuant
−strident	+strident	+strident
−del. release	+del. release	+del. release

While both the stop and the fricative share features with the affricate, it is readily seen that the fricative shares "more" features with the affricate than the stop. I believe that we can establish that the relationship between fricative and affricate as well as the relationship between stop and affricate are subsumed under the notion complement relation, a concept central to the theory of atomic phonology. This will then enable us to formulate a principle which correctly constrains the choice of phonological substitutes in the acquisition of a second language.

Briefly, atomic phonology characterizes two rules as complements, as being in a complement relation, if those shared, i.e., identical, features in the structural descriptions of the two rules are sufficient to define all and only those input representations defined by the two rules together. The complement relation may be illustrated by the following pair of rules:

1.   stop obstruents are voiceless word-finally.

$$\begin{bmatrix} -\text{sonorant} \\ -\text{continuant} \end{bmatrix} \rightarrow [-\text{voice}] \quad / \underline{\quad} \#$$

2.   continuant obstruents are voiceless word-finally.

$$\begin{bmatrix} -\text{sonorant} \\ +\text{continuant} \end{bmatrix} \rightarrow [-\text{voice}] \quad / \underline{\quad} \#$$

precisely the set of input representations defined by the two rules jointly. (For a more complete discussion of complement rules and atomic phonology cf. Dinnsen, 1976a.)

More recently it has been argued that such complement relations obtain between single segments effecting a same structural change (cf. Keel, 1977). It therefore seems plausible that the notion "complement of" may be extended to define certain relationships which obtain between individual phonological segments. Two segments would be defined as complement segments if those identical features shared by the two segments are sufficient to define precisely the two segments alone. To illustrate this we may return to the coronal segments [t], [s], [tˢ]. Note that the affricate and the fricative form a complement relation on the basis of the features identical to the two segments, all features except the specification for the feature [continuant]. Note further that the affricate and the stop form a complement relation on the basis of the shared identical features, all features except the specification for the features [strident] and [del. release]. However, since both [t] and [s] are in a complement relation with the segment to be acquired, [tˢ], the simple notion "complement of" is not sufficient to constrain the choice of the phonological substitute.

I propose that we consider the notion of a *minimal complement segment.* A minimal complement segment would be defined as follows: Given two segments, both of which are complements of a third segment, that segment is the minimal complement which has the fewest nonidentical feature specifications with respect to the third segment. We would thus constrain the choice of a substitute segment to the minimal complement segment within the inventory of the nontarget language. This provides us with a basis for predicting which segment in the learner's inventory will be substituted for the difficult to acquire segment. In formulating *his* hypothesis with regard to the phonological system of the target language the learner seems to analyze those segments not present in his native language as their minimal complements in his own language.

Thus, the learner having the choice between [t] and [s] as substitutes for [tˢ] chooses [s], since [s] has the fewest nonidentical features in common with the affricate. The substitutes for the labial affricate [p^f] pattern the same way: only where the minimal complement segment was not present (Kazakh) was [p] chosen, otherwise [f].

The other phonological substitutions—replacement of velar fricatives by voiceless stop, etc.—follow a similar pattern, although in these cases the choice of substitutes is restricted essentially by the native inventory. Thus the "complement of" notion while sufficient does not appear to be a necessary element in those cases.

In summary, we have surveyed a series of phonological errors—phonological substitutions—in the acquisition of German made by several groups of non-German speakers. While the difficulty in acquiring foreign segments is to a large extent determined by their absence in the native inventory, we find no principled explanation for the parallelity of choice of substitutes for difficult to acquire segments evidenced by students from several language families. Neither contrastive analysis, nor Jakobson's implicational universals of first language acquisition provide an explicit enough framework for predicting substitutes, where plausible choices exist. A possible solution is suggested which extends atomic phonology's concept "complement of" to include relationships which obtain between phonological segments. The choice of phonological substitutes in second language acquisition is then limited to the minimal complement of the difficult to acquire segment within the native inventory. If this characterization of the strategies involved in the learner's acquisition of a phonological system is valid, then the concept "complement of" has broader application than was previously thought. Not only does it play a crucial role in constraining variation on a phonological process; it also functions in second language acquisition as the learner forms his hypotheses regarding the phonological system of the target language.

Chapter 15

Two Birds
with One Stone:
Teaching a
Standard Dialect
to Mixed Classes

Rodolfo J. Cortina
Oliver T. Myers

We are proposing a solution to a highly specialized type of language acquisition problem, because we have a definite need for such a consideration in our own teaching and because we have found no published studies that deal with precisely this situation. Given the following circumstances: a third-year college language skills course (typically composition and conversation), with a mixed student population (those whose first language is English and whose first language is a dialect of the target language), how does one make maximum use of the presence of both categories of student in an integrated class approach (i.e., without dividing the class into two separate groups, or treating the class as a completely homogeneous body)? Theoretical and applied papers alike have concentrated on the beginning stages of second language acquisition;[1] similarly the literature on second dialect acquisition has focused on homogeneous classes.[2] We now wish to explore the problems posed by the actual situation that we have encountered, describe it in general terms, and then suggest a possible solution with specific illustrations where the target language (or target dialect) is New World Standard Spanish (NWSS).

We assume that the class is composed of two basic types of student, in about equal numbers: (1) students whose native language is English and who have achieved their current level of proficiency in FL classes; these are the second language students (SL's), and may be considered fairly homogeneous for our immediate purposes; (2) the second dialect students (SD's), who acquired a given dialect of the classroom standard as their first language, who may or may not have received formal training in their dialect, and/or in the target dialect, and who have been assigned by the academic unit to this level (already an implication of remediation); this group is clearly not homogeneous, but will share more characteristics among themselves than with any of the SL group.

If the course is conducted as a series of one-to-one transactions, there will be no feedback from the performance of any one student on the development of skills by any other. This will also require essentially individualized instruction, with the burden on the instructor to diagnose the initial level of skill on entry, set individualized tasks, and evaluate final performance on the basis of individual progress.[3] We suggest that this is inefficient, both in its use of the instructor's time and in the waste of potential resources in the class.

If the course attempts full participation from all those present, then a dilemma arises with respect to standards. Either the SD's are favored, as when the command of idiom or fluency is the criterion; or the SL's gain an advantage, if the communication of acceptable ideas or the construction of paragraphs is paramount (i.e., nonlinguistic skills or factors), or further, as when the SD's use a dialect of less social prestige than the target. In the latter instance, there could be no utilization of the SD students as a resource, since their usage would have been found to be defective; neither would there be an advantage to relying on their usage as a model, as in the first alternative, since this would effectively prevent a fair evaluation of their work.

Problems in the attitude of the teacher might include (1) a nonnative teacher sees the SD's as threatening, such as when regional vocabulary or idioms are used by the students, outside the experience of the instructor; (2) the teacher is of native background, but of a different social class or from a different dialect area, who might insist that his practices represent the norm.

Student attitudes will vary widely. The SL's most likely are highly motivated (the level is elective, or they are majors), and have positive views toward the culture and peoples of the FL areas, and in mastering the target language they may suffer only temporary cultural dislocation;[4] for them, learning the classroom standard is a wholesome, positive activity, with definite career and personal benefits. For some of the SD's, the attitudinal stance will be similar, as when they view the classroom standard as prestigious, or identify with the speakers of the dialect, or at least when they can freely adopt the stylistic values of the standard with minimal personal loss. For the other SD's, for whom the standard dialect may represent a historically repressive class, or a nationally alien (but not linguistically foreign) culture, a deep antagonism may impede their objective progress toward effective use of the new dialect. The definition of the classroom standard is trivial[5] when only SL's are involved. Somewhat greater precision is required when the class is all SD, but the climate clearly calls for imposition of an arbitrary standard, not always identified as "arbitrary." But in the mixed class, the very nature of the terms "language" and "dialect" must be clarified at every stage, because the instructor is in fact defining the standard by each judgment on the grammaticality of utterances produced by all students, as the types of unwanted sentences will differ on the surface but will have stemmed from similar processes of interference.[6] The arbitrariness of the concepts now comes to the fore: Do Danish and Norwegian differ more than Alabama Black English and Liverpool colloquial? Is Haitian Creole a dialect of French or is it another Romance language? Are there perhaps more similarities between two closely related standards than between their associated colloquials? If the SD has only a colloquial usage experience in his native dialect, the classroom problem then is one primarily of style; the SD may have a formal (not colloquial) knowledge of English, and thus may move more easily between the two formal usages than between his own colloquial and the class standard.[7]

The essence of the problem thus seems to be the definition of the process in the two categories of student: individual differences apart, is second language acquisition essentially different from second dialect acquisition? We believe it is not.[8] In that case, what pedagogical implications are there for mixed classes? We will argue that there are crucial benefits in the use of parallel methods, with mutual observation of the analogous process by one group of the other in the classroom.

The Solution

There are many ways to acquire a second language or dialect, and the way outlined here, we must emphasize, regards the middle level, if one were to divide language acquisition in three stages: introductory, middle, and advanced levels. Language learning appears to be determined by two major variables: the objectives of the learner, and the environmental conditions in which the learning takes place.[9] Finding the locus of the mixed class at the middle level implies that the learner's objectives are to continue to perfect his mastery of the target language or dialect.

For the model to function, it is imperative that the basic course objectives be explained fully and clearly. We see these as being two very general objectives: the acquisition of language skills as specified by the course title and the development of the student's capacity for language analysis. The first must be explained in terms of the relative position of the target language to the language conditions of the class (i.e., standard dialect of a language, formal style), as the second will be conditioned by such a repertory of language varieties. Thus the goals of the teacher will become consonant with those of the students and the class will function as one.

The core of the model lies in utilizing the language conditions of the class as represented by the student population and thus maximizing the effective use of class time. The key approach is one which requires that whatever technique for language acquisition be used for SL students going from the home to the target language must also be employed for the SD students in going from the home to the target dialect, and that both sets of students learn to describe the processes observed in the other group as it engages in class exercises. Since the method of instruction should be, for all practical purposes, identical when working with SL and SD students at this level, though the content of the lessons may occasionally vary for each group, we must insist that whatever method is chosen for the presentation of new material in language acquisition (we favor no one method in particular), we must *also* adopt the teaching procedures which rely on descriptive and contrastive analysis of language. Given the linguistic variety and the method adopted, we contend that the observation of the language acquisition process by one group as it takes place in the other is the most efficient and successful way of approaching a mixed class.

There are three language conditions in the mixed class: (1) the "classroom standard" of the target dialect, (2) the various dialects spoken by the SD students related to the standard, and (3) the various dialects of the nonrelated language spoken by the SL students. The model requires that the course include both the description carried out by the teacher and/or the text of the three sets of language conditions, and the learning of techniques for describing the linguistic phenomena of the course. All students must be expected to be able to describe what actually occurs in all three of the sets. They will then move to identifying and analyzing features from the three sets taken pairwise. This should proceed simultaneously with exercises that demonstrate their use of the standard, as they are to be prepared to identify differences and similarities between the standard and their own dialect in such a way that the course activity will create its own environment for maximizing learning opportunities for all students involved.

The class activity must be directed in part to the isolation of deviations from the standard and the attempt to classify these as dialectal, results of interferences or analogy and/or errors. Deviations should be acceptable within the standard framework if they match an identifiable standard in the set of formal dialects. All students ought to be expected to account for the deviations identified, whether occurring in their group or in the other, and to learn the general criteria for the determination of acceptable deviation such as intelligibility, documented lexicon, etc.

The issue of the teacher's attitude, however, becomes crucial when addressing some of these problems in the mixed classroom.[10] It may be that whereas in the SL student mother-tongue interference would be so glaring that the teacher can easily classify it as an error, in the case of the SD student the teacher may well flag instances where it is difficult to document the claim of acceptability. The danger that arises in such situations is that of having the teacher's idiolect become the classroom standard. Hence an open atmosphere of inquiry must be fostered from the start. As far as practicable, all responses will be delivered to the class as a whole. The instructor must work in the opening weeks of the course to create and develop a climate of warm, interpersonal relationships among all members of the class. The model depends absolutely on an eventual state in which conversation is not inhibited and criticism is accepted by all members of the class, especially across the SL/SD line.

The nature of evaluation must be, therefore, considered very carefully.[11] The teacher will have to evaluate the student's progress both in language acquisition and language analysis. Certainly the latter appears easier than the former, especially at the middle level: it is always easier to measure incremental language acquisition from a base of zero, but since that is only possible at the introductory level a base must be established even if it is not a zero-base. This can be accomplished by collecting from the student samples of his performance from the beginning and the end of the term. The index of progress thus determined would have to be adjusted to the level minima of competence required. Testing the ability to analyze language is indeed easier, and also more rewarding in terms of the model, for the student's developing skills in this area will depend on his capacity to work with students from the other group. In short, the model depends on the teacher's evaluation of student work both on the degree of approximation to the standard and on the ability to describe and analyze given examples of various dialects.

In evaluating the model two important gains must be noted for the students when the model is used: one pedagogical and the other psychological.[12] The first concerns the actual progress of students in the mixed class, and we must claim that given the controlled environment of the classroom, the efficiency in the use of class time, and the parallel treatment of SL and SD students, as well as the maximum use of the language conditions of the class, the acquisition of competency and analytical skills is higher. The second concerns the attitudinal change we have seen experienced when working with the model: the linguistic starting point of all students is considered valid and worthy of objective study. We agree with those who maintain that the original speech is not to be replaced by the standard, bur rather that the standard should be acquired as a more general alternative for wider practicality in communication.[13] We do not advocate remediation nor extirpation of some arbitrary set of "unacceptable" rules or usages, though we tend to be more conventional with written language and follow standard orthographic norms. We classify as errors those individual deviations which are not documented in the dialect group, and we do prescribe customary forms of the dialect to replace such individual variations, as appropriate. The success of this system, as well as the equitable and fair treatment of all students, which is implied in the model, makes such prescription, in our view, a requirement for language teachers.

Illustrations

In the remainder of this paper, we will give a few samples of exercises that illustrate the technique we are proposing. It should be stressed that it is not the particular type of exercise, but rather the parallel use of it that forms part of our argument. It should also be kept in mind that at present there are no textbooks that are designed for this approach, no matter what method is being adopted or what theory of second language acquisition underlies the method.[14] In a practical situation, a conventional SL text could be modified by the use of supplemental examples/explanations/exercises of SD content, for study by all students in the class.[15]

In our class model, we assume that all students can function effectively in formal English, and that the target is New World Standard Spanish at a stylistic level associated with essays and narrative, and with formal conversation and oral communication. The dialects represented among the SD students are most frequently Puerto Rican, Mexican, and Chicano: the latter group very likely will not have acquired a formal use of any dialect in Spanish. At some prior point in the courses, general notions of language variation (regional, social, stylistic) will have been introduced; no previous training in language pedagogy can be assumed.

Pronunciation

The student records a sentence on tape in the class. On the playback, the student comments on the sounds produced, noting those that might be unwanted because of interference with the native tongue; further comments can come from other students in both groups. The student repeats the exercise, noting degree of approximation to the norm. Class discusses range of acceptable variations.

> Example: *Los obreros estaban de huelga.* "The workers were on strike."
> NWSS pronunciation: lo so βré ro ses tá βan de wél ɣa
> or: lo so βré ro ses tá βan de ɣu̯él ɣa

SL student says [lous]; hears diphthong on replay, observes interference from English glide, repeats without glide to yield [los]. SD students should observe nature of English vowels causing erroneous Spanish articulation.

SD student says [dehuérɣa]; hears initial aspiration and /r/ for /l/ on playback, observes interference from home dialect, repeats with /l/, but also /h/; class discusses the range of possibilities found in spoken Spanish: [de ɣu̯él ɣa]; [de hu̯él ɣa]; [de wér ɣa]; [de gu̯él ɣa], etc. Instructor should point out which are acceptable in NWSS and which are regional variants ("unwanted" forms in the classroom context). SD's should perceive which of the acceptable forms may occur in their usage, and learn to make appropriate distinctions. SL's should learn to adopt [dewélɣa] or [de ɣuelga] in their normal speech in NWSS, but will recognize other sounds as possible in regional dialects that they may encounter.

Both groups should thus observe that certain speech habits from their native tongue may interfere with their production of the target, and that certain variants have wider currency ("are more acceptable") than others and thus should be adopted for the classroom standard.

Conversation

The student speaks before the class on a prepared topic. The class comments on pronunciation, grammar, and style. SD student says: [yóselotrúho] ("I brought it to him"), corrects self to say [yóselotrúhe], i.e., corrected error of agreement. Student should then catch difference between dialect [trúhe] and standard [tráhe], and make final standard utterance [yóselotráhe]. SL's should observe difference between error and dialectal variant, both unwanted forms in the context of NWSS. SL student says: [yóselotrayó]; corrects self to say [yóselotraɪ], i.e., corrected error of agreement, but class notes that error of inflection is left uncorrected, and that the verb was inflected by analogy. All thus should observe the process of error production, as it may occur in either group, but always distinguished from dialectal variation.

Translation

The student translates a sentence from a typical FL textbook. The translation is flashed on an overhead projector and the student explains the process followed in achieving the acceptable sentence in (NWSS). Students from both groups SL and SD note difficulties of paraphrase necessary to overcome mother-tongue inter-ference. Class discusses the various ways of rendering the sentence into acceptable NWSS. (Example: *I have found out who wrote the note.*) SL student is able to translate literally, but notices the lack of syntactical parallel and the need for a paraphrase. Student writes *Me he enterado de quién ha escrito la nota.* (I have informed myself of who has written the note.) Class discusses the idiomatic paraphrase and other possible expressions available. (Example: *Me puede muncho que no jui.*) Chicano SD student translates the sentence provided by the teacher and/or taken from supplementary materials, from home to target dialect thus, *Lo siento mucho que no fui.* (I'm sorry I didn't go.) Class discusses the need for paraphrased translation, and the need for stylistic transposition. Class observes that the process of idiomatic paraphrase is the same in the SL as in the SD group. They also note the distance between the original sentence and the translated product in terms of orthographic conventions in NWSS. (Example: *Bamo a bel que diz el reló.*) Puerto Rican SD student rewrites as NWSS to *Vamos a ver qué dice el reloj.* (Let's see what the clock says.) Class observes the lack of paraphrase in the process of rendering the sentence supplied into NWSS. They observe that some orthographic adjustments and phonological changes (the adding of an *s* to *Bamo*, the *l/r* switch in *bel/ver*) and the adding of an *e* to *diz* makes the sentence acceptable in NWSS.

Composition

The student writes a composition on a prepared topic designed by the teacher to test vocabulary, grammar or style or all of these together with organization, coherence, and effective written communication. The teacher flashes the composition on the overhead projector for all the class to see and comment on. SL student writes a composition where a narrative sequence begins *Sr. González quiero venir por verme.* SD's note the lack of verb-subject agreement, the lack of article and the confusion of *para/por* prepositions. SL student supplies the appropriate correction for each instance of error. Class discusses the source of the errors isolating mother-tongue interference in the lack of article and in the *por/para* confusion, but sees the verb subject agreement as either a slip or signal to the student to undertake a paradigm review. SD student writes a composition where the following appears *Su relativo lo eso con abilida.* SL's point out the lack of a verb until they notice that *eso* does not represent a demonstrative, but a verb; *hizo* then is supplied by the SD as he corrects his usage in NWSS. The SL's observe the lack of a final *d* in *abilida*, the teacher enters the discussion by pointing out the NWSS spelling with a silent *h* at the beginning of the word. The teacher may also have to note the use of *relativo* for *pariente* and the concomitant anglicism which neither student group noticed.

Conclusion

Ultimately, of course, our concern should be with language learning rather than with language teaching. The interesting and valuable experience takes place not in the classroom, but internally in the student, whether of the SD or the SL category. The model outlined above for the mixed classroom cannot in and of itself account for the success or failure of language acquisition per se: What it does is to provide a compensatory clearinghouse of language rules, practices and conventions for two very distinct, yet largely heterogeneous student populations. For the SD student the paramount problem is not that of learning a large quantity of material as is the case with the SL student. Rather the heart of the problem lies in the concept of self, the identity of the student, for not until the SD student recognizes that he is really engaging in a process that is essentially the same as that of second language learning, will he be able to begin to make progress. What constitutes that progress is not only the learning of the NWSS, but also the controlled observation of how the SL student acquires a second language. Thus self-improvement is reinforced by the improvement of the others in the class, and his criticism of them is as valuable as theirs is to him. For the SL student, the model mixed class represents an open pursuit of furthering his knowledge of NWSS and gaining more insight into language acquisition processes. On the other hand, the SD student who seeks to "perfect" his Spanish is deluding himself into believing that he knows Spanish already, but needs a little work. His expectations in terms of difficulty of material, grading and the very notion of being able to observe appreciable progress in his own command of NWSS tend to lead him toward failure in the course and disappointment, at best, if not outright hostility for the process, the individuals, and the institutions involved. Even though the distance between the SD student's home and target dialect is minimal, compared to the SL's case, the rate of success in his case is usually lower than the SL's. This is due, very likely, to the attitudinal differences between both sets of learners. The model mixed class helps to contextualize language learning for the SL student. In most cases the SD students play the role of native informants to the SL students and SL learning becomes less foreign in the mixed class. Both groups, SD and SL learners, therefore, benefit from a mixed class, especially when the class employs the model proposed in this paper. The model mixed class becomes a laboratory of language acquisition and of language learning analysis in written and/or oral communication, where cooperation is necessary from all parties for the total success of the enterprise. In this way the mixed class becomes not an obstacle for the language teacher, but a positive setting with unexpectedly ideal conditions.[18]

Notes

In the course of this paper, the authors assert, without proof, that the process of second dialect acquisition is essentially the same as that of second language acquisition. In a separate research project dealing with a wider range of linguistic circumstances, they are proposing to test certain hypotheses relating to language learning in young adults, the results of which could support or challenge the present assumptions.

1. Piepho (1975) states the problem very succinctly: "Linguistic theories and descriptive and analytic 'schools' have contributed more to language teaching in the first two or three years than to the teaching of more advanced skills" (133); he cautions further, and we have seen little to contradict him: "We know but very little about the psychology of second language learning" (136).

2. See Gaarder et al. (1972) for a typical approach (Spanish context). The report refers to mixed classes only briefly and for elementary or secondary school levels.

3. This is essentially what is described in Boring (1977). She acknowledges the very considerable extra work required for the instructor.

4. Cf. studies on anomie in FL students cited in Torrey (1971). She observes: "Learning a language is accepting a culture, and therefore, in some degree, a personal identity" (251-252). A useful discussion is given in Jakobovits (1970).

5. This is "trivial" or "tautological" in the sense that the standard is whatever the text and teacher declare it to be. There is typically no testing of the standard against other models, such as would be represented by the SD's. The conditions produced by a combination of outmoded texts and poorly trained FL teachers, while lamentable, are not addressed in the present paper.

6. The term "unwanted form" as used by George (1972:2) has much to recommend it as more neutral than the usual word "error" with its popular and theological stigmatization.

7. George (1972) discusses "high" and "low" styles in language teaching (178ff). Gomes de Matos (1976), deals with three levels in Brazilian Portuguese, "formal," "neutral," and "informal." Fishman (1972) surveys earlier work on defining styles. For our immediate purpose, we use a bipolar division.

8. Allen (1970) is more concerned with the negative effects of the term "foreign language" when applied to the acquisition of standard American English by speakers of Black English than with a neat distinction between the two processes.

Robinett (1970) gives a very useful discussion of the necessity for adequate teacher training in handling SL or SD classes when standard English is the target. Substantially all of what she points out has relevance here. However, neither she nor Allen considers the advantages or disadvantages of having both SL and SD students in the same class.

9. Parreren (1975) uses these two broad categories to sum up the conditions which may have an influence on the process of learning a second language.

10. We must make clear at this point that though we are assuming a similarity between the process of second language learning and that of second dialect acquisition, we do not and cannot assume that teachers trained in foreign and/or second language teaching can make the transition to second dialect teaching without further training (Robinett, 1970). It has been our experience that those teachers whose training included a certain amount of linguistics and who are therefore more linguistically sophisticated than the average second language teacher can usually make the transition much more readily. But we must also emphasize that the knowledge of linguistics itself, however, is not as important as an objective attitude toward dialectal varieties. The individual and, no less important, the institutional prejudice are the fundamental factors which affect negatively the practice of second dialect teaching.

11. George (1972) discusses error analysis and makes several practical suggestions for teachers. This careful consideration of student work we believe to be essential in the mixed classroom because any reference to standards in the labeling of errors may be creating more problems than it solves unless it is done with full awareness of all the ambiguities implied.

12. These gains are noted as a result of our own observations in our classrooms over a period of five years.

13. Paulston (1971) explores the moral dilemma of the linguist in language maintenance situations where the teaching of a standard dialect is taking place.

14. Our personal preference relies heavily on contrastive analysis, whereby the differences between, e.g., Chicano and NWSS, on one hand, and between English and NWSS, on the other, would be presented as being analogous. In a method which would exclude Chicano, after having defined Chicano as a related but separate linguistic system, only utterances that are grammatical in NWSS would be accepted in the class context; the instructor could feign not to understand either English or Chicano statements until translated into NWSS.

15. There is considerable utility in having SL students produce utterances in several dialects: read paragraphs with Peninsular Standard ("Castilian"), River Plate, Caribbean, etc., phonetic features; write short dialogues in several styles and regional dialects. In particular, the SL's should learn to recognize characteristics of the dialects represented in the class.

16. The examples, however, could have well been drawn from a mixed class of ESL (SL) and Black English (SD) students where the target was standard English.

17. A useful device in this connection is to have the SL's imitate different regional and/or social dialects in English, as well as attempt to produce samples of spoken English with specific "foreign accents." No amount of theoretical awareness can accomplish linguistic objectivity without considerable practical reinforcement.

18. The authors would like to take this opportunity to thank the discussants Irwin Feigenbaum, Bernhard Peters and Linda Haughton for their commentary after the presentation of the paper at the 6th Annual UWM Linguistics Symposium. In addition we thank our other colleagues Pierre Ullman and Marguerite Suárez-Murias for helpful suggestions during the redaction of the paper's final draft. All responsibility for the contents of the paper, however, rests solely with the authors.

Chapter 16

Teaching English Suprasegmentals to Spanish Speakers

Bertha Chela de Rodriguez

Audiocomprehension and a native-like fluency are perhaps one of the most difficult aspects to master in a second language. It is very common and most frustrating for the foreign language learner to find himself unable to divide the native speaker's speech into meaningful utterances even after having covered exhaustively the grammatical structures of the target language. The typical classroom activities, grammatical drills, reading aloud, dictations, etc., help to increase productive control but do not usually develop aural comprehension, nor are any of those activities sufficient to guarantee a pronunciation accurate enough to make the student's speech intelligible and fluent. On the other hand, many foreign language teachers, especially abroad, use a formal, deliberate and repetitive pronunciation in the classroom with the result that the uninhibited pronunciation of the native speaker in the street is quite unintelligible for the student.

Although some work is done on pronunciation in language programs, most of it is usually left to be picked up by imitation or passive listening, especially the suprasegmentals. Unfortunately however, most adult students learning a second language are inexperienced listeners; in only few cases can they achieve a native-like fluency by mere imitation and "unconscious" listening. F. L. Billows (1961:34) recommends passive listening as one of the best ways to get an insight into the language. He gives as an example an Austrian musician who had lived in Ankara for five years and spoke Turkish like a native. For the first two years, this musician had been among Turks a great deal but had only spoken to those who understood German. After a time, when he needed to use Turkish, he did so with ease and eventually without an accent. Billows specifies, however, the advantage this Austrian musician had over the average language student, i.e., the fact that he had already developed a musician's capacity for attentive listening: most of our language students are novice listeners and will hear new sounds in terms of their own phonetic habits. So an important task of the foreign language teacher is to teach the student to "hear" and to do it correctly in the new language.

Intensive, deliberate work on pronunciation is also often left aside on the grounds that a native-like fluency is neither possible nor desirable as a goal in most cases; but even if we are aiming at the minimum requirements for intelligibility in a foreign language, i.e., having a comfortable, intelligible pronunciation and being able to understand the native speaker's informal speech, intensive, deliberate work both on segments and suprasegmentals has to be carried out. Very few language programs deal with suprasegmental accuracy as an objective and it is usually these features that help us divide the native speaker's speech into meaningful utterances. English suprasegmentals are frequently neglected because they are more difficult to describe and analyze than segments and this is also one of the aspects in which the English teacher who is not a native speaker has the most difficulty himself.

The Learning Process

There are several aspects to be considered when planning pronunciation lessons. First of all there should be a presentation of the segment or suprasegmental to be drilled. If necessary a minimum of technical explanation should be included; the adult student usually welcomes these explanations since he likes to understand what he is doing. For this presentation the teacher should also predict the difficulties in advance by a point-by-point comparison of the structure of the native language and the target language. This contrastive analysis is important since merely by pedagogical experience and intuition it is not possible to develop a full awareness of the ways in which two phonetic systems differ. Such an analysis will help the teacher pinpoint the segments and suprasegmentals which do not occur in the native language and those which are different according to their distribution in the system.

From the technical explanations one should not move on straight into the articulatory drills without having the student identify the new feature first. Leon (1966:59) tells us that:

> *Phonetic habits cannot be mastered solely through articulatory drills. . . . The control of sound production is probably much more auditory than articulatory. . . . As long as the sound has not been heard correctly, it cannot be reproduced correctly except by chance.*

Pronunciation exercises must be drilled intensively, and the language laboratory becomes an indispensable tool in the teaching of foreign languages. But unless the student's ear is trained beforehand, he will only hear his inaccurate pronunciation played back to him repeatedly and not be in a position to evaluate it, maybe even thinking that he *is* giving an accurate imitation. Enough listening practice will enable the student to discriminate between accurate and inaccurate speech and consequently to hear and correct his own mistakes.

Some of the Problems

When choosing a suitable model for student imitation, Leon (1966:61) suggests two possibilities—either the uninhibited pronunciation of the man in the street or the overcareful diction of the teacher; "the final objective would probably be the former for audiocomprehension and the latter for sound production." Gimson (1970:302) also recommends that the foreign learner aim at a careful colloquial style of English in his own speech but at the same time to be aware of the features which characterize the rapid colloquial or familiar style that he is likely to hear from native speakers. For an accurate colloquial style on the part of the student, such features as word and sentence stress, proper rhythm and intonation should be mastered before he can be said to have reasonably fluent speech. Features of assimilation, elision, etc., which occur in rapid speech are important for audiocomprehension but not essential for the student to produce.

The difficulty that the Spanish speaker finds in recognizing and producing certain words is due both to the reduction of vowel sounds to /ə/ or to syllabic consonants and to the different position of the stress. Many Spanish speakers only recognize the word *cotton* /ˈkɑtn̩/, for example, if the two syllables are made roughly equal in length and the second receives its full vowel value and is made to rhyme with the first: */ˈkɔtɔn/.

Accurate teaching of stress and rhythm is significant because they usually exert considerable influence on other matters of pronunciation. Many of the most important signals of grammatical meaning are given by words that occur in unstressed syllables and are, therefore, particularly likely to be missed, so that the sentence *I would have mentioned this before* may well be heard as *I have mentioned this before* or even *I mentioned this before* because the *I would have* in the first utterance is usually reduced in rapid colloquial speech to *I'd've*.

The shifting of stress that is used in English for emphasis or grammatical contrast and which frequently places a heavy stress on forms usually unstressed is another source of difficulties for the Spanish speaker. Compare the following English sentences with their Spanish equivalents:

A. That's his car.   Ese es su coche.
B. That's not his car.   Ese no es su coche.
C. That's not *his* car.   No es el coche de él.

The emphasis given to the possessive adjective in example (C) in English does not have a point-by-point translation in Spanish as in the previous two cases. Spanish relies instead on grammatical or lexical devices. This is specially difficult for Spanish speakers when auxiliaries are used to emphasize a statement, for example:

I'm going to New York tomorrow.   Voy a Nueva York mañana.
I *am* going to New York tomorrow.   Sí voy a Nueva York mañana.

The rhythm in the two languages is also quite distinct: Although Spanish syllables receiving primary stress or sentence stress are longer than other syllables, they are not as long as similar syllables in English. Spanish rhythm tends to give each syllable approximately the same duration. The phrases will thus be proportionately longer or shorter depending on the number of syllables they contain. Consider the following sentences:

> El problema es difícil.
> El problema no es difícil.
> El problema no es muy difícil.

Spanish may be said to have syllable-timed rhythm. English rhythm, on the other hand, depends more on stress. Compare for example the time it takes to pronounce the following sentences:

> If I *talk* to him he'll *do* it.
> If I *talked* to him he would *do* it.
> If I had *talked* to him he would have *done* it.

In English there is a tendency to try to equalize the time between stressed syllables: the greater the number of unstressed syllables between the two stressed syllables, *talk* and *do*, the greater seems to be the speed of delivery of the sentences. So in English it is normal for many syllables to cluster around one primary stress. It is important to point out these differences to the Spanish speaker learning English and to lead him through numerous exercises both for comprehension and production since, as far as pronunciation is concerned, this is one of the main causes for being misunderstood and for his difficulty in audiocomprehension. Allen (1954) gives useful exercises to practice the rhythm of English. He first shows graphically how the English pattern he is going to practice looks, for example:

and then gives sentences for production to match this pattern, such as:

> What are you doing?
> Bring me another.
> Open the window.

Features of assimilation, elision, etc., which occur especially at word boundaries should also be included when planning pronunciation lessons since the student is going to encounter them in rapid colloquial speech and will be confused unless he knows what is happening with the words that have been familiar to him in other situations where deliberate formal speech has been used. The extent of variation that we are going to find at word boundaries depends, of course, upon the speed of the utterance, i.e., in slow speech we will tend to preserve a form nearer to that of the isolated word. So a group of words such as:

I can try and borrow some money from her

would be pronounced in the following way for the student's production

/aɪ kən 'traɪ ən 'bɔro səm ˋ mʌnɪ frəm hər/

but for listening practice it should also be presented as:

/aɪ kn 'traɪm 'bɔro sm ˋ mʌnɪ frəm ər/

Gimson (1970:302) tells us that the foreign learner does not necessarily have to attempt to produce in his speech such phonetic variations unless he wants his speech to be a perfect reproduction of that of the native speaker; but he must know of their existence, for otherwise he will find it difficult to understand much of ordinary colloquial English. Some of the most important phonetic variations at word boundaries listed by Gimson are:

1.   Assimilatory tendencies which involve a variation in the place of articulation, changes which are normal in colloquial speech and of which the native speaker is usually unaware. Word final /t, d, n, s, z/ readily assimilate to the place of the following word initial obstruents: *that pen* /ðæppɛn/, *good boy* /gubbɔɪ/, *ten players* /tɛmplerz/, *this shop* /ðɪʃʃɑp/, *those young men* /ðoʒjʌŋmɛn/, *has she?* /hæʒɪ/. Although the sense of an utterance may be determined by the context, the assimilation of the final alveolars to the place of the following word initial obstruent may confuse the comprehension of the foreign learner.

2.   Coalescence of /t, d, s, z/ with /j/ at word boundaries, e.g.:

/t/   +   /j/   — *What you want* /wətʃuwɔnt/
/d/   +   /j/   — *Would you* /wudʒə/
/s/   +   /j/   — *In case you need it* /ɪŋkeʃunidɪt/
/z/   +   /j/   — *Has your letter come?* /hæʒɔr 'lɛtər 'kʌm/

This coalescence is especially noticeable in question tags, e.g., *didn't you?, could you?*, etc. To make sure the student is hearing these variations one could test them through phonetic transcriptions which will also help him visualize the processes more clearly. One should remember however that the ability to transcribe these features proves that the student can perceive the phonetic variations but not that he can produce them.

Another of the phonetic variations present in rapid colloquial speech that Gimson enumerates (1970:297) and which might confuse the student, is that of elision: "Initial /ə/ is often elided, particularly when followed by a continuant and preceded by a word final consonant ..., e.g.: *not alone* /nɒtl̩ləʊn/, *get another* /getn̩ʌðə/, *run along* /rʌnl̩ɒŋ/." The syllabic consonant seems to compensate for the loss of /ə/.

When dealing with the different intonation patterns in English, the language teacher dealing with Spanish speakers should consider the different levels of pitch between the native and target language. Basically there are four levels of pitch in English, i.e., Low (1), Normal (2), High (3), Emphatic (4), and only three in Spanish, i.e., Low (1), Normal (2), Emphatic (3) (Stockwell and Bowen, 1965:25). The intonation patterns of the two languages are obviously going to be different. Matter-of-fact statements in English usually have the intonation pattern /231/ whereas in Spanish it would be /211/, e.g.:

I'm from Venezuela.   Soy de Venezuela.

The pattern /231/ is used in Spanish for emphatic statements, whereas the English equivalent would be /241/:

Yes, but why?   Sí, pero por qué?

If the Spanish speaker uses the pattern /211/ in normal matter-of-fact situations, e.g.:

What's for dinner?   What are you doing now?

the native speaker of English will react negatively since this pattern is used in uncolored, indifferent utterances in English. On the other hand, Stockwell and Bowen suggest to the English student who finds it difficult to master this pattern in Spanish, to say it as if he were a little angry, otherwise if he answered a question such as *De dónde es Ud.?* with the matter-of-fact intonation pattern of English /231/ for example, *Soy de Nueva York*, he will make the statement emphatic and the interrogator may well think he is irritated by the question (1965:31).

Testing Perception of English Suprasegmentals

One of the ways of measuring the accuracy of the student's auditory perception of suprasegmentals is by means of phonetic transcriptions of phrases, sentences, dialogues, etc., which will include the necessary features of stress and intonation. However, teaching the student to transcribe accurately is not an easy procedure and sometimes we might misjudge the student's discriminatory abilities by his lack of control in handling the phonetic symbols. Furthermore, we might take more time teaching the student to transcribe properly than to discriminate and produce the sounds correctly.

I would like to suggest some exercises, besides phonetic transcriptions, for both drilling and testing suprasegmentals. The exercises are based mainly on minimal contrasts usually found when dealing with segments but which I believe can also be of great use in the perception, discrimination and production of some of the difficult and more subtle features of the English suprasegmentals.

I tested the exercises on ten Spanish-speaking students who ranged from beginners to advanced; the exercises which turned out to be more difficult were so for both levels and in some cases there was better discrimination and perception from students who had had less exposure to the language. By means of this test, I wanted to corroborate the point made earlier in the article, namely, that most language courses are no preparation for developing a perceptive ear; such an achievement requires first an understanding that ear training is a skill to be handled on its own and not as the result of reading, writing and speaking instruction. Like these latter skills it requires deliberate and systematic work as part of the language program.

Of the ten students tested, five were beginners (three males and two females) and five advanced (two males and three females). Their average age was 24 and the level of their English proficiency was estimated on the basis of their level in Intensive English courses which they either were attending or had attended. They were all volunteers.

In the first part of the test (given in full in the Appendix) I dealt with word-stress. Sixteen words (ten cognates) were presented and the student had to identify the primary stress and mark the appropriate column, e.g.:

	1st syllable	2d syllable	3rd syllable
fortunate	x		
tradition		x	

In exercise B, the students were to discriminate pairs of sentences which differed only in one unstressed syllable and were therefore particularly likely to be confused. One of the two sentences was read and the students had to identify the correct one by writing a or b next to the numbers 1 to 4.

The two sentences on the left in exercise C were read four and three times respectively, changing the position of the primary stress each time. The student had to identify the primary stress in the sentences by marking the correct responses on the right, e.g.:

1. (I don't want to buy a *brown* coat.)   But Mary does.   4
2. (I don't want to *buy* a brown coat.)   Buy a jacket then.   3
3. (I don't want to buy a brown *coat*.)   Yes, I know you hate brown.   1
4. (*I* don't want to buy a brown coat.)   Why don't you rent one then. 2

Exercise D, which consisted in underlining the most important words in the sentence, did not turn out to be a good exercise since it also confused the native speakers whom I tested in order to measure the efficiency and clarity of the test; therefore I left it out in most of the cases. A similar exercise, however, should be devised, for it is important that a Spanish speaker hear the differences between the English rhythm and that of Spanish before he is asked for oral production.

In exercise E, I wanted to see whether the student could hear and interpret the different levels of pitch in the B utterances, i.e., the dialogue was read twice changing the level of pitch of response B and the student was asked to underline one of the three possible interpretations given below.

The eight sentences in exercise F had either a fall or rise at the end and the student was asked to interpret the attitude of the speaker for the first three imperatives and to distinguish a question from a confirmation for the last five. They responded by underlining one of the two possibilities.

The instructions were always given in Spanish and except for C, were kept to a minimum without any other clarifying examples or previous practice. For C, however, the explanation was quite detailed; even differences between the shifting of stress in English and the changes needed in the structure in Spanish to obtain the same result were explicitly pointed out. This was obviously a completely new concept for nine of the students, and I had to give a different example with the responses in order to show the procedure.

Test items were read directly to the students, who were to mark or number the correct unit on hearing the stimulus. The stimulus was repeated up to three times if requested by the student.

The results of the test are given below in three tables, one for each group tested. The horizontal division gives the letters of the different exercises tested (exercise D was left out for the reasons explained previously). Vertically, the division indicates the number of correct and incorrect responses obtained; for example, for test A there was a possibility of 80 correct responses for each group:

Beginners

	A	B	C	E	F	Total
Correct	51	71	8	19	21	170
Incorrect	29	9	27	21	19	105
Total	80	80	35	40	40	275

Advanced

	A	B	C	E	F	Total
Correct	68	70	7	27	25	197
Incorrect	12	10	28	13	15	78
Total	80	80	35	40	40	275

Native speakers

	A	B	C	E	F	Total
Correct	80	80	35	35	39	269
Incorrect	0	0	0	5	1	6
Total	80	80	35	40	40	275

Although the sample for this preliminary study was inadequate for satisfactory statistical evaluation of the results, several things are suggestive:

1.   The virtually perfect responses of the native control group show that the tests do in fact reflect ability to discriminate suprasegmentals. They did not, however, distinguish between the two groups of Spanish speakers. The most likely explanation, it would seem, is that the two groups are not really very different with respect to the ability in question, and that our present course of instruction does not teach this ability as well as we might wish.

2.   The tests varied greatly in difficulty. On test B, both beginners and advanced scored nearly as well as native speakers, whereas on test C, which also gave native speakers no problems, both Spanish-speaking groups did very poorly. It is interesting to note that test B involves the effect of stress on segments, rather than stress itself.

Suggestions for Further Research

The exercises presented here could be used to train a group of students and then compare the results with those of an untrained group. Other language groups, besides Spanish, could also be tested. Various exercises should be compared for efficacy and made more complex according to the level of the students and the listening practice they have had. Furthermore, once the student is familiar with this kind of ear-training exercises, the stimulus could be given without allowing the student to visualize what is being read aloud to him. In this way, he would not either corroborate or cancel the first impressions of the ear.

Appendix

Stress, rhythm and intonation: A test to measure the Spanish speaker's auditory perception of English suprasegmentals.

A.   Word-stress

		First syllable	Second syllable	Third syllable
1.	fortunate			
2.	tradition			
3.	determine			
4.	attitude			
5.	intervene			
6.	capital			
7.	assistance			
8.	quantity			
9.	difficult			
10.	immediate			
11.	talkative			

12.	unusual	
13.	yesterday	
14.	newspaper	
15.	overlook	
16.	regardless	

Sentence-stress and rhythm

B.   Contractions

1.   a.   We'll talk to him   (tomorrow.)
      b.   We talk to him   (every day.)
                                    1.
                                    2.
                                    3.
                                    4.

2.   a.   I'll cut it for you.
      b.   I've cut it for you.
                                    1.
                                    2.
                                    3.
                                    4.

3.   a.   They come to see you   (every day.)
      b.   They've come to see you (twice already.)
                                    1.
                                    2.
                                    3.
                                    4.

4.   a.   You've stayed   (there several times.)
      b.   You'd've stayed   (if she had been there.)
                                    1.
                                    2.
                                    3.
                                    4.

C.   Shifting of stress

1.   I don't want to buy a brown coat.   But Mary does _____.
                                            Buy a jacket then   _____.
                                            Yes, I know you hate brown   _____.
                                            Why don't you rent one then? _____.

2.   Why is Mary wearing that hat?   Because the other one is dirty _____.
                                            Because she doesn't like veils _____.
                                            Because Jane decided not to
                                                  wear it_____.

D.   Underline the most prominent words.

1.   He talked to you about it, didn't he?
2.   She only eats twice a day.
3.   He can understand them.
4.   I would have spoken to him if I had seen him.
5.   We aren't English but they are.
6.   They're not very clever with it, are they?

Intonation

E.   Different pitch-levels. (Comments refer *only* to b.)

1.   a. What are you doing?
      b. I'm writing a letter.

1. Unfriendly   1. Unfriendly
2. Normal   2. Normal
3. Emphatic   3. Emphatic

2.   a. Here's your book.
      b. Thank you.

1. Indifferent   1. Indifferent
2. Normal   2. Normal
3. Emphatic   3. Emphatic

3.   a. What did you think of him?
      b. Charming.

1. Sarcastic   1. Sarcastic
2. Normal   2. Normal
3. Emphatic   3. Emphatic

4.   a. How is your job?
      b. It's just great.

1. Sarcastic   1. Sarcastic
2. Normal   2. Normal
3. Emphatic   3. Emphatic

F.   Fall vs. Rise

1.   Pass me the salt!

1. Abrupt, ordering
2. Friendly, requesting

2.   Open the window!

1. Abrupt, ordering
2. Friendly, requesting

3.   Take the blue one!

1. Abrupt, ordering
2. Friendly, requesting

4.   That's not the way to do it.

1. asking
2. affirming

5.   That's it.

1. asking
2. affirming

6.   He's coming later.

1. asking
2. affirming

7.   It's cold, isn't it?

1. asking
2. affirming

8.   You're Venezuelan, aren't you?

1. asking
2. affirming

Bibliography

Abrahams, Roger D., and Rudolph Troike. 1972. *Language and cultural diversity in American education.* N.Y.: Prentice-Hall.

Adjemian, Christian. 1976. On the nature of interlanguage systems. *Language learning* 26:297-320.

Akmajian, Adrian. 1972. Getting tough. *Linguistic inquiry 3*:373-377.

————. 1977. The complement structure of perception verbs in autonomous syntax. In *Formal syntax*, A. Akmajian, P. Culicover and T. Wasow (eds.). N.Y.: Academic Press.

Allen, Virginia French. 1970. A second dialect is not a foreign language. In *Linguistics and the teaching of a standard English to speakers of other languages or dialects,* James E. Alatis (ed.), Monograph Series on Languages and Linguistics, no. 22. Washington, D.C.: Georgetown Univ. Press, 189-202.

Allen, W. S. 1954. *Living English speech.* London: Longman.

Aronoff, M. 1976. *Word formation in generative grammar.* Cambridge, Mass.: M.I.T. Press.

Austin, Tim. 1976. How to get by: The passive in language acquisition. *Proceedings of the Northeastern Linguistic Society.* Montreal: Univ. of Montreal.

Bach, Emmon. 1974. Explanatory inadequacy. In *Explaining linguistic phenomena*, D. Cohen (ed.). Washington, D.C.: Hemisphere, 153-171.

Bailey, N.; C. Madden; and S. Krashen. 1974. Is there a "natural sequence" in adult second language learning? *Language learning 24*:235-243.

Baker, C. 1976. What's not on the other hand in American Sign Language. In *Papers from the Twelfth Regional Meeting of the Chicago Linguistic Society,* Univ. of Chicago.

Baker, R. G., and P. T. Smith. In press. Sound patterns and spelling patterns in English. To appear in *The Stirling psychology of language conference,* R. N. Campbell and P. T. Smith (eds.), *Vol. II.* N.Y.: Plenum Press.

Battison, R.; H. Markowicz; and J. Woodward. 1975. A good rule of thumb: Variable phonology in American Sign Language. In *New ways of analyzing variation in English,* R. Shuy and R. Fasold (eds.), II. Washington, D.C.: Georgetown Univ. Press.

Bellugi-Klima, U. 1968. Linguistic mechanisms underlying child speech. In *Proceedings of the conference on language and language behavior,* E. M. Zale (ed.). N.Y.: Appleton-Century-Crofts.

Bellugi, U., and E. Klima. 1972. The roots of language in the sign talk of the deaf. *Psychology today.* June: 61-64, 76.

————. 1975. Aspects of sign language and its structure. In *The role of speech in language,* J. Kavanagh and J. Cutting (eds.). Cambridge, Mass.: M.I.T. Press.

Bennett, W. A. 1974. *Applied linguistics and language learning.* London: Hutchinson Education Ltd.

Bernstein, Basil. 1970. A sociolinguistic approach to socialization: With some reference to educability. In *Language and poverty,* Frederick Williams (ed.). Chicago: Markham Publishing Company.

Bever, T. 1970. The cognitive basis for linguistic structures. In *Cognition and the development of language,* J. R. Hayes (ed.). N.Y.: John Wiley & Sons.

Billows, G. L. 1961. *The techniques of language teaching.* London: Longman.

Bloom, L. 1973. *One word at a time: The use of single-word utterances before syntax.* The Hague: Mouton.

Boring, Phyllis Z. 1977. The point system: An approach to individualization in advanced language courses. *Foreign language annals 10*:91-94.

Bowerman, M. 1973. *Early syntactic development: A cross-linguistic study with special reference to Finnish.* Cambridge, England: Cambridge Univ. Press.

Bowerman, M. In press. Words and sentences: Uniformity, individual variation, and shifts over time in patterns of acquisition. In *Communicative and cognitive abilities: Early behavioral assessment,* F. D. Ninifie and L. L. Lloyd (eds.). Baltimore, Md.: Univ. Park Press.

Boyes-Braem, P. 1973. A study of the acquisition of the dez in American Sign Language. Working paper, Salk Institute for Biological Studies, La Jolla, California.

Braine, M. 1976. *Children's first word combinations.* Monographs of the Society for Research in Child Development, ser. no. 164, vol. 41, no. 1.

Broen, P. 1972. The verbal environment of the language learning child. *American speech and hearing monograph.* No. 17.

Brown, R. 1968. The development of *wh* questions in child speech. *Journal of verbal learning and verbal behavior* 7:279-290.

———. 1973. *A first language: The early stages.* Cambridge, Mass.: Harvard Univ. Press.

Brown, R., and U. Bellugi. 1964. Three processes in the child's acquisition of syntax. *Harvard educational review 34*:133-151.

Brown, R.; C. Cazden; and U. Bellugi. 1973. The child's grammar from I to III. Reprinted in *Studies of child language development,* C. A. Ferguson and D. I. Slobin (eds.). N.Y.: Holt, Rinehart and Winston, from Minnesota symposia on child psychology, vol. 2. J. P. Hill (ed.). Univ. of Minnesota Press, Minneapolis, 1968.

Brown, R., and C. Hanlon. 1970. Derivational complexity and order of acquisition in child speech. In *Cognition and the development of language,* J. R. Hayes (ed.). N.Y.: John Wiley & Sons, Inc.

Brown, R.; R. A. Salerno; and J. Sachs. 1972. *Some characteristics of adults' speech to children.* Report no. 6, Language Acquisition Laboratory, Univ. of Connecticut.

Buium, N.; J. Rynders; and J. Turnure. 1973. Early maternal linguistic environment of normal and non-normal language-learning children. In *Proceedings,* 81st Annual Convention, APA.

Canale, M.; R. Mougeon; M. Bélanger; and S. Ituen. 1977. Aspects de l'usage de la préposition *pour* en français-ontarien: interférence et/ou généralisation? *Working papers on bilingualism 12*:62-73.

Cancino, Herlindo; Ellen Rosansky; and John Schumann. 1975. The acquisition of the English auxiliary by native Spanish speakers. *TESOL quarterly 9*:421-430.

Carroll, John B. 1965. The prediction of success in intensive foreign language training. In *Training research and education,* Robert Glazer (ed.). N.Y.: John Wiley & Sons.

Carroll, John B.; P. Davies; and B. Richman. 1971. *The American Heritage word frequency book.* Boston: Houghton Mifflin.

Chai, D. T. 1967. *Communication of pronominal referents in ambiguous English sentences for children and adults.* Ann Arbor: Univ. Microfilms.

Chomsky, Carol. 1969. *The acquisition of syntax in children from 5 to 10.* Cambridge, Mass.: M.I.T. Press.

———. 1971. Linguistic development in children from 6 to 10. U.S. Department of Health, Education, and Welfare: Office of Education: ERIC Document Reproduction Service No. ED 059 196.

Chomsky, N. 1957. *Syntactic structures.* The Hague: Mouton.

———. 1964a. On the notion "rule of grammar." In *The structure of language,* J. Fodor and J. Katz (eds.). Englewood Cliffs, N.J.: Prentice-Hall.

———. 1964b. Formal discussion of Miller, W., and Ervin, S. The development of grammar in child language. In *The acquisition of language,* U. Bellugi and R. Brown (eds.). Monographs of the Society for Research in Child Development, ser. no. 92, vol. 29, no. 1, 35-39.

———. 1965. *Aspects of the theory of syntax.* Cambridge, Mass.: M.I.T. Press.

———. 1967. Some general properties of phonological rules. *Language 43*:102-128.

———. 1970. Remarks on nominalization. In *Readings in English transformational grammar,* R. A. Jacobs and P. S. Rosenbaum (eds.). Waltham, Mass.: Ginn and Company.

Chomsky, N. 1973. Conditions on transformations. In *A Festschrift for Morris Halle*, S. Anderson and P. Kiparsky (eds.). N.Y.: Holt, Rinehart and Winston, 232-286.
———. 1975. *Reflections on language*. N.Y.: Pantheon Books.
Chomsky, N., and M. Halle. 1968. *The sound pattern of English*. N.Y.: Harper & Row.
Clark, E. V. 1971. Review of C. Chomsky's *The acquisition of syntax in children from 5 to 10. Language 47*:742-749.
———. 1973. What's in a word? On the child's acquisition of semantics in his first language. In *Cognitive development and the acquisition of language*, T. E. Moore (ed.). N.Y.: Academic Press.
Clark, H. H. 1973. Space, time, semantics and the child. In *Cognitive development and the acquisition of language*, T. E. Moore (ed.). N.Y.: Academic Press.
Clark, R.; S. Hutcheson; and P. Van Buren. 1974. Comprehension and production in language acquisition. *Journal of linguistics 10*:39-54.
Corder, S. P. 1967. The significance of learners' errors. *International review of applied linguistics 5*:161-170.
Cramer, P. 1968. *Word associations*. N.Y.: Academic Press.
Cromer, R. 1970. Children are nice to understand: Surface structure clues for the recovery of a deep structure. *British journal of psychology 61*:397-408.
———. 1972. The learning of surface structure clues to deep structure by a puppet show technique. *Quarterly journal of experimental psychology 24*:66-67.
Curtiss, S.; V. Fromkin; S. Krashen; D. Rigler; and M. Rigler. 1974. The linguistic development of Genie. *Language 50*:528-554.
Dale, P. 1976. *Language development*. 2d ed. N.Y.: Holt, Rinehart and Winston.
Davis, Philip W. 1973. *Modern theories of language*. Englewood Cliffs, N.J.: Prentice-Hall.
Derwing, B. L. 1973. *Transformational grammar as a theory of language acquisition*. Cambridge, England: Cambridge Univ. Press.
Dickerson, Lonna. 1975. The learner's inter-language as a system of variable rules. *TESOL quarterly 9*:401-407.
Dickerson, Wayne B. 1976. The psycholinguistic unity of language learning and language change. *Language learning 26*:215-231.
Dingwall, W. O. 1969. Secondary conjunction and universal grammar. *Papers in linguistics 1*:207-230.
Dinnsen, D. A. 1976a. Some preliminaries to atomic phonology. In *Papers from the twelfth regional meeting of The Chicago Linguistic Society*, S. Mufwene, C. Walker and S. Steever (eds.). Chicago: Univ. of Chicago, 133-144.
———. 1976b. Some formal and empirical issues in atomic phonology. Paper read at the 1976 Mid-America Conference. Minneapolis, Minnesota.
Dinnsen, D. A., and F. R. Eckman. 1976. The atomic character of phonological processes. In *Phonologica*, W. U. Dressler and O. Pfeiffer with T. Herok (eds.), 1976. Innsbruck: Innsbrucker Beiträge zur Sprachwissenschaft.
Dougherty, R. 1970. A grammar of coordinate conjoined structures: I. *Language 46*:850-898.
———. 1971. A grammar of coordinate conjoined structures: II. *Language 47*:298-339.
Drach, K. 1969. The language of the parent: A pilot study. In *The structure of linguistic input to children*, Working Paper no. 14, Language Behavior Research Laboratory, Univ. of California, Berkeley.
Dulay, H. C. and M. K. Burt. 1974a. Errors and strategies in child second language acquisition. *TESOL quarterly 8*:129-136.
———. 1974b. A new perspective on the creative construction process in child second language acquisition. *Language learning 24*:253-278.
———. 1974c. Natural sequences in child second language acquisition. *Working papers on bilingualism 3*:45-66.
———. 1974d. You can't learn without goofing. In *Error analysis*, J. C. Richards (ed.). London: Longman.

Eaton, H. (ed.). 1940. *An English-French-German-Spanish word frequency dictionary.* N.Y.: Dover Publications.

Echeverria, Max. 1975. *Late stages in the acquisition of Spanish syntax.* Unpublished doctoral dissertation, Univ. of Washington.

Eckman, F. 1977. Contrastive analysis and universal grammar. In *Proceedings of the 1976 Mid-America Linguistics Conference,* K. Houlihan, L. Hutchinson, and A. MacLeish (eds.). Minneapolis: Univ. of Minnesota, 69-79.

Ellenberger, R.; D. Moores; and R. Hoffmeister. 1975. Early stages in the acquisition of negation by a deaf child of deaf parents. Minneapolis research report no. 94, Univ. of Minnesota Research Development and Demonstration Center in Education of Handicapped Children.

Ellenberger, R., and M. Steyaert. In press. A child's representation of action in American Sign Language. To appear in *Understanding language through sign language research,* P. Siple (ed.). N.Y.: Academic Press.

Emonds, Joseph. 1970. *Root and structure-preserving transformations.* Unpublished doctoral dissertation, M.I.T.

Ervin-Tripp, S. M. 1971. An overview of theories of grammatical development. In *The ontogenesis of grammar,* D. Slobin (ed.). N.Y.: Academic Press.

———. 1974. Is second language learning like the first? *TESOL quarterly 8*:111-127.

Essen, A. J. van, and J. P. Menting, with T. Heronmueller (eds.). 1975. *The context of foreign language learning.* Assen, The Netherlands: Van Gorcum and Company.

Farwell, C. 1973. The language spoken to children. *Papers and reports in child language development,* no. 5. Stanford Univ.

Ferguson, C. A. 1964. Baby-talk in six languages. *American anthropologist 66*:103-113.

———. 1971. Absence of copula and the notion of simplicity: A study of normal speech, baby talk, foreigner talk, and pidgins. In *Pidginization and creolization in language,* D. Hymes (ed.). Cambridge, England: Cambridge Univ. Press.

———. 1975. Toward a characterization of English foreigner talk. *Anthropological linguistics 17*:1-14.

Ferguson, C., and D. Slobin (eds.). 1973. *Studies of child language development.* N.Y.: Holt, Rinehart and Winston.

Fischer, S. 1973. Verb inflections in American Sign Language and their acquisition by the deaf child. Paper presented at the 1973 Meeting of the Linguistic Society of America.

Fishman, J. 1966. The implications of bilingualism for language teaching and language learning. In *Trends in language teaching,* Albert Valdman (ed.). N.Y.: McGraw-Hill.

———. 1972. *Sociolinguistics: A brief introduction.* Rowley, Mass.: Newbury House.

Fodor, J.; T. Bever; and M. Garrett. 1975. *The psychology of language.* N.Y.: McGraw-Hill.

Fodor, J.; M. Garrett; and T. Bever. 1968. Some syntactic determinants of sentential complexity, II: Verb structure. *Perception and psychophysics 3*:453-460.

Forner, M. 1976. The *why* and *because* of comprehension in language acquisition. Paper presented at the Second Annual Minnesota Regional Conference on Language and Linguistics, Minneapolis, Minnesota, May 14-15, 1976. To appear in *Minnesota working papers in linguistics and philosophy of language,* no. 4.

———. 1978. The mother as LAD: Interaction between order and frequency of parental input and child production. (This volume.)

Foss, D. J. 1968a. An analysis of learning in a miniature linguistic system. *Journal of experimental psychology 76*:450-459.

———. 1968b. Learning and discovery in the acquisition of structured material: Effects of number of items and their sequence. *Journal of experimental psychology 77*:341-344.

Fowler, M., and I. Tasniya. 1952. *The total distribution of the sounds of Siamese.* Madison: Univ. of Wisconsin Press.

Fox, Robert P. (ed.). 1973. *Essays on teaching English as a second language and as a second dialect*. Champaign-Urbana, Ill.: National Council of Teachers of English.

Fraser, C., and N. Roberts. 1975. Mothers' speech to children of four different ages. *Journal of psycholinguistic research 4*:9-16.

Frederick, W. C.; L. S. Golub; and S. L. Johnson. 1970. Analysis of the *Linguistic Ability Test*, grades 4 and 6. Madison, Wisc.: Wisconsin Research and Development Center for Cognitive Learning, ERIC Document Reproduction Service No. ED 040 401.

Friedman, L. 1975. Space, time and person reference in American Sign Language. *Language 51*:940-961.

———. 1976a. The manifestation of subject, object, and topic in the American Sign Language. In *Subject and topic*, C. Li (ed.). N.Y.: Academic Press.

———. 1976b. *Phonology of a soundless language*. Ph.D. dissertation, Univ. of California, Berkeley.

Gaarder, A. Bruce et al. 1972. Teaching Spanish in school and college to native speakers of Spanish. *Hispania 55*:619-631.

Gee, J. 1977. Comments on Akmajian. In *Formal syntax*, A. Akmajian, P. Culicover and T. Wasow (eds.). N.Y.: Academic Press.

George, H. V. 1972. *Common errors in language learning: Insights from English*. Rowley, Mass.: Newbury House.

Gillis, Mary, and Rose-Marie Weber. 1976. The emergence of sentence modalities in the English of Japanese-speaking children. *Language learning 26*:77-94.

Gimson, Alfred Charles. 1970. *An introduction to the pronunciation of English*. London: Edward Arnold.

Gleason, J. B. 1973. Code-switching in children's language. In *Cognitive development and the acquisition of language*, T. E. Moore (ed.). N.Y.: Academic Press.

Gleitman, L. 1969. Coordinating conjunctions in English. In *Modern studies in English*, D. Reibel and S. Schane (eds.). Englewood Cliffs, N.J.: Prentice-Hall.

———. 1975. Let me do it alone, Mommy. Keynote address delivered at the First Annual Boston University Conference on Language Acquisition, Boston, Mass., October 2-3, 1975.

Gomes de Matos, Francisco. 1976. Usos no português do Brasil: uma lista de referência. *Hispania 59*:891-892.

Goodluck, H., and Roeper, T. The acquisition of perception verbs. (This volume.)

Gough, P. 1967. The limitations of imitation. In *New directions in elementary English*, A. Frazier (ed.). Champaign-Urbana, Ill.: National Council of Teachers of English.

Granowsky, S., and W. Krossner. 1970. Kindergarten teachers as models for children's speech. *The journal of experimental education 38*:4, 23-28.

Gruber, J. 1967. Topicalization in child language. *Foundations of language 3*:37-65.

Guess, D., and D. M. Baer. 1973. An analysis of individual differences in generalization between receptive and productive language in retarded children. *Journal of applied behavior analysis 6*:311-329.

Halle, M. 1964. Phonology in generative grammar. In *The structure of language*, J. A. Fodor and J. J. Katz (eds.). Englewood Cliffs, N.J.: Prentice-Hall.

———. 1973. Stress rules in English: A new version. *Linguistic inquiry 4*:451-464.

Hankamer, J. 1971. *Constraints on deletion in syntax*. Unpublished doctoral dissertation, Yale University.

Harries, J. 1973. Coordination reduction. *Stanford University working papers on language universals 11*:139-209.

Hatch, E. 1974. Second language learning-universals? *Working papers in bilingualism*, no. 3. Toronto: Ontario Institute for Studies in Education.

———. 1976. Discourse analysis and second language acquisition. Paper presented at the conference on second language learning and teaching. July, 1976. SUNY at Oswego.

Hebrard, P., and R. Mougeon. 1975. La langue parlée entre les parents et les enfants. *Working papers on bilingualism 7*:52-70.

Hockett, C. 1966. The problem of universals in language. In *Universals of Language*, 2d. ed., J. Greenburg (ed.). Cambridge, Mass.: M.I.T. Press.

Hoemann, H. 1975. The transparency of meaning of sign language gestures. *Sign language studies* 7:151-161.

Huang, J. 1970. A Chinese child's acquisition of English syntax. Unpublished M.A. thesis. Univ. of California, Los Angeles.

Hüdepohl, K. E. 1961. Schwierigkeiten der Aussprache im Deutschunterricht an Brasilianer. *Deutschunterricht für Ausländer 11*:151-155.

Hunt, K. W. 1970. Syntactic maturity in school-children and adults. *Monographs for the Society for Research in Child Development 35*:1 (serial no. 134).

Hurford, J. 1975. A child and the English question formation rule. *Journal of child language* 2:299-301.

Hutchinson, L. 1974. Grammar as theory. In *Explaining linguistic phenomena*, D. Cohen (ed.).Washington, D.C.: Hemisphere Publishing Corp.

———. 1978. Axiom, theorem and rule. In *Evidence and argumentation in linguistics*, T. Perry (ed.). Berlin: Walter De Gruyter & Co.

Huttenlocher, J. 1975. Encoding information in sign language. In *The role of speech in language*, J. Kavanagh and J. Cutting (eds.). Cambridge, Mass.: M.I.T. Press.

Hyman, L. M. 1975. *Phonology: Theory and analysis.* N.Y.: Holt, Rinehart and Winston.

Ingram, D. 1972. The acquisition of questions and its relation to cognitive development in normal and linguistically deviant children: A pilot study. Papers and reports in child language development, no. 4, Stanford University.

———. 1975. If and when transformations are required. In *Developmental psycholinguistics: Theory and applications*, D. P. Dato (ed.). Georgetown Round Table on Languages and Linguistics, 1975. Washington, D.C.: Georgetown Univ. Press.

Inoue, K. 1969. *A study of Japanese syntax.* The Hague: Mouton.

Iowa tests of basic skills. 1971. N.Y.: Houghton Mifflin.

Itoh, H. 1973. *A Japanese child's acquisition of two languages.* Unpublished M.A. thesis, Univ. of California, Los Angeles.

Jackendoff, R. S. 1972. *Semantic interpretation in generative grammar.* Cambridge, Mass.: M.I.T. Press.

———. 1975. *Tough* and the trace theory of movement. *Linguistic inquiry* 6:437-446.

Jakobovits, Leon A. 1970. *Foreign language learning: A psycholinguistic analysis of the issues.* Rowley, Mass.: Newbury House.

Jakobson, R. 1968. *Child language, aphasia and phonological universals.* The Hague: Mouton.

Jenkins, L. 1976. Chomsky and second language learning: The extended standard theory. Paper presented at the First Annual Boston Univ. Conference on Language Development. October, 1976.

Jensen, A. 1969. How much can we boost IQ and scholastic achievement? *Harvard Educational Review 39*:1-123.

John, Vera P., and S. Moskovits. 1970. Language acquisition and development in early childhood. In *Linguistics in school programs*, A. H. Marckwardt (ed.). Chicago: National Society for the Study of Education.

Jones, Randall L., and Bernard Spolsky (eds.). 1975. *Testing language proficiency.* Arlington, Va.: Center for Applied Linguistics.

Keel, W. D. 1977. Phonological variation in the dialects of NE Switzerland. In *Proceedings of the 1976 Mid-America Linguistics Conference*, R. L. Brown et al. (eds.). Minneapolis: Univ. of Minnesota.

Keenan, E. 1973. Variation in universal grammar. Paper presented at the second Georgetown conference on new ways of handling variation in English, 1973.

Kegl, J., and R. Wilbur. 1976. Where does structure stop and style begin? Syntax, morphology, and phonology vs. stylistic variation in American Sign Language. In *Papers from the twelfth regional meeting of the Chicago Linguistic Society*, Univ. of Chicago.

Kelleher, T. R. 1973. Testing, teaching, and retesting syntactic structures in children from 5 to 10. *Linguistics 115*:15-38.

Kessel, F. S. 1970. The role of syntax in children's comprehension from ages six to twelve. *Monographs of the Society for Research in Child Development 35*:6, serial no. 139.

Keyser, S. J., and P. M. Postal. 1976. *Beginning English grammar.* N.Y.: Harper & Row.

Kiparsky, P. 1968. Linguistic universals and linguistic change. In *Universals in linguistic theory*, E. Bach and R. Harms (eds.). N.Y.: Holt, Rinehart and Winston.

Klein, R. 1974. *Word order:.Dutch children and their mothers.* Master's thesis, Institute for General Linguistics, Univ. of Amsterdam.

Klima, E. S. 1964. Negation in English. In *The structure of language*, J. A. Fodor and J. J. Katz (eds.). Englewood Cliffs, N.J.: Prentice-Hall.

Klima, E. S., and U. Bellugi. 1966. Syntactic regularities in the speech of children. In *Psycholinguistic papers*, J. Lyons and R. J. Wales (eds.). Edinburgh: Edinburgh Univ. Press.

Kobashigawa, B. 1969. Repetitions in a mother's speech to her child. Working paper 14, Language-Behavior Research Lab., Univ. of California, Berkeley.

Koutsoudas, A. 1971. Gapping, conjunction reduction and coordinate deletion. *Foundations of language 7*:337-386.

Kramer, P. E.; E. Koff; and A. Luria. 1972. The development of competence in an exceptional language structure in older children and young adults. *Child development 43*:121-130.

Kühnel, H. 1971. Phonetische Probleme im Deutschunterricht für Araber. *Deutsch als Fremdsprache 8*:54-55.

Kuno, S. 1967-68. And to To, Ni, Ya. *Kotoba-No Uchuu*, December 1967, January and February 1968. Tokyo.

———. 1973. *The structure of the Japanese language.* Cambridge, Mass.: M.I.T. Press.

Lacy, R. 1972a. Development of Sonia's negations. Working paper, Salk Institute for Biological Studies, La Jolla, California.

———. 1972b. Development of Pola's questions. Working paper, Salk Institute for Biological Studies, La Jolla, California.

Lambert, W. E. 1956. Developmental aspects of second language acquisition: I. Associational fluency, stimulus provocativeness, and word-order influence: II. Associational stereotype, associational form, vocabulary commonness, and pronunciation: III. A description of developmental changes. *Journal of social psychology*, February 1956, 83-104.

Lambert, Wallace E.; R. C. Gardner; H. C. Barik; and K. Tunstall. 1962. Attitudinal and cognitive aspects of intensive study of a second language. *Journal of abnormal and social psychology 66*:358-368.

Landes, J. 1975. Speech addressed to children: Issues and characteristics of parental input. *Language learning 25*:355-379.

Lange, D. 1971. Schwierigkeiten in der Aussprach für Thailändische Studenten. *Zielsprache Deutsch 2*:176-185.

Langendoen, D. T. 1975a. The relation of competency to performance. In *Developmental psycholinguistics and communicative disorders*, D. Aronson and R. Reiter (eds.). N.Y.: Annals of the New York Academy of Sciences.

———. 1975b. Acceptable conclusions from unacceptable ambiguity. In *Testing linguistic hypotheses*, D. Cohen and J. Wirth (eds.). Washington, D.C.: Hemisphere Press.

Larsen-Freeman, D. 1975. The acquisition of grammatical morphemes by adult ESL students. *TESOL quarterly 9*:409-419.

———. 1976. An explanation for the morpheme acquisition order of second language learners. *Language learning 26*:125-134.

Lasnik, Howard, and Robert Fiengo. 1974. Complement object deletion. *Linguistic inquiry 5*:535-572.

Law, M. 1973. Assumptions in linguistics and the psychology of learning made in current modern language courses. *Praxis des neusprachlichen Unterrichts 20*:231-238.

Legum, Stanley E. 1975. Strategies in the acquisition of relative clauses. Southwest Regional Laboratory technical note. Los Alamitos, Calif.: SWRL.

Lennart, Levin. 1972. *Comparative studies in foreign language teaching.* Stockholm: Almqvist and Wiksell.

Lenneberg, Eric. 1967. *Biological foundations of language.* N.Y.: John Wiley & Sons.

Leon, Pierre. 1966. Teaching pronunciation. In *Trends in language teaching,* Albert Valdman (ed.). N.Y.: McGraw-Hill.

Leopold, W. 1953. Patterning in children's language learning. *Language learning 5*:1-14.

Lerchner, G. 1971. Zum Aufbau eines Phonetikunterrichts des Deutschen für Irakische Studierende auf der Grundlage einer kontrastiven Phonemanalyse von Irakischem Arabisch und Deutsch. *Deutsch als Fremdsprache 8*:161-172.

Liberman, M., and A. Prince. 1977. On stress and linguistic rhythm. *Linguistic inquiry 8*:249-336.

Littlewood, W. T. 1973. A comparison of first language acquisition and second language learning. *Praxis des neusprachlichen Unterrichts 20*:343-348.

Loban, W. 1966. *Problems in oral English: Kindergarten through grade nine.* Champaign-Urbana, Ill.: Research report no. 5, National Council of Teachers of English.

Luria, A. R. 1973. Basic problems of neurolinguistics. In *Current trends in linguistics,* Thomas A. Sebeok (ed.), *Volume 12.* The Hague: Mouton.

Lust, B. 1977. Conjunction reduction in child language. *Journal of child language 4*:257-287.

Macnamara, J. 1970. Review of C. Chomsky's *The acquisition of syntax in children from 5 to 10. General linguistics 10*:164-173.

———. 1971. The cognitive strategies of language learning. *Preprints of the conference on child language.* Les Presses de l'Université Laval.

Maling, J. 1972. On gapping and the order of constituents. *Linguistic inquiry 3*:101-108.

Malmberg, B. 1970. Probleme der Ausspracheschulung. *Zielsprache Deutsch 1*:2-12.

Maratsos, M. 1974a. *The use of definite and indefinite reference in young children.* Cambridge, England: Cambridge Univ. Press.

———. 1974b. How preschool children understand missing complement subjects. *Child development 45*:700-706.

———. 1978. New models in linguistics and language acquisition. In *Linguistic theory and psychological reality,* M. Halle, J. Bresnan, and G. A. Miller (eds.). Cambridge, Mass.: M.I.T. Press.

Maratsos, M., and R. Abramovitch. 1975. How children understand full, truncated and anomalous passives. *Journal of verbal learning and verbal behavior 14*:145-157.

Maratsos, M., and S. Kuczaj. 1976. Is not n't? A study in syntactic generalization. In *Papers and reports on child language development,* E. S. Anderson and S. Veach (eds.). Stanford, Calif.: Stanford Univ. Department of Linguistics, no. 12, 157-168.

McIntire, M. 1974. *A modified model for the description of language acquisition in a deaf child.* Unpublished master's thesis, Univ. of California, Los Angeles.

McNeill, D. 1966a. The creation of language by children. In *Psycholinguistic papers,* J. Lyons and R. Wales (eds.). Edinburgh: Edinburgh Univ. Press.

———. 1966b. Developmental psycholinguistics. In *The genesis of language,* F. Smith and G. Miller (eds.). Cambridge, Mass.: M.I.T. Press.

———. 1970. *The acquisition of language: The study of developmental psycholinguistics.* N.Y.: Harper & Row.

Mendenhall, W., and M. Ramey. 1973. *Statistics for psychology.* North Scituate, Mass.: Duxbury Press.

Milan, John P. 1974. The development of negation in English by a second language learner. *TESOL quarterly 8*:137-143.

Miller, W. 1973. The acquisition of grammatical rules by children. In C. Ferguson and D. Slobin (eds.).

Mougeon, R.; M. Bélanger; M. Canale; and S. Ituen. 1977. L'usage de la préposition *sur* dans le français d'un groupe d'élèves franco-ontariens bilingues. *Montreal working papers in linguistics 8.*

Mougeon, R.; M. Canale; and M. Bélanger. To appear. Rôle de la société dans l'acquisition et le maintien du français par les élèves franco-ontariens. In the proceedings of the "Conference sur l'apprentissage et l'enseignement du français," held at Collège Universitaire Saint-Jean, The University of Alberta, September 6-11, 1977.

Mougeon, R., and P. Hebrard. 1975a. L'acquisition et la maîtrise de l'anglais parlé par les jeunes bilingues de Welland. Final report prepared for the Secretary of State, Ottawa.

———. 1975b. Rapport sur l'acquisition et la maîtrise de l'anglais parlé par les jeunes bilingues de Sudbury. Final report prepared for the Secretary of State, Ottawa.

Moulton, W. G. 1962. *The sounds of English and German.* Chicago: Univ. of Chicago Press.

Muraki, M. 1970. Does Japanese violate Ross' metarules of gapping? *Papers in linguistics 3:* 419-430.

Myerson, R. 1976. *A study of children's knowledge of certain word formation rules.* Unpublished Harvard dissertation.

Nakau, M. 1971. *Sentential complementation in Japanese.* Unpublished doctoral dissertation, M.I.T.

Nelson, K. 1973. *Structure and strategy in learning to talk.* Monographs of the Society for Research in Child Development, no. 149.

Nelson, K.; G. Carskaddon; and J. Bonvillian. 1973. Syntax acquisition: The impact of experimental variation in adult verbal interaction with children. *Child development 44:*497-504.

Newkirk, D. 1975. Some phonological distinctions between citation-form signing and free pantomime. Working paper, Salk Institute for Biological Studies.

O'Donnell, R. C.; R. C. Norris; and W. J. Griffin. 1967. *Syntax of kindergarten and elementary schoolchildren: A transformational analysis.* Champaign-Urbana, Ill.: Research report no. 8. National Council of Teachers of English.

Okubo, A. 1968. *Yooji Gengo-no Hattatsu.* (Development of young children's language.) Tokyo-do-Shoten.

Olds, H. F., Jr. 1968. *An experimental study of syntactical factors influencing children's comprehension of certain complex relationships.* Cambridge, Mass.: Harvard Univ. Center for Research and Development of Educational Differences.

Oller, J. W., Jr., and N. Inal. 1971. A cloze test of English prepositions. *TESOL quarterly 5:*315-326.

Ortmann, W. D. 1971. Lehrerumfrage zu Ausspracheproblemen deutschlernender Ausländer. *Zielsprache Deutsch 2:*174-175.

Osser, Harry. 1970. Biological and social factors in language development. In *Language and poverty,* Frederick Williams (ed.). Chicago: Markham Publishing Company.

Palermo, D. S., and D. L. Molfese. 1972. Language acquisition from age five onward. *Psychological bulletin 78:*409-428.

Palermo, D. S., and M. Parrish. 1971. Rule acquisition as a function of number and frequency of exemplar presentation. *Journal of verbal learning and verbal behavior 10:*44-51.

Parreren, C. F. van. 1975. First and second language learning compared. In A. J. Van Essen and J. P. Menting, with T. Heronmueller (eds.), 1975.

Paulston, C. B. 1971. On the moral dilemma of the sociolinguist. *Language learning 21:*175-182.

Paulston, C. B., and M. N. Bruder. 1976. *Teaching English as a second language.* Cambridge, Mass.: Winthrop Publishers, Inc.

Perlmutter, David. 1971. *Deep and surface structure constraints in syntax.* N.Y.: Holt, Rinehart and Winston.

Peters, Stanley. 1972. The projection problem: How is a grammar to be selected? In *Goals of linguistic theory,* Stanley Peters (ed.). Englewood Cliffs, N.J.: Prentice-Hall.

Peters, Stanley, and R. W. Ritchie. 1973. On the generative power of transformational grammars. *Information sciences* 6:49-83.

Pfuderer, C. 1969. Some suggestions for a syntactic characterization of baby talk style. In *The structure of linguistic input to children*. Working paper no. 14, Language Behavior Research Laboratory, Univ. of California, Berkeley.

Phillips, J. 1970. *Formal characteristics of speech which mothers address to their young children*. Unpublished Ph.D. dissertation, Johns Hopkins University.

———. 1973. Syntax and vocabulary of mothers' speech to young children: Age and sex comparisons. *Child development* 44:182-185.

Piepho, Hans-Eberhard. 1975. Differences and similarities between linguistic description for its own sake and linguistic description with a view to language teaching. In A. J. van Essen and J. P. Menting, with T. Heronmueller (eds.), 1975.

Postal, Paul. 1971. *Cross-over phenomena*. N.Y.: Holt, Rinehart and Winston.

Postal, Paul, and John Ross. 1971. Tough movement si, tough deletion no! *Linguistic inquiry* 2:544-545.

Pulte, W. 1971. Gapping and word order in Quechua. In *Papers from the seventh regional meeting of the Chicago Linguistic Society*. Chicago: Univ. of Chicago.

Rabinowitsch, A. I. 1971. Ausspr255cheschwierigkeiten im Deutschen für kasachische Schüler. *Deutsch als Fremdsprache* 8:238-242.

Ramig, C. J. 1974. *The relationship between reading comprehension and listening comprehension among second, third, fourth and fifth graders on eight different sentence types*. Unpublished doctoral dissertation, Univ. of Wisconsin, Madison.

Ravem, R. 1974. The development of *wh*-questions in first and second language learners. In *Error analysis*, J. Richards (ed.). London: Longman.

Remick, H. 1971. *The maternal environment of linguistic development*. Unpublished Ph.D. dissertation, Univ. of California, Davis.

Robinett, Betty Wallace. 1970. Teacher training for English as a second dialect and English as a second language: The same or different? In *Linguistics and the teaching of standard English to speakers of other languages or dialects*, James E. Alatis (ed.). Monograph series on languages and linguistics, no. 22. Washington, D.C.: Georgetown Univ. Press.

Roeper, T. 1972. *Approaches to a theory of language acquisition with examples from German children*. Unpublished Ph.D. dissertation, Harvard University.

———. 1973. Theoretical implications of word order, topicalization and inflections in German language acquisition. In C. Ferguson and D. Slobin (eds.), 1973.

———. 1974. Deep structures in the acquisition of German stress phonology. Unpublished paper, Univ. of Massachusetts.

———. 1976. Three relations between semantics and syntax in child language. In *Baby talk and infant speech*, W. von Raffler-Engel (ed.). N.Y.: Humanities Press.

———. 1977. Linguistic universals and the acquisition of gerunds. In *Papers in the structure and development of child language*, H. Goodluck and L. Solan (eds.). Amherst, Mass.: Univ. of Massachusetts Occasional Papers in Linguistics.

Rosansky, E. J. 1976. Methods and morphemes in second language acquisition research. *Language learning* 26:409-426.

Rosenbaum, P. S. 1967. *The grammar of English predicate complement constructions*. Cambridge, Mass.: M.I.T. Press.

Ross, J. R. 1968. *Constraints on variables in syntax*. Bloomington, Ind.: Indiana Univ. Linguistics Club.

———. 1970. Gapping and the order of constituents. In *Progress in linguistics*, M. Bierwisch and K. Heidolph (eds.). The Hague: Mouton.

Rūķe-Draviņa, V. 1973. On the emergence of inflection in child language: A contribution based on Latvian speech data. In C. Ferguson and D. Slobin (eds.), 1973.

Sachs, J., and J. Devin. 1976. Young children's use of age-appropriate speech styles in social interaction and role playing. *Journal of child language* 3:81-98.

Sachs, J.; R. Brown; and R. Salerno. 1972. Adults' speech to children. Paper presented at the International Symposium on First Language Acquisition, Florence, Italy.

Sag, I. 1976. *Deletion and logical form.* Unpublished Ph.D. dissertation, M.I.T.

Sanches, M. 1968. *Features in the acquisition of Japanese grammar.* Unpublished doctoral dissertation, Stanford University.

Sanders, G. 1975. *Invariant ordering.* The Hague: Mouton.

Sanders, L. J. 1971. The comprehension of certain syntactic structures by adults. *Journal of speech and hearing research 14*:739-745.

Savić, S. 1975. Aspects of adult-child language communication: The problem of question acquisition. *Journal of child language 2*:251-260.

Scherer, George A. C., and Michael Wertheimer. 1964. *A psycholinguistic experiment in foreign-language teaching.* N.Y.: McGraw-Hill.

Scollen, R. T. 1974. *One child's language from one to two: The origins of construction.* Unpublished Ph.D. dissertation, Univ. of Hawaii.

Scott, Margaret Sue, and G. Richard Tucker. 1974. Error analysis and English language strategies of Arab students. *Language learning 24*:69-97.

Selinker, L. 1972. Interlanguage. *IRAL 10*:209-231.

———. 1974. Interlanguage. In *Error analysis,* J. Richards (ed.). London: Longman.

Selinker, L.; M. Swain; and G. Dumas. 1975. The interlanguage hypothesis extended to children. *Language learning 25*:139-152.

Shatz, M., and R. Gelman. 1973. The development of communication skills: Modifications in the speech of young children as a function of listener. *Monographs for The Society for Research in Child Development 38*:5, serial no. 152.

Sheldon, A. 1974. The role of parallel function in the acquisition of relative clauses in English. *Journal of verbal learning and verbal behavior 13*:272-281.

———. 1977. The acquisition of relative clauses in French and English: Implications for language learning universals. In *Current themes in linguistics: Bilingualism, experimental linguistics, and language typology,* F. Eckman (ed.). Washington, D.C.: Hemisphere Publishing Corp.

Sinclair, A.; H. Sinclair; and O. de Marcellus. 1971. Young children's comprehension and production of passive sentences. *Archives de Psychologie 41*:161, 1-22.

Sinclair, J.; J. Berthoud-Papandropoulou; J. P. Bronckart; J. Chipman; E. Ferreiro; and E. Rappe Du Cher. 1976. Recherches en psycholinguistique génétique. *Archives de Psychologie 44*:171, 157-175.

Slobin, D. 1971a. Developmental psycholinguistics. In *A survey of linguistic science,* W. O. Dingwall (ed.). College Park, Md.: Univ. of Maryland Linguistics Program.

———. 1971b. *Psycholinguistics.* Glenview, Ill.: Scott, Foresman and Company.

———. 1973. Cognitive prerequisites for the development of grammar. In C. Ferguson and D. Slobin (eds.), 1973.

Slobin, D., and C. Welsh. 1973. Elicited imitation as a research tool in developmental psycholinguistics. In C. Ferguson and D. Slobin (eds.), 1973.

Smith, P. T., and R. G. Baker. 1976. The influence of English spelling patterns on pronunciation. *Journal of verbal learning and verbal behavior 15*:267-285.

Smith, Philip D., Jr. 1970. *A comparison of the cognitive and audiolingual approaches to foreign language instruction.* Philadelphia: The Center for Curriculum Development.

Snow, C. 1972. Mothers' speech to children learning language. *Child development 43*:549-565.

———. 1974. Mothers' speech research: An overview. Paper presented at the conference on language input and acquisition. Boston, Mass., September 6-8, 1974.

Solan, L. 1976. The acquisition of the *easy-to-please* construction. Unpublished paper, Univ. of Massachusetts.

Spolsky, B. 1978. *Educational Linguistics.* Rowley, Mass.: Newbury House.

Statts, Arthur W. 1971. Linguistic mentalistic theory versus an explanatory S-R learning theory of language development. In *The ontogenesis of grammar*, D. Slobin (ed.). N.Y.: Academic Press.

Stearns, S. W. 1973. Review of C. Chomsky's *The acquisition of syntax in children from 5 to 10. Studies in linguistics 23*:105-109.

Stern, H. H. 1967. *Foreign languages in primary education: The teaching of foreign or second languages to younger children*. London: Oxford Univ. Press.

Stockwell, Robert P., and J. Donald Bowen. 1965. *The sounds of English and Spanish*. Chicago: Univ. of Chicago Press.

Stockwell, R. P.; P. Schachter; and B. H. Partee. 1973. *The major syntactic structures of English*. N.Y.: Holt, Rinehart and Winston.

Strevens, P. 1971. Two ways of looking at error-analysis. *Zielsprache Deutsch 2*:1-6.

Stubbs, J. B., and G. R. Tucker. 1974. The cloze test as a measure of English proficiency. *Modern language journal 58*:239-241.

Suter, Richard W. 1976. Predicators of pronunciation accuracy in second language learning. *Language Learning 26*:233-253.

Swain, M. K. 1975. *Changes in errors: Random or systematic*. Toronto: Ontario Institute for Studies in Education.

Tai, J. H-y. 1969. *Coordination reduction*. Bloomington, Ind.: Indiana Univ. Linguistics Club.

———. 1971. Identity deletion and regrouping in coordinate structures. In *Papers from the seventh regional meeting of the Chicago Linguistic Society*. Chicago: Univ. of Chicago.

Tanz, C. M. 1976. *Studies in the acquisition of deictic terms*. Unpublished doctoral dissertation, Univ. of Chicago.

Tarone, E.; A. D. Cohen; and G. Dumas. 1976. A closer look at some interlanguage terminology: A framework for communication strategies. *Working papers on bilingualism 9*:76-90.

Tarone, E.; M. Swain; and A. Fathman. 1976. Some limitations to the classroom applications of current second language acquisition research. *TESOL quarterly 10*:19-32.

Tavakolian, S. 1975. The structural analysis of complex sentences and the determination of functional relations by preschoolers. Unpublished paper, Univ. of Massachusetts, Amherst.

———. 1977. *Structural principles in the acquisition of complex sentences*. Unpublished doctoral dissertation, Univ. of Massachusetts, Amherst.

Taylor, Barry P. 1974. Towards a theory of language acquisition. *Language learning 24*:23-35.

Torrey, Jane W. 1971. Second language learning. In *The learning of language*, Carroll E. Reed (ed.). N.Y.: Appleton-Century-Crofts.

Upshur, John. 1968. Four experiments on the relation between foreign language teaching and learning. *Language learning 18*:111-124.

Valdman, A. 1975. Learner systems and error analysis. In *Perspective: A new freedom*, G. A. Jarvis (ed.). The ACTFL Review of Foreign Language Education, number 7.

Watt, W. 1970. On two hypotheses concerning psycholinguistics. In *Cognition and the development of language*, J. R. Hayes (ed.). N.Y.: John Wiley & Sons.

———. 1972. Competing economy criteria. School of Social Science, *Social sciences working papers*, no. 5. Univ. of California, Irvine.

Wilber, R., and M. Jones. 1974. Some aspects of the bilingual/bimodal acquisition of Sign and English by three hearing children of deaf parents. In *Proceedings of the tenth regional meeting of the Chicago Linguistics Society*, R. Fox and S. Bruck (eds.). Chicago: Chicago Linguistics Society.

Wilkins, D. A. 1972. *Linguistics in language teaching*. Cambridge, Mass.: M.I.T. Press.

Williams, E. 1975. Small clauses in English. In *Syntax and semantics volume 4*, J. Kimball (ed.). N.Y.: Academic Press.

Zierrer, E. 1961. Lautbildungsschwierigkeiten spanischsprachiger Peruaner. *Deutschunterricht für Ausländer 11*:26-29.